MARVEL MASTERWORKS
PRESENTS

THE UNCANNY
X·MEN

VOLUME 1

COLLECTING
GIANT-SIZE X-MEN No. 1
& THE X-MEN Nos. 94-100
CHRIS CLAREMONT • DAVE COCKRUM
WITH LEN WEIN

Collection Editor
Cory Sedlmeier

Book Design
Nickel DesignWorks

Senior Vice President of Sales
David Gabriel

Editor in Chief
Joe Quesada

Publisher
Dan Buckley

Executive Producer
Alan Fine

MARVEL MASTERWORKS: THE UNCANNY X-MEN VOL. 1. Contains material originally published in magazine form as GIANT-SIZE X-MEN #1 and X-MEN #94-100. First printing 2009. ISBN# 978-0-7851-3702-3. Published by MARVEL PUBLISHING, INC., a subsidiary of MARVEL ENTERTAINMENT, INC. OFFICE OF PUBLICATION: 417 5th Avenue, New York, NY 10016. Copyright © 1975, 1976 and 2009 Marvel Characters, Inc. All rights reserved. $24.99 per copy in the U.S. (GST #R127032852); Canadian Agreement #40668537. All characters featured in this issue and the distinctive names and likenesses thereof, and all related indicia are trademarks of Marvel Characters, Inc. No similarity between any of the names, characters, persons, and/or institutions in this magazine with those of any living or dead person or institution is intended, and any such similarity which may exist is purely coincidental. **Printed in the U.S.A.** ALAN FINE, EVP - Office Of The Chief Executive Marvel Entertainment, Inc. & CMO Marvel Characters B.V.; DAN BUCKLEY, Chief Executive Officer and Publisher - Print, Animation & Digital Media; JIM SOKOLOWSKI, Chief Operating Officer; DAVID GABRIEL, SVP of Publishing Sales & Circulation; DAVID BOGART, SVP of Business Affairs & Talent Management; MICHAEL PASCIULLO, VP Merchandising & Communications; JIM O'KEEFE, VP of Operations & Logistics; DAN CARR, Executive Director of Publishing Technology; JUSTIN F. GABRIE, Director of Publishing & Editorial Operations; SUSAN CRESPI, Editorial Operations Manager; ALEX MORALES, Publishing Operations Manager; STAN LEE, Chairman Emeritus. For information regarding advertising in Marvel Comics or on Marvel.com, please contact Mitch Dane, Advertising Director, at mdane@marvel.com. For Marvel subscription inquiries, please call 800-217-9158. **Manufactured between 10/23/09 and 11/11/09 by R.R. DONNELLEY, INC., SALEM, VA, USA.**

10 9 8 7 6 5 4 3 2 1

MARVEL MASTERWORKS
CREDITS

THE
UNCANNY X-MEN
GIANT-SIZE X-MEN No. 1 & THE X-MEN Nos. 94-100

Writers: **Chris Claremont** (Nos. 94-100)
Len Wein (*Giant-Size X-Men No. 1;* Nos. 94, 95)
Bill Mantlo (No. 96)

Penciler: **Dave Cockrum**

Inkers: Dave Cockrum (*Giant-Size X-Men No. 1;* No. 100)
Bob McLeod (No. 94)
Sam Grainger (Nos. 95-98)
Frank Chiaramonte (No. 99)

Letterers: John Costanza (*Giant-Size X-Men No. 1*)
Tom Orzechowski (No. 94)
Karen Mantlo (No. 95)
Dave Hunt (No. 96)
Annette Kawecki (Nos. 97, 100)
Joe Rosen (No. 98)
Irving Watanabe (No. 99)

Editors: Len Wein & Marv Wolfman

Collection Cover Art: Gil Kane, Dave Cockrum & Dean White

Color Reconstruction: Wesley Wong (*Giant-Size X-Men No. 1;* Nos. 94-97)
Tom Mullin (Nos. 98-100)
Michael Kelleher (Covers)

Art Reconstruction: Dale Crain & Michael Kelleher

Special Thanks: Ralph Macchio, Tom Brevoort & Mark Beazley

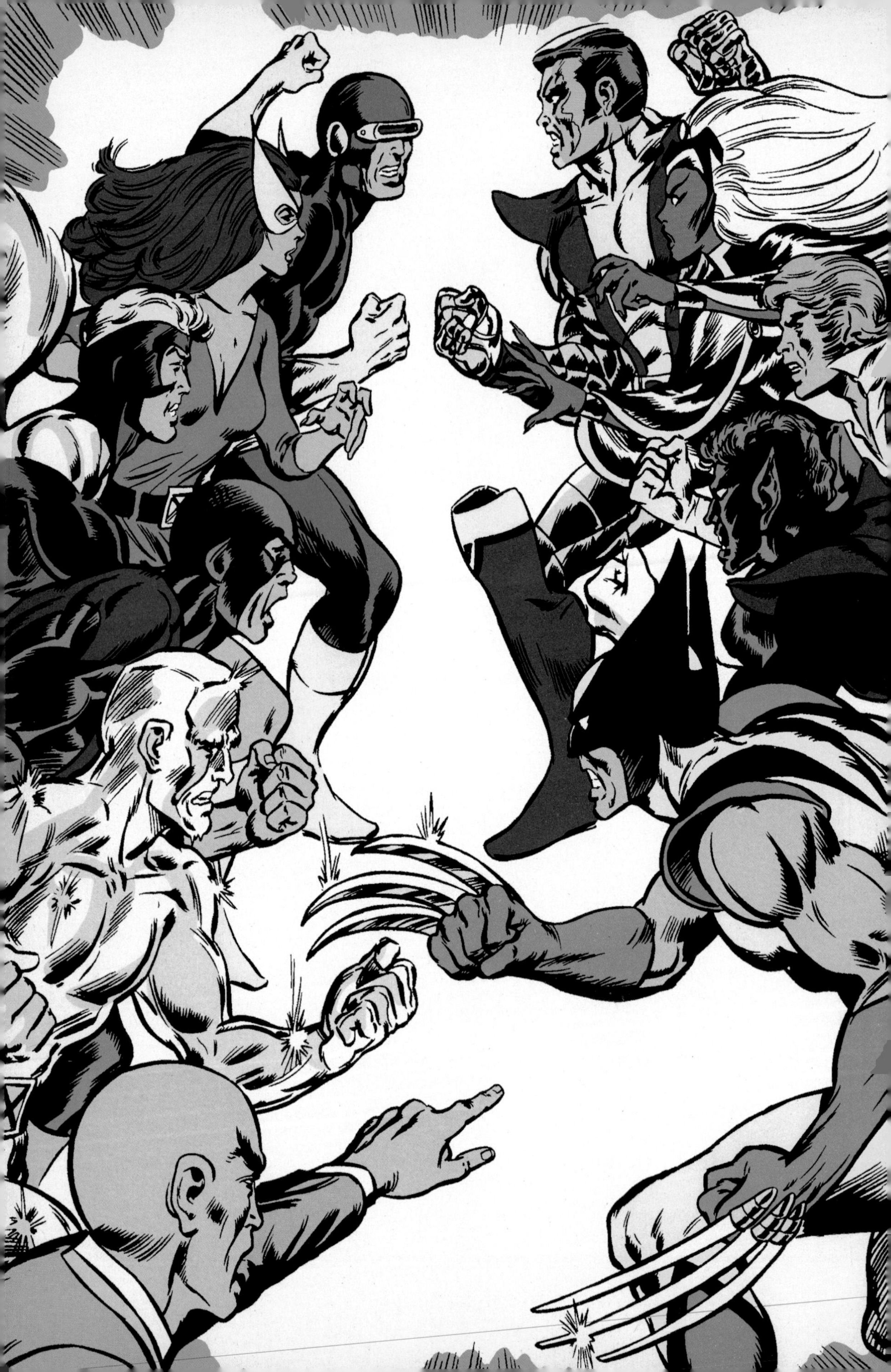

MARVEL MASTERWORKS
CONTENTS

INTRODUCTION
BY CHRIS CLAREMONT

It's always better in memory.

That's the way of it, with the passage of time. The bad sort of slips more and more out of focus, the good becomes richer and more resonant. The realities of the present materially affect perceptions of all that came before. Which is by way of saying that none of what follows is even meant to be objective.

The differences between now and then are, in some ways, too extraordinary to be credible. Now, being the age when the *X-Men*—and the associated books of its canon—bestride the comics publishing world like (dare I say it) a Colossus. When *Uncanny X-Men* is used by one of the major distributors—as it has been for well over a decade—as the benchmark sales level against which all other titles are judged. When the X-titles have been described by Marvel as the equivalent of the third or fourth largest comics publishers in the United States.

Then—in 1974, when all this came together—it was a whole other story. For one thing, a great many of the book's current audience weren't even born. For another, pretty much everyone today responsible for producing the books was still in grade school, if that. A whole generation of creators and readers who've grown up in the shadow of this title's phenomenal success.

Thing is, when the new series was launched, success was defined by those who worked on it as simple survival. *X-Men* in those days was a bimonthly mid-list title, sort of a cult favorite with an extremely checkered career behind it, achieving some heights of critical fame but only marginal sales. Indeed, the series was slated for outright cancellation in the late '60s; however, thanks to the comparative success of the last string of original issues—by Roy Thomas, Neal Adams and Tom Palmer—the decision was made instead to continue the book as a reprint.

Marvel was a whole other place as well, ensconced in a moderate suite of offices on Madison Avenue, struggling to sustain a burgeoning black-and-white magazine line as well as the bread and butter color titles. Today, it's a place of Executive Editors and Managing Editors and Line Editors, with a vast array of associates and assistants and interns, as befits a billion dollar operation. Then, there was Editor-in-Chief Len Wein, Associate Editor Chris Claremont (yup, me), and a literal handful of staff. No less chaotic than now, but a whole lot smaller in scale.

That was one of our advantages, and a phenomenal one in its way. Len, together with Dave Cockrum, created the new X-Men. Marv Wolfman, who succeeded Len as Editor-in-Chief, was one of his best friends. I was second in command to both of them. It allowed for a freewheeling editorial relationship that proved to be as much a collaboration as the one between first Len and Dave and then, almost right off the bat, between myself and Dave. By the same token, because Len and Marv knew my capabilities as a writer, and Dave's as a penciler, we were trusted to do our jobs to the best of our ability. And, because there were no real expectations for the book, we were left alone. Effectively no interference, unless there was a major problem, or we asked for help. The chain of command was short enough, and direct enough, that any glitches could be worked out quickly and informally and with a minimum of hassle, or hard feelings.

Finally, there was the inestimable joy of creating a concept, virtually from scratch. Len and Dave laid the foundation, in a debut issue that remains a marvel (so to speak) of power and storytelling clarity, introducing its characters and situations with an eloquence and economy that many titles today might do well to emulate. Everyone was brought on stage and introduced to the audience; everything else, from that point on, was up for grabs.

How did I feel at the assignment? Excited. Happy. Eager. I was working on characters that looked intensely cool, with an artist whose work I'd admired ever since his stint on DC's *Legion of Super Heroes*. It was my first legitimate super-hero series. And though I didn't realize it until I'd been on the book awhile, we were operating in such a comparative backwater of the Marvel Universe—again, on a title fueled more by hope than true expectations—that no real limitations were placed on our work. In essence, Dave and I could do whatever we wanted.

How long since anyone's had that kind of freedom, anywhere in mainstream comics?

Len set the tone for the series, with what was originally structured as *Giant-Size X-Men* #2, his last as plotter, my first script. (While Dave and I were working on the book, the decision was made to revert the title to the standard 32-page format and a bimonthly schedule, which necessitated some frantic restructuring of plot and layout—another aspect of the series that appears to have lasted to the present day. So *Giant-Size* #2 became *X-Men* #s 94 & 95, picking up the numbering where the reprints left off.) He wanted to show, as dramatically as possible, that this team operated under a deadlier set of realities than their predecessors—or, for that matter, any other super heroes. Thunderbird changed that. It demonstrated to the new X-Men right off the bat that they were vulnerable, and suggested to the audience that this was a book where anything could happen. *X-Men* #s 94 & 95 laid the groundwork for the Phoenix storyline that was to follow—forty odd issues later—but those are anecdotes for another introduction.

My first original issue—where I handled plot and script—was #96: "Night of the Demon." Most notable, in memory, for being the first (of many) stories written on the road, during a sabbatical I was taking in England. It also established, beyond all doubt, probably my most notorious character paradigm: the really handsome woman with the really big gun. I mean, who else but the X-Men would have a housekeeper (Moira MacTaggart) who, on her first day at work, would be attacked by a bloodthirsty demon and respond by grabbing an M-16 from the armory and cutting loose?

At the same time, Dave and I also introduced the Sentinels storyline. You see, we found ourselves in something of a scheduling bind. Tradition—not to mention the practicalities of the marketplace—demanded that we have some Big Event to celebrate the landmark Hundredth issue, even though the new book would be seven issues old at that point. Subtract the first two issues, needed to cover the story of *Giant-Size* #2, and we had only five in which to do the job. So, not only were Dave and I trying to get a solid handle on these (mostly) newborn characters, we were trying to come up with an issue that would knock the readers' proverbial socks off. We wanted the threat to come from within the *X-Men* canon, but we didn't want to use Magneto, the series' premier villain. For one thing, he'd been reduced to infancy by Len in an issue of *Defenders*; for another, both Dave and I wanted to re-intro him in circumstances where we felt we didn't have to rush. The Sentinels were big, classic, easily recognizable and didn't require much explanation.

In #94, Len established that Jean Grey was leaving the team, along with Angel, Beast and Iceman. The pencils were done, there was no time to make changes, I wrote the scene as drawn. But I was also determined to bring her back to the book and the team as quickly as possible. The first book I saw when I first came to work for Marvel in 1969 as a gofer was also Neal Adams' first as *X-Men* penciler, with his breathtaking rendition of all the characters. I was smitten with Jean pretty much from that moment; I wasn't about to lose her. The only thing I asked of Dave was that we reorient her from the Scarsdale Upper Middle Class Republican WASP look she affected in #95 to something a tad more downtown and funky. In *X-Men* #97, he obliged.

By then, the creative elements of the book were starting to fall into place. From the opening scene of "My Brother, My Enemy!" we established that the scope of the title was in no way confined to the Earth. We were also getting into the habit of causing all manner of major property damage, especially at Kennedy Airport (which I'm sure they appreciated). The characters were coming more and more into focus, with elements such as Wolverine idly cutting a tic tac toe grid on an antique table, Nightcrawler's innate Errol Flynn like flamboyance, Colossus's ongoing culture shock and the growing friendship between Jean and Storm. We also established Storm as being the one member of the team who would stand up to Wolverine when his temper was flaring and, through sheer force of personality, get him to back down. There was even one classic coloring goof, long since corrected. In the final panel, we see a villain (presumably the Shi'ar Emperor) watching another villain (Steven Lang) watching the X-Men on video screens. Originally, the X-Men were shown in color, but Lang was shown in black & white, with Emperor delineated in color. Someone belatedly wondered how someone could watch something in color on a black & white screen? Oopsie.

With #98, celebrating the team's first X-Mas together, creators and book hit their stride. The romance between Scott and Jean was established in full flower and the characterizations of the other X-Men grew that much richer in concert. It was also the moment where we established—in a deliberately understated throwaway scene—that Wolverine's claws were a part of him, rather than being a function of the gloves as they'd originally been intended. We took the team to the edge of space, put them into the fight of their young lives and closed on a cliffhanger whose repercussions still form an integral part of the canon to this day, better than fifteen years later.

What defined the *X-Men* when Dave and I began? Passion, mostly. Between Dave and I and the characters, between the characters themselves, ultimately between the book and its readers. This was a series about people who grow into friends, and further into friends who care deeply about each other. All the relationships were interlocking levels of friendship—the X-Men for themselves, Moira MacTaggart and Peter Corbeau for Charles Xavier. The moments where the characters became the most vulnerable were those when they were attacked through affection and love, for those friends, the ultimate expression of this being Jean Grey's decision to sacrifice her life to save the man—and friends—she loves. These were people who believed in each other, which consequently allowed the readers to believe in them.

What makes these issues—sloppy as their construction may be in places and, to my eye that looks at the script from the vantage of twenty years experience, hellaciously overwritten—special is that they were the beginning. Somewhere, Dave and I tapped into the mother lode—and for those readers with us at the same time there was the chance to see all those relationships grow. As Dave and I honed our craft, as individuals and a team, so did the characters make their initially halting and occasionally clumsy steps into becoming a team, and ultimately a family. I think when fans speak of how much more some like those early issues than any of the more recent run, they speak to the establishment of relationships that today are taken as a matter of course. The characters had only just met then, as opposed to having been together for longer than many readers' and some creators' lifetimes. There was the marvel of discovery to every aspect of the book. All in an environment that held precious few restrictions.

Every writer—every creator, I'll wager—has that series which occupies a special place in heart and memory. I grew up professionally with the *X-Men*: it was a significant part of my life for virtually the entire length of my association with Marvel. To paraphrase David Letterman, I would like to think that the work I did—the standards that were set, both creatively and commercially—in association with John Byrne and Louise Simonson, among many others, inspires the same pride in Marvel that it did in me. As I am the better for my seventeen years' tenure on this title, so is Marvel.

Things change, the wheel turns, relationships don't always endure. The *X-Men* are history for me now, the creative responsibilities for these titles passed on to other hands. I'm sure, over time, stories will be crafted that will be equal to the best of what's come before; some may even surpass them, though I hope that'll take some doing. But no matter how good the book gets in the future, or what new and greater benchmarks it achieves, there's one thing that belongs forever to Len Wein and Dave Cockrum and myself, and for which we should be excused some measure of pardonable pride. We were here first. In those moments, for this book, we were the best there were at what we did. And what we did was damn fine.

1993

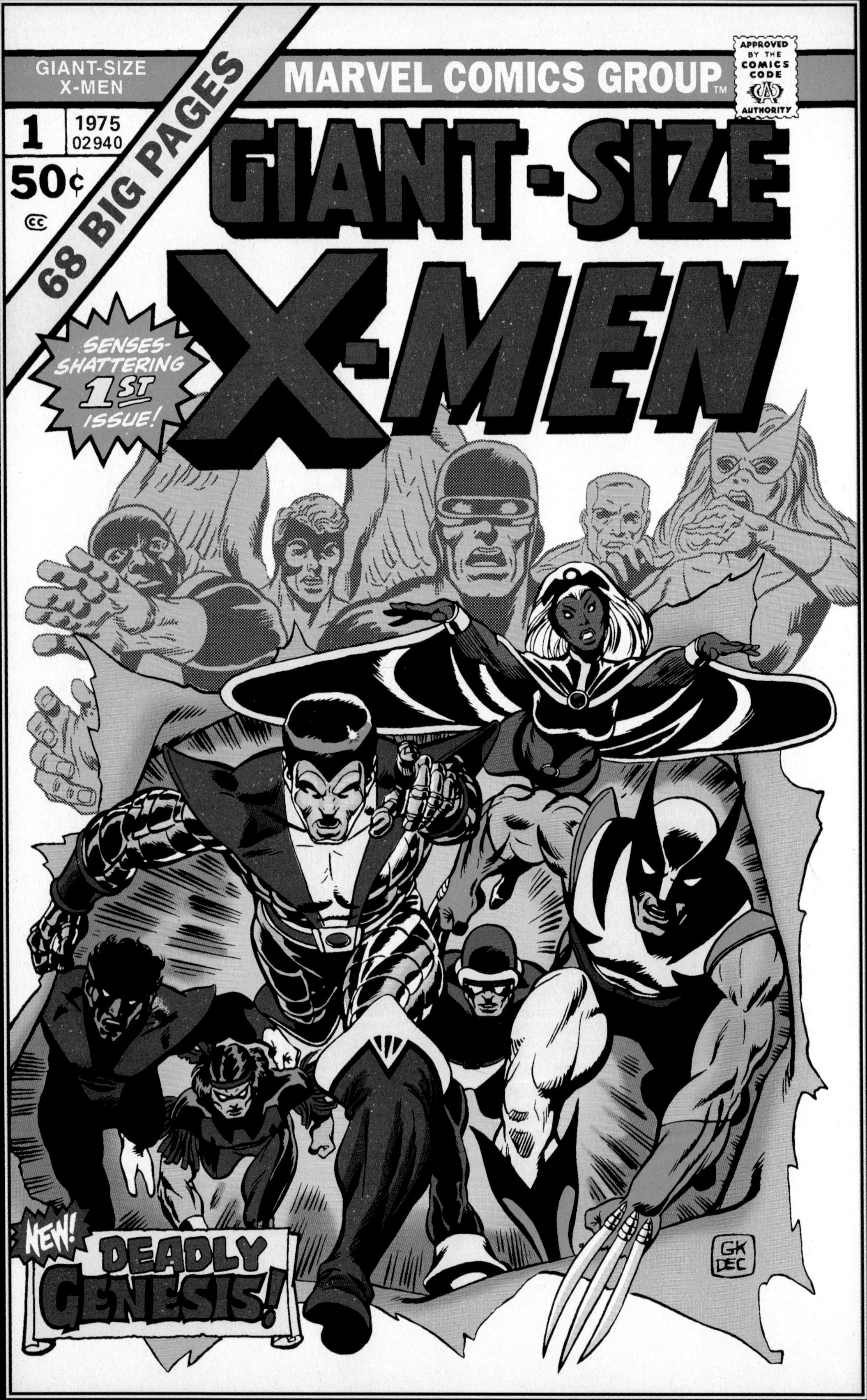
GIANT-SIZE
X-MEN
MARVEL COMICS GROUP
APPROVED BY THE COMICS CODE AUTHORITY
1
1975
02940
50¢
68 BIG PAGES
GIANT-SIZE
X-MEN
SENSES-SHATTERING 1ST ISSUE!
NEW!
DEADLY GENESIS!
GK
DEC

Stan Lee PRESENTS:

THE UNCANNY X-MEN!™

LEN WEIN WRITER EDITOR & DAVE COCKRUM ILLUSTRATOR | GLYNIS WEIN colorist | JOHN COSTANZA letterer
– CO-CREATORS –

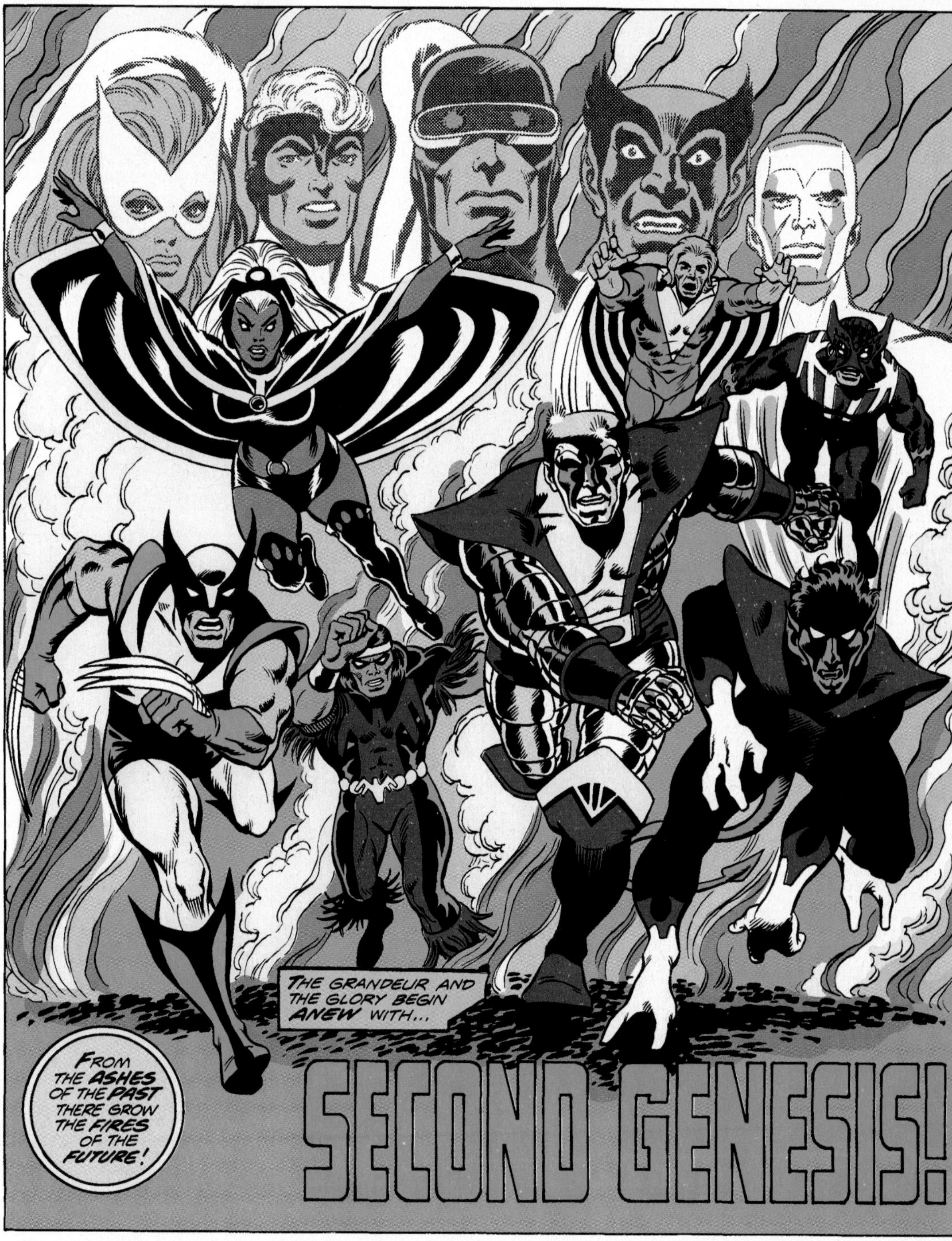

THE GRANDEUR AND THE GLORY BEGIN ANEW WITH...
FROM THE ASHES OF THE PAST THERE GROW THE FIRES OF THE FUTURE!
SECOND GENESIS!

WINZELDORF, GERMANY: NESTLED DEEP IN THE BAVARIAN ALPS, THIS TINY VILLAGE HAS HARDLY *CHANGED* OVER THE CENTURIES.

IN WINZELDORF, LIFE IS GENTLE, *PEACEFUL*--

--FOR *NOTHING* EVER HAPPENS HERE TO *DISTURB* THE DOMES-TIC...

...TRANQUILITY?

THIS WAY, MEN! THE *MONSTER* WENT *THIS* WAY!

MONSTER, IS IT?

THE *FOOLS!* IT IS *THEY* WHO ARE THE *MONSTERS*--

--THEY WITH THEIR MINDLESS *PREJUDICES!*

PERHAPS THINGS WOULD BE SIMPLER--*SAFER*--IF I HAD STAYED WITH *DER JAHRMARKT*--

--BUT THE LIFE OF A *CARNIVAL FREAK* IS NOT FOR ME--NOT FOR *KURT WAGNER!*

LET THEM *COME* IF THEY MUST--LET THEM TRY TO *KILL* ME--!

AT LEAST IF I *DIE,* IT WILL BE AS A *MAN!*

IRONICALLY, THE ASTONISH-ING *LEAP* ALONE LENDS *DOUBT* TO KURT WAGNER'S HUMANITY...

WE'VE *GOT* HIM NOW!

COME *DOWN,* MONSTER! COME DOWN--OR WE'LL *BURN* YOU DOWN!

...AND HIS *HIDEOUS HOWLING,* LIKE THAT OF A *BAYING BEAST, DENIES* IT COMPLETELY!

GO *AWAY,* YOU FOOLS! I HAVE DONE *NOTHING!*

BUT THE ONLY *RESPONSE* THE CORNERED MISFIT RE- CEIVES IS ONE HE HAD *HARDLY EXPECTED*...

THEY'RE UTTERLY *MAD!* THEIR THREAT WAS *SERIOUS!*

THEY'LL DESTROY THEIR ENTIRE *VILLAGE* TO MAKE CERTAIN THAT THEY DESTROY *ME!*

AND FOR WHAT *REASON?* I CAME AMONG THEM ONLY TO *LEARN* --

-- YET ALL I'VE LEARNED THUS FAR ARE THE WAYS OF BLIND, UNREASON- ING *VIOLENCE!*

WELL, IF THAT IS *ALL* THAT THOSE WHO DWELL IN THE *NORMAL* WORLD HAVE TO *TEACH* ME --

-- I WILL SHOW THEM THAT I LEARN MY LESSONS *WELL!*

THWAMM!

VERY WELL INDEED!

CHOK!

HOWLING WILDLY, KURT WAGNER PLUNGES THRU THE THICK OF THE *MOB* --

-- UNTIL THE SHEER *WEIGHT* OF ITS NUMBERS CARRIES HIM *DOWN!*

WE *HAVE* HIM! WE *HAVE* HIM!

QUICKLY -- BRING THE *STAKE!*

NOW, MONSTER-- WE WILL BE *RID* OF YOU!

NOW WE WILL...

STOP!

AND, REMARKABLY... THEY *DO!*

VAS--? TH-THEY'RE NOT *MOVING!*

WHAT HAS *HAPPENED* TO THEM?

I HAPPENED TO THEM, KURT WAGNER. MY NAME IS *CHARLES XAVIER!*

YOU DID... *THIS* TO THEM? BUT *HOW--? WHY?*

I HEARD YOU SAY YOU'D COME HERE TO *LEARN,* MY FRIEND. I AM A *TEACHER.* I RUN A *SCHOOL* FOR GIFTED YOUNGSTERS SUCH AS YOU.

A SCHOOL FOR *MUTANTS!*

MUTANT? YES... I HAVE *HEARD* THE WORD.

YOU ARE A MUTANT, KURT.

I CAN HELP YOU FIND YOUR TRUE *POTENTIAL.*

CAN YOU HELP ME TO BE *NORMAL?*

AFTER TONIGHT'S MISFORTUNE, KURT-- WOULD YOU TRULY *WANT* TO BE?

PERHAPS *NOT.* I WANT ONLY TO BE A *WHOLE* KURT WAGNER!

IF YOU CAN MAKE ME *THAT,* TEACHER... I WILL *GO* WITH YOU.

QUEBEC, CANADA: FEW PEOPLE KNOW OF THIS SECLUDED MILITARY INSTALLATION.

FEWER STILL KNOW OF ITS TRUE PURPOSE.

IT IS THE HOME BASE OF A SPECIAL GOVERNMENTAL AGENCY-- AND ITS VERY SPECIAL AGENT.

THE AGENT CIPHER-CODED WEAPON X...

THEY'RE WAITING FOR YOU IN THE CONFERENCE ROOM, SIR.

LET THEM WAIT. IT'S GOOD FOR THE SOUL.

...BUT BETTER KNOWN TO US AS-- THE WOLVERINE!

ALL RIGHT, GENTS-- I'M HERE!

NOW WHO'S THIS BIGWIG YOU WANT ME TO MEET?

I AM THE BIGWIG, WOLVERINE. PROFESSOR CHARLES XAVIER AT YOUR SERVICE.

AM I SUPPOSED TO BE IMPRESSED?

APPARENTLY THE TOP BRASS IS IMPRESSED, WOLVERINE. ALL I KNOW IS THAT THE PROFESSOR IS HERE TO MAKE YOU SOME SORT OF OFFER!

AN OFFER, EH? OKAY, PROF-- YOU'VE PIQUED MY CURIOSITY. WHAT'S THE DEAL?

I'LL COME STRAIGHT TO THE POINT THEN.

I KNOW OF YOUR RECENT BATTLE WITH THE HULK *-- AND, MOREOVER, I KNOW OF YOUR POWERS.

*IN HULK #181. --LEN.

YOU, MY FRIEND, ARE A MUTANT-- AND I HAVE NEED OF MUTANTS--

--DESPERATE NEED!

BUT WHAT ABOUT MY POSITION *HERE*--?

I'M OFFERING YOU A CHANCE TO BECOME A *FREE AGENT*--

--A CHANCE TO LEARN TO PUT YOUR POWERS TO THEIR *GREATEST* USE!

A CHANCE TO GET OUT FROM UNDER THE *RED TAPE* AND *RIGMAROLE*, EH?

ALL RIGHT, PROFESSOR -- YOU'VE *FOUND* YOUR MAN! *WHAT*--?

NOT SO *FAST*, FELLA!

THE GOVERNMENT HAS INVESTED A GREAT DEAL OF TIME AND MONEY TURNING YOU INTO WHAT YOU ARE *NOW!*

YOU TRY *WALKING OUT* ON US-- AND I'LL HAVE YOU *LOCKED UP!*

UH-HUH.

IT SEEMS YOU DIDN'T GET MY *MEANING*, FRIEND.

THIS IS STILL A *FREE COUNTRY*, ISN'T IT?

SNIKT!

SO I'M *RESIGNING* MY COMMISSION--

--EFFECTIVE *IMMEDIATELY!*

KRRIIIPP!

UNLESS, OF COURSE, YOU HAVE ANY FURTHER *OBJECTIONS?*

I DIDN'T *THINK* SO.

BELIEVE ME, MISTER-- YOU HAVEN'T HEARD THE *LAST* OF THIS!

ANY TIME YOU *WANT* ME, YOU KNOW WHERE TO COME *LOOKING!*

COME ON, PROF-- LET'S *GO!*

NASHVILLE, TENNESSEE: A VISITOR TO THE GRAND OL' OPRY FINDS HE HAS A VISITOR OF HIS OWN...

BEGORRA! 'TIS PROFESSOR X HIMSELF NOW.

BANSHEE-- I MUST TALK WITH YOU.

SHORTLY, IN THE BANSHEE'S SHABBY QUARTERS...

SO THAT'S THE STORY, IS IT? THEN SURE AN' I'LL HELP YE, PROFESSOR.

'TWILL BE NICE TO TREAD THE STRAIGHT AN' NARROW...FER A CHANGE.

KENYA, EAST AFRICA: ATOP A LONELY KNOLL, THERE STANDS A GREAT STONE PORTAL.

MEN COME TO IT IN HUMILITY, THEIR VOICES RAISED IN PRAISE AND SONG-- AND PRAYERFUL SUPPLICATION.

"ORORO, GREAT GODDESS OF THE STORM," THE VOICES CRY, "COME UNTO US AND EASE OUR BURDEN!"

AND WITH THE HOLLOW PEAL OF THUNDER AND THE MOAN OF LONELY WINDS --

-- THE STORM GODDESS COMES!

I AM HERE, MY CHILDREN. WHAT DO YOU WISH OF ME?

THERE IS DROUGHT UPON THE LAND, BLESSED ONE. OUR CROPS WITHER, OUR GRASSES PARCH.

TEN GOATS AND CHICKENS SHALL WE SLAY IN YOUR HONOR-- IF YOU WILL ONLY BRING US RAIN!

HER EYES ARE CRYSTAL BLUE, AND OLDER THAN TIME. THEY SPARKLE AS SHE ANSWERS...

SAVE YOUR BEASTS, MY CHILDREN, YOU NEED THEM MORE THAN I.

I WILL DO AS YOU PLEAD.

HER LIQUID EYES GROW DARK THEN-- AND THE SKY GROWS DARK AS WELL.

7

ONCE MORE, THE HOWLING WINDS COME UP--

--AND SWEEP THE STORM GODDESS *AWAY!*

SHE SOARS ALOFT LIKE AN EBON BIRD, LIGHTNING LANCING FROM HER FINGERTIPS, THE GLOW OF *LIFE* SHINING FULL UPON HER *FACE.*

SHE IS *HAPPY* HERE-- ONLY TRULY HAPPY *HERE* AMONG THE ELEMENTS--

--AND THE RAGING SKY, *TOUCHED* BY HER HAPPINESS...

...*WEEPS.*

WHEN THE STORM GODDESS RETURNS TO *EARTH* AT LAST, HER JOY IS SHARED BY *ALL.*

A MOST *IMPRESSIVE* DISPLAY, ORORO... TRULY *BEAUTIFUL.*

WH-WHO ARE *YOU?* WHAT *BUSINESS* HAVE YOU IN ORORO'S LAND?

I AM CALLED *XAVIER*--

--AND I HAVE COME TO MAKE YOU AN OFFER I *PRAY* YOU WILL NOT *REFUSE.*

AN...*OFFER?* WHAT HAVE *YOU* TO OFFER A *GODDESS?*

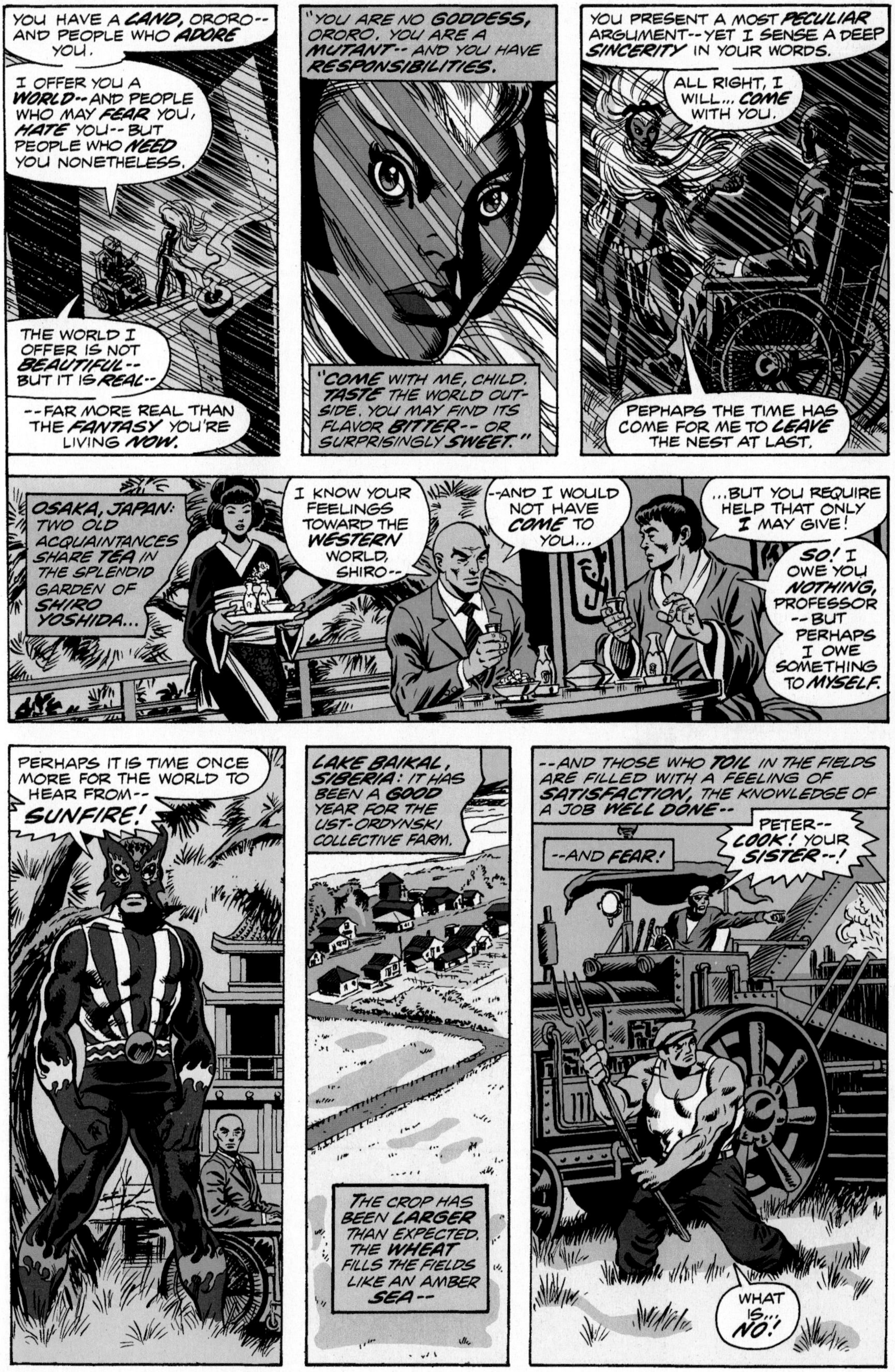

YOU HAVE A LAND, ORORO-- AND PEOPLE WHO ADORE YOU.
I OFFER YOU A WORLD--AND PEOPLE WHO MAY FEAR YOU, HATE YOU--BUT PEOPLE WHO NEED YOU NONETHELESS.
THE WORLD I OFFER IS NOT BEAUTIFUL--BUT IT IS REAL--
--FAR MORE REAL THAN THE FANTASY YOU'RE LIVING NOW.
"YOU ARE NO GODDESS, ORORO. YOU ARE A MUTANT--AND YOU HAVE RESPONSIBILITIES.
"COME WITH ME, CHILD. TASTE THE WORLD OUTSIDE. YOU MAY FIND ITS FLAVOR BITTER--OR SURPRISINGLY SWEET."
YOU PRESENT A MOST PECULIAR ARGUMENT--YET I SENSE A DEEP SINCERITY IN YOUR WORDS.
ALL RIGHT, I WILL... COME WITH YOU.
PEPHAPS THE TIME HAS COME FOR ME TO LEAVE THE NEST AT LAST.
OSAKA, JAPAN: TWO OLD ACQUAINTANCES SHARE TEA IN THE SPLENDID GARDEN OF SHIRO YOSHIDA...
I KNOW YOUR FEELINGS TOWARD THE WESTERN WORLD, SHIRO--
--AND I WOULD NOT HAVE COME TO YOU...
...BUT YOU REQUIRE HELP THAT ONLY I MAY GIVE!
SO! I OWE YOU NOTHING, PROFESSOR--BUT PERHAPS I OWE SOMETHING TO MYSELF.
PERHAPS IT IS TIME ONCE MORE FOR THE WORLD TO HEAR FROM--SUNFIRE!
LAKE BAIKAL, SIBERIA: IT HAS BEEN A GOOD YEAR FOR THE UST-ORDYNSKI COLLECTIVE FARM.
THE CROP HAS BEEN LARGER THAN EXPECTED. THE WHEAT FILLS THE FIELDS LIKE AN AMBER SEA--
--AND THOSE WHO TOIL IN THE FIELDS ARE FILLED WITH A FEELING OF SATISFACTION, THE KNOWLEDGE OF A JOB WELL DONE--
--AND FEAR!
PETER--LOOK! YOUR SISTER--!
WHAT IS...NO!

PETER RASPUTIN LOOKS UP FROM HIS WORK--AND HIS EYES GROW WIDE WITH *HORROR!*

HE DISCERNS IT ALL IN AN INSTANT; THE RUNAWAY *TRACTOR*-- THE *CHILD* PLAYING BLINDLY IN ITS PATH--

--AND, WITHOUT HESITATION, PETER RASPUTIN IS *RUNNING*, LEGS PUMPING, HEART POUNDING--

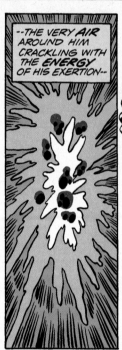

--THE VERY *AIR* AROUND HIM CRACKLING WITH THE *ENERGY* OF HIS EXERTION--

--ENERGY *RELEASED* IN A MOST *ASTONISHING* MANNER!

THE ARMORED MA-CHINE BEARS RELENT-LESSLY DOWN UPON THE UNWITTING CHILD..

--AS AN ARMORED *COLOSSUS* SNATCHES HER FROM ITS PATH!

THERE IS NO *TIME* FOR PETER RASPUTIN TO MOVE *OUT* OF HARM'S WAY--

--THUS HE STANDS HIS *GROUND* AS THE RAMPANT TRACTOR PLUNGES *TOWARD* HIM --

--AND HE WONDERS HOW HIS POOR NEIGHBORS WILL EVER *AFFORD* TO BUY ANOTHER!

KWA-THOOM!

THAT, THOUGH, IS A WORRY FOR *ANOTHER* DAY.

THIS DAY WILL BE FILLED WITH PROBLEMS *ENOUGH.*

PETER RASPUTIN, I WISH TO *TALK* TO YOU.

THAT *VOICE* IN MY *HEAD--!* WHO--?

BY NOW, WE *KNOW* THE ANSWER TO THAT QUESTION--

--SO MOMENTS *LATER...*

YOU WANT ME TO GO WITH YOU... TO *AMERICA?*

BUT IF I POSSESS SUCH *POWER* AS YOU SAY-- DOES IT NOT BELONG TO THE *STATE?*

POWER SUCH AS YOURS BELONGS TO THE *WORLD,* PETER-- TO BE USED FOR THE GOOD OF *ALL.*

AND BELIEVE ME-- YOUR POWERS ARE *NEEDED!*

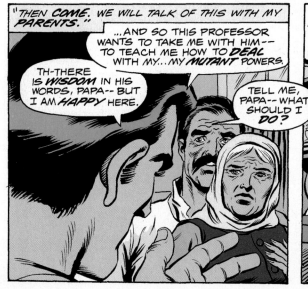

"THEN *COME.* WE WILL TALK OF THIS WITH MY *PARENTS.*"

...AND SO THIS PROFESSOR WANTS TO TAKE ME WITH HIM-- TO TEACH ME HOW TO *DEAL* WITH MY... MY *MUTANT* POWERS.

TH-THERE IS *WISDOM* IN HIS WORDS, PAPA-- BUT I AM *HAPPY* HERE.

TELL ME, PAPA-- WHAT SHOULD I *DO?*

DO AS YOUR *HEART* TELLS YOU, MY SON, IT WILL NOT *BETRAY* YOU.

MY HEART TELLS ME TO *STAY,* PAPA--

--BUT MY *CONSCIENCE* TELLS ME OTHERWISE.

I *MUST* GO, PAPA.

THEN IT IS *RIGHT* THAT YOU *DO.*

DOSVIDANYA, PETER, OUR *LOVE* GOES WITH YOU.

DO NOT *WORRY*, MAMA--I WILL *WRITE* YOU.

GOOD-BYE, PAPA--I WILL MAKE YOU *PROUD.*

WE ARE *ALREADY* PROUD... MY SON.

CAMP VERDE, ARIZONA: JOHN PROUDSTAR DOES NOT *LIKE* THE RESERVATION. HE DOES NOT LIKE TO WATCH THE OLD ONES, SITTING SLUMPED AGAINST THEIR DOORSTEPS, DREAMING DREAMS OF *GLORY* LONG GONE.

JOHN PROUDSTAR IS AN *APACHE*--AND HE IS *ASHAMED* OF HIS PEOPLE.

THE APACHE WERE MEANT TO BE HUNTERS, WARRIORS-- NOT SAD-EYED SIMPERING *SQUAWS.*

THEY WERE MEANT TO RUN *FREE* THRU THE CRISP PLAINS GRASSES, THE *WIND* BLOWING WILDLY THRU THEIR HAIR.

ONCE NOTHING COULD STAND BEFORE THE APACHE.

THE BISON THAT COVERED THESE PLAINS FELL LIKE *RAIN* BEFORE APACHE *SKILL,* APACHE *BRAVERY*--

--BUT NEVER DID ANY BISON FALL LIKE-- *THIS!*

THERE, HORNED ONE-- DO YOU *SEE?*

THERE IS STILL A *MAN* AMONG THE APACHE!

THOOM!

AND SUCH A MAN HAVE I COME *LOOKING* FOR, JOHN PROUDSTAR.

HUH??

NOW HOW IN BLAZES DID A *CRIPPLE* GET WAY OUT *HERE*? NOT THAT IT *MATTERS* MUCH.

YOU'VE GOT FIVE SECONDS TO *VAMOOSE*, WHITE-EYES! I DON'T *WANT* COMPANY--ESPE-CIALLY *YOURS*!

DON'T BE TOO *HASTY*, MY YOUNG FRIEND.

I'VE COME TO HELP YOU *FULFILL* YOUR DREAM-- TO GIVE *PRIDE* BACK TO YOUR PEOPLE.

YOU ARE *SPECIAL*, JOHN PROUDSTAR. YOU ARE A *MUTANT*.

AND YOU ARE *NEEDED*.

AND *YOU* CAN STUFF A *CACTUS*, CUSTER!

THE WHITE MAN NEEDS *ME*? THAT'S *TOUGH*!

I OWE HIM NOTHING BUT THE *GRIEF* HE'S GIVEN MY PEOPLE!

NOW *BEAT* IT!

I OFFER YOU A CHANCE TO HELP THE *WORLD*-- AND YOU TURN YOUR *BACK* ON ME?

THEN PERHAPS WHAT THEY SAY IS *TRUE*!

PERHAPS THE APACHE *ARE* ALL FRIGHTENED SELFISH *CHILDREN*!

HO-KAY... THAT *DOES* IT!

AIN'T *NOBODY* THAT CALLS ME A *COWARD*, MISTER!

I'M AS GOOD AS THE *NEXT* GUY-- HELL, I'M *BETTER*!

YOU GIVE ME A CHANCE-- I'LL *PROVE* IT!

AND YOU WILL *HAVE* YOUR CHANCE, JOHN. I *PROMISE* YOU THAT.

BUT WILL *YOU*-- WILL *ANY* OF MY NEW *X-MEN* BE EQUAL TO THE TASK THAT LIES BEFORE YOU?

OR WILL YOU CARRY THE *WORLD* DOWN INTO *RUIN*?

CHAPTER II "...AND WHEN THERE WAS ONE!"

WESTCHESTER, NEW YORK: THE SCHOOL HAD SEEMED A LATTER-DAY *TOWER OF BABEL* AT FIRST-- BUT A TELEPATHIC *CRASH COURSE* IN THE ENGLISH LANGUAGE HAD CLOSED THE *COMMUNICATION GAP* IN MERE MINUTES.

NOW PROFESSOR CHARLES XAVIER SITS, SOMBERLY *STUDYING* HIS COLORFULLY-COSTUMED *HOUSE-GUESTS*--

--AND WHATEVER *THOUGHTS* HE MIGHT HAVE AT THIS POINT ARE *HIS* ALONE TO KNOW.

IN ALL MY LIFE, SUCH *CLOTHING* AS THIS I HAVE NEVER *SEEN!*

THE COSTUME IS *BEAUTIFUL,* AND THE FIT--*PER-FECT!* BUT HOW DID YOU...?

THE UNIFORMS ARE CONSTRUCTED FROM *UNSTABLE MOLECULES,* WHICH *ADJUST* THEMSELVES WHERE NECESSARY.

I OBTAINED THEM FROM A MAN NAMED *REED RICHARDS,* AND I'M CERTAIN YOU'LL LEARN *MORE* OF HIM AND HIS FRIENDS LATER.

BUT RIGHT *NOW...*

RIGHT *NOW* YOU WILL TELL US WHY YOU *DRAGGED* US HERE, PROFESSOR!

I, FOR ONE, AM SWIFTLY LOSING MY *PATIENCE!*

SUNFIRE, *PLEASE*--

--IT WAS NOT MY INTENTION TO *WASTE* YOUR TIME.

I'VE MERELY AWAITED THE *ARRIVAL* OF ONE WHO CAN *EXPLAIN* THE SITUATION FAR *BETTER* THAN I.

MY FRIENDS, ALLOW ME TO PRESENT *SCOTT SUMMERS*--

--THE MAN CALLED *CYCLOPS!*

HE WILL FILL YOU IN ON THE *DETAILS.*

THE "*DETAILS*", PEOPLE, ARE DEPRESSINGLY *SIMPLE!*

YOU HAVE BEEN CALLED HERE BECAUSE-- *THE X-MEN HAVE DISAPPEARED!*

YOU SEVEN ARE OUR *ONLY* HOPE OF... BUT I'M GETTING *AHEAD* OF MYSELF.

COME ON. I MAY AS WELL *SHOW* YOU WHERE IT ALL *BEGAN!*

THIS IS *CEREBRO*, OUR SPECIALLY-DESIGNED *MUTANT-DETECTOR!*

IT'S THRU *THIS* MECHANISM THAT WE DISCOVERED ALL OF *YOU*--

--AND *LOST* MY CLOSEST *FRIENDS!*

15

WE'D ALL ANSWERED THE *SIGNAL-ALARM* WITHIN SECONDS: THE PROFESSOR, ANGEL, ICEMAN, MARVEL GIRL, LORNA DANE, MY BROTHER HAVOK, AND MYSELF...

WHAT *IS* IT, SIR? CEREBRO HAS NEVER REACTED SO *VIOLENTLY* BEFORE.

WHAT IT *IS*, SCOTT, IS-- *INCREDIBLE!*

APPARENTLY, CEREBRO HAS DETECTED A *NEW* MUTANT ON THE ISLAND OF *KRAKOA* IN THE SOUTH PACIFIC--

--A MUTANT SO *POWERFUL* AS TO *DEFY* CLASSIFICA-TION!

IT SEEMS YOU ALL HAVE *WORK* TO DO, SCOTT...

FIND THAT MUTANT-- *QUICKLY*-- BEFORE SOMEONE *ELSE* FINDS HIM *FIRST!*

YOU HEARD THE PROFESSOR, X-MEN-- IT'S *TRAVELIN' TIME!*

"SHORTLY AFTER, OUR SPECIALLY-DESIGNED *STRATO-JET* ARCED HIGH OVER THE PATCHWORK COUNTRY-SIDE--

"--STREAKING TOWARDS AN UNKNOWN *CONFRON-TATION*--

"--BUT AT *THAT* MOMENT, OUR MINDS WERE ON *OTHER* THINGS.

WISH WE COULD'VE CONTACTED THE *BEAST!* HANK McCOY'S DEXTEROUS DIGITS MIGHT BE--EH--*HANDY* ON A JOB LIKE THIS.

HANK *GRADUATED* THE X-MEN, JEAN. IF HE HASN'T GOT *TIME* FOR US NOW, THAT'S *HIS* BUSINESS.

16

RIGHT NOW WE'VE GOT BUSINESS OF OUR *OWN* TO WORRY ABOUT.

THAT'S *KRAKOA* DEAD AHEAD!

YEECH--YOU'D NEED A SUPER-POWER JUST TO *SURVIVE* ON THAT DESOLATE MUD-BAR.

ENOUGH *BANTER!* STRAP IN FOR *LANDING!*

"WE TOUCHED DOWN MOMENTS LATER, OUR *VTOL* * JETS LOWERING US TO EARTH AS GENTLY AS AN INFANT IS LOWERED INTO ITS CRADLE--

*VERTICAL TAKE-OFF AND LANDING. --ENCYCLOPEDIC LEN.

"--BUT WE WERE *NOT* INFANTS--AND THIS WAS DEFINITELY NO *CHILD'S GAME!*

I THINK WE TOOK THE *WRONG* BUS, GANG. THIS PLACE SURE DOESN'T LOOK LIKE *CLEVELAND.*

ALL THE *INSECTS* IN THE AIR-- THE OVERGROWN *JUNGLE*--!

ON SECOND THOUGHT, MAYBE THIS *IS* CLEVELAND.

I TOLD YOU *BEFORE,* ICEMAN--*SHELVE* THE SNAPPY PATTER!

WE HAVE A *DIFFICULT* JOB AHEAD OF US, FINDING THAT NEW *MUTANT*--!

MAYBE AN *IMPOSSIBLE* ONE, CYKE--WHEN YOU CONSIDER WE HAVE *NO* IDEA WHAT WE'RE *LOOKING* FOR!

POINT *TAKEN,* ANGEL. LET'S *FAN OUT* AND SEE IF...

BEHIND US-- L-LOOK! IT'S...IT'S...

QUICK, EVERYBODY-- *SCATTER!*

GET *MOVING* BEFORE WE...

"I'M ASHAMED TO SAY I NEVER EVEN *SAW* WHAT *HIT* US!

"MY HEAD WAS A THROBBING MASS OF PAIN AND SCREAMING IMAGES WHEN I STRUGGLED *AWAKE* LORD KNOWS HOW LONG AFTERWARD.

"I DIDN'T REALIZE *WHERE* I WAS, NOR DID I REALLY *CARE*. ALL THAT *CONCERNED* ME WAS...

MY *FRIENDS!* WHAT HAPPENED TO THE OTHER *X-MEN?*

"AND *WORSE*, WHAT HAD HAPPENED TO *ME?*

MY *EYES!* DEAR HEAVEN, MY *EYES--!!*

THEY'RE *UNCOVERED!* THEY'RE...

THEY'RE... NORMAL... *POWERLESS!*

HOWEVER HARD I TRY, I *CAN'T* PROJECT MY *OPTIC BLASTS!*

DID YOU HEAR ME, WORLD? I CAN'T... *HUH?*

"THAT'S WHEN I DISCOVERED I WAS BACK ON THE *STRATO-JET*--

"--AND I *WASN'T* IN CONTROL!

AUTOMATIC PILOT IS *JAMMED!* CAN'T TURN THIS CRATE BACK TO THE *ISLAND*--!

"I SPENT THE NEXT FIVE MINUTES POUNDING FUTILELY ON THE *CONTROL PANEL*, THEN RESIGNED MYSELF TO THE SITUATION AND SAT BACK IN MY SEAT.

"I WASN'T *HAPPY* BY THE TIME I REACHED *WESTCHESTER*--

SLAMM!

PROFESSOR --I'M *BACK!*

CYCLOPS!? WHAT--? WH-WHERE ARE THE *OTHERS?*

"--NOT *HAPPY* AT ALL!

"THE PROFESSOR WAS NO HAPPIER THAN *I* AFTER I *TOLD* HIM...

DO YOU MEAN TO TELL ME THE OTHER X-MEN ARE *STILL* ON THAT ISLAND--

--AND YOU HAVE NO IDEA WHAT'S *HAPPENED* TO THEM?

I KNOW *NOTHING*, PROFESSOR-- EXCEPT THAT *SOMETHING* ON KRAKOA *CURED* MY EYES AND DEPOSITED ME BACK IN THAT...

HUH? WHAT IS IT, PROFESSOR? WHY ARE YOU *LOOKING* AT ME LIKE THAT?

YOUR *EYES,* SCOTT-- THEY'RE *GLOWING* AGAIN--?

QUICKLY, SCOTT-- GRAB SOME *PROTECTIVE* LENSES! YOUR OPTIC POWERS HAVE *RETURNED!*

NO-- NOT *AGAIN!* DON'T LET IT HAPPEN *AGAIN!*

"BUT I SHOULD HAVE KNOWN BETTER THAN TO EVEN *ASK!*"

"THE OPTIC ENERGIES THAT HAD *CURSED* ME SINCE MY EARLY TEENS WERE *BACK* AGAIN--"

"--WITH A *VENGEANCE!*"

"AND THIS TIME THEY WERE SO *STRONG,* EVEN I COULD NOT CONTROL THEM! "

CROOM!

SKAKK!

THE PROFESSOR *MODIFIED* ONE OF MY OLD VISORS TO CONTAIN MY INCREASED POWER--

--THEN LEFT ME HERE TO *RETRAIN* MYSELF WHILE HE WENT IN SEARCH OF *YOU!*

AND HE *FOUND* US! SO *NOW* WHAT?

SO NOW WE GO *BACK* TO KRAKOA TO FIND THE ORIGINAL X-MEN--

--AND THE *MUTANT* THAT DEFEATED US!

INCORRECT, CYCLOPS! NOW *YOU* GO BACK TO KRAKOA-- NOT *I!*

I WILL HAVE NO *PART* IN THIS FOOL'S ERRAND!

WHAT--?

I DON'T *UNDERSTAND*, SUNFIRE-- WE OFFER YOU A CHANCE TO *HELP* YOUR FELLOW MUTANTS AND...

I DO NOT EVEN *LIKE* MY FELLOW MUTANTS, CYCLOPS!

I CERTAINLY WILL NOT RISK MY *LIFE* TO HELP THEM!

I FEEL SORRY FOR YOU, SUNFIRE-- BUT I DON'T HAVE TIME TO WASTE *ARGUING*!

THE *REST* OF US HAVE A JOB TO DO-- AND WE'RE GOING TO DO IT!

MOMENTS LATER, THE STRATO-JET STREAKS SKYNARD--AND THERE IS ONLY ONE EMPTY SEAT ON BOARD...

IT SEEMS I HAVE HAD MY FIRST TASTE OF *MUTANT CAMARAD-ERIE*-- AND I MUST SAY, CYCLOPS--

-- I DID NOT *LIKE* IT!

MAYBE YOU DIDN'T *NOTICE*, SISTER-- BUT THIS GROUP AIN'T EXACTLY A *MUTUAL ADMIRATION SOCIETY!*

"WE'RE ALL INVOLVED IN THIS *FIASCO* FOR OUR *OWN* REASONS, GIRLY-- AN' PATTING EACH OTHER ON THE BACK AIN'T ONE OF... *HUH*?"

"HEY, ONE-EYE-- THERE'S SOMETHING *FOLLOWIN'* US!"

"I *SEE* IT, GERONIMO! IT'S..."

"WELL, I'LL BE JIGGERED, ONE-EYE-- THE *JAP*!"

ARE YOU GOING TO *OPEN* THE HATCH, CYCLOPS--

OR DO YOU EXPECT ME TO *FLY* ALL THE WAY TO KRAKOA BY *MYSELF*?

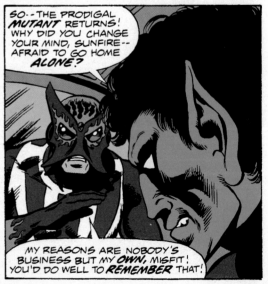

SO-- THE PRODIGAL *MUTANT* RETURNS! WHY DID YOU CHANGE YOUR MIND, SUNFIRE-- AFRAID TO GO HOME *ALONE*?

MY REASONS ARE NOBODY'S BUSINESS BUT MY *OWN*, MISFIT! YOU'D DO WELL TO *REMEMBER* THAT!

CHAPTER II. ASSAULT FORCE!

AN *HOUR* PASSES -- TWO HOURS -- UNTIL THE FORSAKEN ATOLL CALLED *KRAKOA* LOOMS FULL BEFORE THE VIEWPORTS...

SO THAT'S WHERE YOU *MISLAID* YOUR PARTNERS, HUH?

CAN'T SAY MUCH FOR YOUR TASTE IN *VACATION SPOTS*, SUMMERS!

"AND *I* CAN'T SAY MUCH FOR *YOUR* SENSE OF HUMOR, WOLVERINE! NOR *YOURS*, THUNDERBIRD!"

"THE NAME IS *PROUDSTAR*, ONE-EYE!"

"NOT *ANYMORE!* THE PROFESSOR HAS GIVEN YOU ALL *CODE-NAMES*, GROUP! YOU MIGHT AS WELL START GETTING *USED* TO THEM!"

"NOW THE *ASSAULT TEAMS* WILL BE AS FOLLOWS:"

"*STORM*, YOU AND *COLOSSUS* WILL COME IN FROM THE *NORTH!*"

"*BANSHEE* AND THE *WOLVERINE* WILL MOVE ACROSS FROM THE *EAST!*"

'TIS A PLEASURE TA BE *WORKIN'* WITH YE, LADDY.

WHOOPEE.

"*SUNFIRE* AND THE *NIGHTCRAWLER* WILL START SEARCHING FROM THE *SOUTH!*"

NO -- NOT *HIM!*

I DID NOT *HEAR* CYCLOPS GIVING YOU A *CHOICE*, MAN.

THUNDERBIRD AND I WILL HANDLE THE *WEST* END OF THE ISLAND!

NOW GET *READY*, SOUTH TEAM -- YOUR *DROP* IS COMING UP!

I DON'T MUCH LIKE THE *TONE* OF YOUR VOICE, CYCLOPS!

"WE CAN ARGUE ABOUT IT WHEN YOU GET *BACK!* NOW -- GO!"

"*EAST TEAM* -- GO!"

CRIPES! DO YOU HAVE TO *SCREECH* LIKE THAT?

"*NORTH TEAM* --"

THAT IS *OUR* SIGNAL, STORM!

COLOSSUS -- NO!

YOU *FOOL*-- YOU CANNOT *FLY*!

OF *COURSE* NOT-- BUT I CAN *LAND* WITH THE *BEST* OF THEM!

THE CHICK AND THE *RUSSKIE* HAVE *LANDED*-- AND IT LOOKS LIKE THEY'RE *ARGUING*--

--WHICH IS ABOUT *PAR* FOR THIS OUTFIT!

WE'RE GOING DOWN *NEXT*, THUNDERBIRD-- *STRAP IN*!

ONCE MORE, THE STRATO-JET'S *VTOL* SYSTEM LOWERS IT TO EARTH-- AND THOUGH HE TRIES, THE MAN CALLED *CYCLOPS* CANNOT SUP-PRESS A *SHUDDER*.

HOW MANY *MORE* WILL WE LOSE *THIS* TIME, HE WONDERS MORBIDLY. WILL I EVEN *LIVE* LONG ENOUGH TO FIND OUT?

BUT HE'S A *PROFESSIONAL*, THIS STAR-CROSSED MUTANT. THE *QUESTIONS* FOLLOW HIM AS HE STEPS OUT UPON THE LANDSCAPE--

--BUT HE LEAVES HIS *FEAR* IN THE SHIP.

EAST IS *THAT* WAY, THUNDERBIRD-- AND THE SOONER WE GET *STARTED*, THE SOONER WE'LL *GET* THERE!

YES *SIR*, GENERAL ONE-EYE *SIR*! I JUST HOPE YOU'RE NOT LEADING ME INTO ANOTHER *LITTLE BIG HORN*!

IT'D BE JUST MY LUCK TO BE THE FIRST *INDIAN* TO GET *MASSA-CREED* BY...

HOLD IT! I LEFT THE MINI-CEREBRO UNIT BACK IN... *HUH*?

I DON'T *BELIEVE* IT!

DON'T BELIEVE *WHAT*?

THE STRATO-JET--!

IT'S-- *GONE*!

22

BUT THAT'S *IMPOSSIBLE!* THE GROUND DOESN'T JUST OPEN UP AND *SWALLOW* A JET PLANE *WHOLE--!*

ABSOLUTELY RIGHT!

AND STRANGE *TEMPLES* DON'T SUDDENLY SPRING UP OUT OF *NOWHERE--*

"--BUT ONE *HAS!*"

HUH? THAT JOINT WASN'T THERE WHEN WE *LANDED!*

EXACTLY! AND SINCE IT SEEMS AS GOOD A SPOT AS ANY TO START *SEARCH-ING--*

LET'S GO!

GRUMBLING IN ANNOYANCE, THE MUTANT NOW RELUCTANT-LY CALLED THUNDERBIRD FOLLOWS HIS *CYCLOPEAN* COMPANION INTO THE VER-DANT *UNDER-BRUSH.*

JOHN PROUD-STAR HAS NEVER MUCH *LIKED* THE JUNGLE--

--AND APPARENT-LY, THE FEELING IS *MUTUAL!*

THE VINES-- THEY'RE *ALIVE--!!*

A CONDITION WE WON'T *SHARE* MUCH LONGER--

--UNLESS WE *DO* SOMETHING-- *FAST!*

GOT ANY *SUGGESTIONS* IN PARTICULAR, ONE-EYE?

SKRAK

ZZAZZH

NOT *REALLY,* THUNDER-BIRD!

FOR A *BEGINNER,* YOU'RE DOING PRETTY WELL ON YOUR *OWN!*

WITHIN MOMENTS, THE TWO YOUNG X-MEN HAVE LEFT THE STRANGLING *CREEPER* VINES FAR BEHIND THEM-- --AND IT IS NOT TERRIBLY *DIFFICULT* TO DETERMINE *WHICH* WAY THEY HAVE *GONE.*

FOURTEEN MINUTES LATER...

WELL, *WE'VE* MADE IT IN *REASONABLE* SHAPE!

I WONDER HOW THE *OTHERS* ARE FARING?

23

WELL, MINUTES EARLIER ON THE ISLAND'S *NORTH* SIDE...

ODD-- I DO NOT RECALL SEEING THAT *TEMPLE* BEFORE.

COME, COLOSSUS-- LET US BEGIN OUR SEARCH *THERE!*

WHATEVER YOU *SAY,* ORORO. YOU ARE SO *UNLIKE* THE GIRLS IN MY... *EH?* THAT *SOUND...?*

AN AVA-LANCHE!

QUICKLY, COLOSSUS-- PERHAPS WE CAN STILL *OUTRUN* IT!

He может быть! THIS LANDSLIDE CANNOT *BE* OUTRUN, ORORO!

IT HAS *CHANGED* ITS DIRECTION TO *FOLLOW* US!

THOSE MAD *ROCKS* CAN NO LONGER *HURT* ME, ORORO--

THEN IF WE CANNOT *AVOID* A CONFRONTATION, WE MUST STAND OUR GROUND-- AND *DEFEND* OURSELVES!

KHUMP!

--BUT FOR THREATENING *YOU,* I SHALL *CRUSH* THEM!

"I AM NO LONGER *THREAT-ENED.*"

I *THANK* YOU, PETER-- BUT THERE IS *NO* NEED TO *PROTECT* ME!

AND SHORTLY...

STORM... COLOSSUS... GLAD YOU MADE IT IN *ONE* PIECE.

BARELY, CYCLOPS ...JUST *BARELY.* I ONLY HOPE THE *OTHERS* ARRIVE SAFELY AS WELL.

24

AND ON THE ISLAND'S *EAST* SIDE...

SAINTS, LADDY--WILL YE LOOK AT THE *SIZE* O' THEM BEASTIES!

LOOKS LIKE THE LOCAL *WELCOMING* COMMITTEE, IRISH--

--BUT A *HANDSHAKE* FROM ONE OF THEM CAN BE *FATAL*!

GOOD THING THEN THEY'RE NOT THE *ONLY* ONES AROUND HERE WITH BIG, SHARP *CLAWS*, ISN'T IT?

THE WOLVERINE HAS *CLAWS* OF HIS *OWN*--

--AND, IRISH, HE LIKES TO *USE* THEM!

SKRAK

HEY--ARE YOU JUST GOING TO STAND AROUND *GAWKING*, IRISH--OR ARE YOU GOING TO *HELP* ME?

BUT THE ERIN-BORN MUTANT IS ALREADY *ALOFT*--AND THOUGH HIS *SONIC SCREAM* IS NOT NEARLY SO *FLAMBOYANT* AS HIS COMPANION'S SLASHING *TALONS*--

--IT IS NONETHELESS EQUALLY *EFFECTIVE*!

EEEEEE

SPRAKT!

THE BATTLE IS *VIOLENT*--BUT *BRIEF*!

WELL, LADDY-- SURE'N IT LOOKS LIKE WE'VE *DONE* FER THE BEASTIES! WE'D BEST BE GETTIN' ON TO THAT *TEMPLE* WE SPIED A TOUCH BACK.

YEAH. *SURE*. THERE'S NOTHING TO KEEP US *HERE*... ANY *MORE*.

AND *SOON*...

FAITH! 'TIS GOOD T' BE *SEEIN'* YE ALL AGAIN. 'TWAS A MOMENT THERE I HAD ME *DOUBTS*.

AND YOU WERE *NOT ALONE*.

WHILE ON THE ISLAND'S *SOUTH SIDE*...

THESE *BIRDS* SEEM DETERMINED TO *PREVENT* US FROM REACHING THAT STRANGE *TEMPLE* AHEAD, SUNFIRE!

A REMARKABLE *OBSERVATION*, MISFIT! YOU HAVE A POSITIVE *TALENT* FOR STATING THE *OBVIOUS!*

SPREEE

YOUR *SARCASM* IS UNCALLED FOR, SUNFIRE! I BEGIN TO THINK THE *MUTANT* COMMUNITY IS NO MORE *HOSPITABLE* THAN THE HUMAN... *EH?*

THAT *BIRD*--ABOUT TO *RAKE* ME WITH ITS *TALONS*--!

A BURST OF *FLAME*-- THE STENCH OF *BRIMSTONE*-- AND THE MUTANT CALLED *NIGHTCRAWLER*--

--IS SUDDENLY *ELSEWHERE!*

HIS *LAUGH* IS LITTLE MORE THAN A HIDEOUS *HOWL!*

YOUR *MANNER* SEEMS MUCH LIKE THAT OF THE *BEASTS* YOU SO *RESEMBLE*, MISFIT!

HOW *APPROPRIATE!*

BUT *SUNFIRE* HAS NO NEED OF SUCH *PARLOR TRICKS* AS YOURS!

I MUCH PREFER THE *DIRECT* APPROACH!

YOUR "*DIRECT* APPROACH," IT APPEARS, HAS LEFT US WITHOUT *OPPONENTS*, SUNFIRE!

THEN I SUGGEST WE GET ON TO THAT *TEMPLE*, MISFIT... ASSUMING, OF COURSE, YOU CAN *KEEP UP* WITH ME!

AND FINALLY...

CYCLOPS! HAVE WE KEPT YOU *WAITING* LONG?

NOT AT *ALL!* JUST GOT HERE *OURSELVES!*

HMMM-- IT APPEARS WE'RE GOING TO HAVE TO *EARN* THE DUBIOUS PRIVILEGE OF GETTING IN THERE!

DOOR'S SEALED *TIGHT*-- AND IT'S ABOUT A *FOOT THICK!*

SUNFIRE... STORM... COLOSSUS... LOOKS LIKE THE TIME HAS COME FOR YOUR FIRST *PRACTICAL LESSON* IN THE ART OF BEING AN *X-MAN!*

AND SINCE WE ARE *ALL* FINALLY HERE, I THINK IT'S ABOUT TIME WE FOUND OUT WHAT'S *INSIDE* THIS TUMBLEDOWN *TEMPLE!*

I'VE GOT A GUT FEELING SOMEONE *LURED* US HERE FOR PRECISELY THAT *PURPOSE*--

--AND I'D HATE TO *DISAPPOINT* THEM *NOW!*

THE LESSON IS ENTITLED *"BREAKING AND ENTERING"*-- AND ALTHOUGH THE NEOPHYTE X-MEN LACK THE *FINESSE* OF THEIR PREDECESSORS--

KWA ROOM!

--THEY CERTAINLY GET AN *'A'* FOR *EFFORT!*

STILL SLIGHTLY *ASTONISHED* BY THEIR OWN ABILITIES, THE YOUNG MUTANTS STEP CAUTIOUSLY INTO THE STYGIAN *DARKNESS*--

OH...MY...GOD...

--AND FIND THEIR *HEARTS* SWELLING HEAVY IN THEIR *THROATS!*

OH, MY *DEAR* GOD-- IT'S TH-THE OTHER *X-MEN*--!

AND SOMETHING SEEMS TO BE... *FEEDING* ON THEM!

WELL, DON'T JUST STAND THERE *STARING* AT THEM--!

IN PITY'S NAME-- *SET THEM FREE!*

CRIPES! WHAT'S GOING ON? AS SOON AS WE PULLED THESE *TUBES* LOOSE--

--THE PLACE STARTED SHAKING ITSELF *APART!*

QUICKLY THEN-- *CARRY* WHOEVER IS *CLOSEST* TO YOU--

--AND LET'S GET *OUT* OF HERE BEFORE THIS TEMPLE COMES *DOWN* AROUND OUR EARS!

KROOM!

AND EVEN AS THE ARCANE TEMPLE TOPPLES INTO RUIN BEHIND THEM...

HEY-- THEY'RE COMING AROUND! MUST NOT HAVE BEEN AS BAD AS...

WHY, CYCLOPS? WHY DID YOU COME *BACK* FOR US?

HUH?

YOU *FOOL*-- DON'T YOU *UNDERSTAND?*

IT *WANTED* YOU TO COME BACK--AND BRING *OTHERS* WITH YOU! IT WAS ALL A *TRAP*-- AND NOW IT'S--

--*TOO LATE!*

THE *GROUND*-- REARING *UP* AROUND THE FALLEN *TEMPLE*--!?!

OF *COURSE!* HAVEN'T YOU REALIZED *YET?*

WE CAME TO THIS ISLAND TO LOOK FOR A *MUTANT*...

"--BUT THE MUTANT IS THE ISLAND ITSELF!"

KKRRAWRR

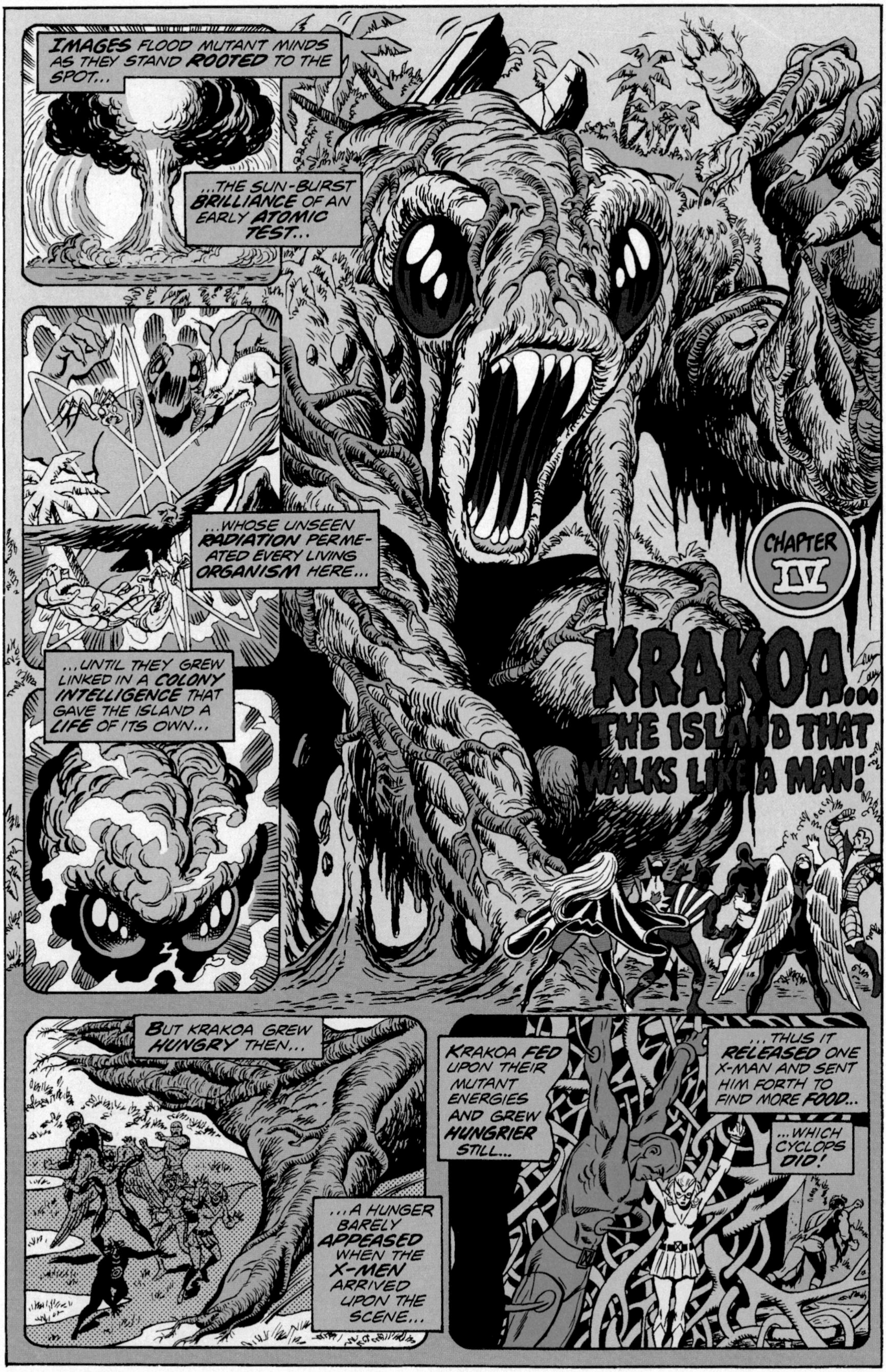
IMAGES FLOOD MUTANT MINDS AS THEY STAND ROOTED TO THE SPOT...
...THE SUN-BURST BRILLIANCE OF AN EARLY ATOMIC TEST...
...WHOSE UNSEEN RADIATION PERMEATED EVERY LIVING ORGANISM HERE...
...UNTIL THEY GREW LINKED IN A COLONY INTELLIGENCE THAT GAVE THE ISLAND A LIFE OF ITS OWN...
CHAPTER IV
KRAKOA... THE ISLAND THAT WALKS LIKE A MAN!
BUT KRAKOA GREW HUNGRY THEN...
...A HUNGER BARELY APPEASED WHEN THE X-MEN ARRIVED UPON THE SCENE...
KRAKOA FED UPON THEIR MUTANT ENERGIES AND GREW HUNGRIER STILL...
...THUS IT RELEASED ONE X-MAN AND SENT HIM FORTH TO FIND MORE FOOD...
...WHICH CYCLOPS DID!

...AND NOW WE WILL GO *HUNGRY* NO LONGER!

FILTHY MONSTER, YOU *USED* ME-- LIKE A LOUSY *JUDAS GOAT* LEADING LAMBS TO THE *SLAUGHTER*--!

YES, WE *USED* YOU, EYELESS ONE-- AS WE USED THE LEG-LESS ONE WHO GATHERED YOU ALL *TOGETHER*--

--AT THE COMMAND OF A *VOICE* ONLY *HIS* MIND COULD HEAR!

BUT THE TIME FOR EXPLANATIONS IS *PAST!*

NOW IT IS TIME FOR *KRAKOA* TO FEED!

SCATTER, X-MEN-- QUICKLY--! *UUNNGH!*

ZZZ KKK AK

YOU *LILY-LIVERS* WANT TO SCATTER, THAT'S *SWELL*--

--BUT THE *WOLVERINE* IS GOING OUT FOR *BLOOD!*

WHUMP!

ASSUMING, OF COURSE, THIS VEGETARIAN MONSTROSITY *HAS* ANY--

--WHICH IS *DOUBTFUL!*

YOUR SOLAR BLASTS HAVE *NO EFFECT* ON THE THING, SUNFIRE!

NOR DO MY BOLTS OF *LIGHTNING!*

BUT WE MUST *FIGHT ON*-- WHATEVER THE *RISK!*

30

MERE **WORDS** COULD NEVER BEGIN TO DESCRIBE THE SHEER UNBRIDLED **SAVAGERY** OF THE BATTLE THAT FOLLOWS--

--SO WE WON'T EVEN **ATTEMPT** IT HERE!

SUFFICE IT TO SAY THAT THE CONFLICT GOES WILDLY **ON** UNTIL...

SCOTT--**STOP!** YOU'RE GOING ABOUT THIS ALL **WRONG!**

HUH? PRO-FESSOR--!?!

I'VE BEEN MENTALLY **MONITORING** YOUR BATTLE THUS FAR--

--STUDYING THIS **LIVING ISLAND**--

--AND I BELIEVE I'VE DISCOVERED IT'S SOLE **WEAK POINT!**

NOW THIS IS MY **PLAN**...

IN AN INSTANT, PRO-FESSOR CHARLES XAVIER'S MENTAL COM-MANDS ARE PROJECTED HALFWAY AROUND A **WORLD**--

--THEN HE CLOSES HIS **EYES**--STEELS HIMSELF FOR THE COMING **ORDEAL**--

--CONCENTRATES--

--AND THE **BATTLE** IS JOINED!

KRRRRAMMMRRR

31

IT IS A WAR FOUGHT ON *TWO* FRONTS-- AS PROFESSOR X WAGES DEADLY MENTAL COMBAT WITH A CRAZED *COMMUNITY INTELLECT*-- WHILE HIS STUDENTS RACE TO CARRY OUT HIS *PLAN*...

HIGH ABOVE KRAKOA, SHE *HOVERS*--

AT CYCLOPS' COMMAND, THE EYES OF THE MUTANT CALLED STORM GROW *DARK* ONCE MORE--

--AND SHE SOARS ALOFT ON THE WINGS OF THE *WIND!*

--SLOWLY SUMMONING TO HER THE TEMPEST'S FULL ELECTRONIC FURY--

--THEN SUDDENLY *TRANSMITTING* THOSE SEETHING ENERGIES TO THE LITHE YOUNG *WOMAN* WHO WAITS ANXIOUSLY BELOW--

--THUS *RESTORING* THE MIGHTY *MAGNETIC POWERS* OF THE GIRL CALLED *LORNA DANE!*

--AND LORNA DANE *SCREAMS* IN ANGUISH AS HER PHYSICAL LIMITS ARE *REACHED*--

--AND *EXCEEDED!*

WITHIN MOMENTS, THE CIRCUIT IS COMPLETED--

DON'T *STOP!* LORD, WHATEVER YOU DO-- *DON'T STOP!*

YOU'VE GOT TO *CALL IT OFF*, SCOTT! LORNA CAN'T *TAKE* THAT KIND OF PUNISHMENT!

SHE'LL BE *KILLED!*

ALEX-- I *CAN'T!*

I CAN'T SACRIFICE A *WORLD* TO SAVE ONE *WOMAN*, ALEX--

--EVEN IF SHE *IS* THE WOMAN YOU *LOVE!*

I SWEAR TO YOU--BROTHER OR *NO* BROTHER, IF SHE *DIES*...

THE REMAINDER OF HAVOK'S ANGRY OUTBURST IS *SLAIN* BY THE CRACKLING ROAR OF THE THUNDROUS *DOWN-POUR*--

--EVEN AS THE TORRENTIAL WATERS LEND *LIFE* TO SOMETHING *ELSE!*

CYCLOPS, THE ISLAND'S MIND HAS SUDDENLY GROWN MORE *FORCEFUL!*

KR
WRAAR

BEGORRAH! THE BLINKIN' *BEASTIE'S* GETTIN' *STRONGER* NOW!

BUT *HOW*--?

I--I CAN'T MAINTAIN MY *ASSAULT* ANY LONGER--!

FORGIVE ME, SCOTT...

...BUT I FEAR... YOU'RE... ON... YOUR... OWN...

FOOLS! YOU BROUGHT *RAIN* FROM THE SKY TO *DESTROY* US--

--BUT IT SERVES ONLY TO *RE-PLENISH* US--

--AND GIVE US *STRENGTH* TO DESTROY *YOU!*

BUT AS BEFORE, THE X-MEN *ARGUE* THAT POINT--

--QUITE *STRONGLY!*

WE CAN'T HOLD THAT THING OFF *FOREVER*, SCOTT! IF THE PROFESSOR'S PLAN DOESN'T *WORK*...

WE'LL *KNOW* IF IT WORKS SOON ENOUGH, JEAN! GET EVERY-BODY *BACK!*

WE'RE READY TO *BEGIN!*

WITH THAT, A SOLEMN SCOTT SUMMERS *TURNS*--TO FIND THAT THE FIGURE OF LORNA DANE HAS BECOME *LOST* WITHIN A *CORUSCATING* INCANDESCENT TOWER OF SHEER *MAGNETIC FORCE.*

HIS MUTANT EYES *NARROW*-- AND A SINGLE *WORD* FORMS UPON HIS LIPS:

NOW!

33

WITH ALMOST-INDE-SCRIBABLE FORCE, LORNA'S MAGNETIC ENERGIES ERUPT *DOWNWARD*--

--THRU *FIVE* MILES OF *OCEAN*--

--THRU *FOUR THOUSAND* MILES OF THE EARTH'S ANCIENT *CRUST*--

--*DOWN*--TO THE VERY MOLTEN *CENTER* OF THE PLANET ITSELF--

--WHERE ITS EFFECTS ARE *IMMEDIATE*--AND *VIOLENT*!

WH-WHAT IS *HAPPENING* TO US? WHY DO WE FEEL SO *STRANGE*?

OUR MIND *HURTS* SO... CAN'T RETAIN OUR *HUMANOID* FORM...!

PLEASE... *HELP* US...

IT'S *WORKING*-- EXACTLY AS THE PROFESSOR *SAID* IT WOULD!

WE'VE ONLY GOT *SECONDS* TO CLEAR OUT OF HERE--BEFORE THE *END*!

LORNA'S TOO *WEAK* TO RUN FOR IT! I'LL...*EH?*

THE LADY DOESN'T NEED *YOUR* HELP, HOTSHOT! SHE'S IN *GOOD* HANDS FOR A CHANGE!

WHY, YOU *LITTLE*...

ARGUE *LATER*-- NOW JUST *MOVE IT*!

AND MOVE IT, THEY DO-- AS FEW OTHER BEINGS ON EARTH POSSIBLY *COULD*!

HOLY *CROW*! WILL YA TAKE A LOOK AT THE *BEACH* UP AHEAD?

THIS WHOLE FREAKIN' *ISLAND* IS BREAKIN' UP *AROUND* US!

AND WITHOUT OUR *STRATO-JET*, THERE'S NO WAY WE CAN GET *FAR* ENOUGH FROM THE ISLAND BEFORE... *HUH?*

NEVER LET IT BE SAID WE *ICEMEN* AREN'T GOOD FOR *SOME-THING*, ANGEL!

EVERYBODY GET *ABOARD*-- AND *FAST*!

34

SWIFTLY, THE DESPERATE X-MEN CLAMBER ABOARD THE CRUDE *ICERAFT*, THEN HANG ON FOR DEAR *LIFE*--

--AS THE MUTANT POWERS OF CYCLOPS AND HAVOK *PROPEL* THE MAKE-SHIFT VESSEL *AWAY* FROM KRAKOA WITH THE SPEED OF A HURTLING *HYDROPLANE!*

BEHIND THEM, THE WORLD CONVULSES IN *CARNAGE*-- AS THE *RESULTS* OF LORNA DANE'S ENERGY-BOLT BECOME *APPARENT* AT LAST--

--FOR HER ELECTRICALLY-CHARGED BURST HAS CUT *ACROSS* THE PLANET'S PRIMARY LINES OF MAGNETIC FORCE-- *SEVERING* THEM--

--AND FOR AN INSTANT ABOUT THE ISLAND KRAKOA-- *GRAVITY CEASES TO EXIST!*

THEN THE EARTH-FORCES COME VIOLENTLY *TOGETHER*--AND THE EFFECT IS THE SAME AS SQUEEZING WET *SOAP* THRU A *FIST!*

KRAKOA'S *DEATH-CRIES* RING FOR LONG SECONDS IN THE MINDS OF THE AWESTRUCK X-MEN--

--THEN A NEW, MORE *FRIGHTENING* REALITY INTRUDES UPON THE SCENE...

BRACE YOURSELVES, EVERYONE-- THERE'S *TROUBLE* AHEAD!

"THE *OCEAN* IS RUSHING TO FILL IN THE SPACE KRAKOA JUST *VACATED*--

"--AND *WE'RE* CAUGHT IN THE *WHIRLPOOL!*"

QUICKLY, BOBBY-- THROW AN AIR-TIGHT *ICE-DOME* OVER THIS RAFT!

IT'S OUR ONLY CHANCE TO *SURVIVE* THIS MISERABLE *MAELSTROM!*

VORACIOUSLY, THE GREAT ICE-BUBBLE IS *SUCKED* INTO THE WILDLY-SWIRLING *MAW*--

--AND THOSE WITHIN ARE BATTERED ALMOST *SENSE-LESS* AGAINST ITS COLD, UNFEELING *WALLS.*

THEY VOICE THEIR *PAIN* ENTHUSIASTI-CALLY--

--AND THEN THEY ARE *GONE!*

THE SEETHING WATERS SWIRL *CLOSED* ABOVE THEIR HEADS-- AND FOR A TIME THE SEA IS *CALM.*

THE MINUTES PASS INTER-MINABLY-- THEN THE HUGE GLEAMING BUBBLE *BURSTS* THE WATER'S SURFACE--

--AND IS *ITSELF* BURST IN TURN BY A BEAM OF *SCARLET FURY!*

FRESH *AIR*... A WARM *SUN*... DID YOU EVER SEE ANYTHING MORE *BEAUTI-FUL?*

YEAH-- *THAT!* ALMOST *FORGOT* THE OL' STRATO-JET IS *WATERTIGHT!*

PADDLE ON *OVER* WHILE I GO *OPEN* THE HATCH!

SHORTLY, AS THE STRATO-JET STREAKS SKY-WARD...

SORRY WE DON'T HAVE *SEATS* FOR *ALL* OF YOU-- BUT THIS PLANE WASN'T *DESIGN-ED* TO CARRY SO MANY *MUTANTS!*

WHICH BRINGS US TO OUR *NEXT* LITTLE PROBLEM,...

WHAT ARE WE GOING TO DO WITH *THIRTEEN* X-MEN?

WE'LL FIND OUT *NEXT ISSUE...*

WHEN THE DOOMSMITH STRIKES!

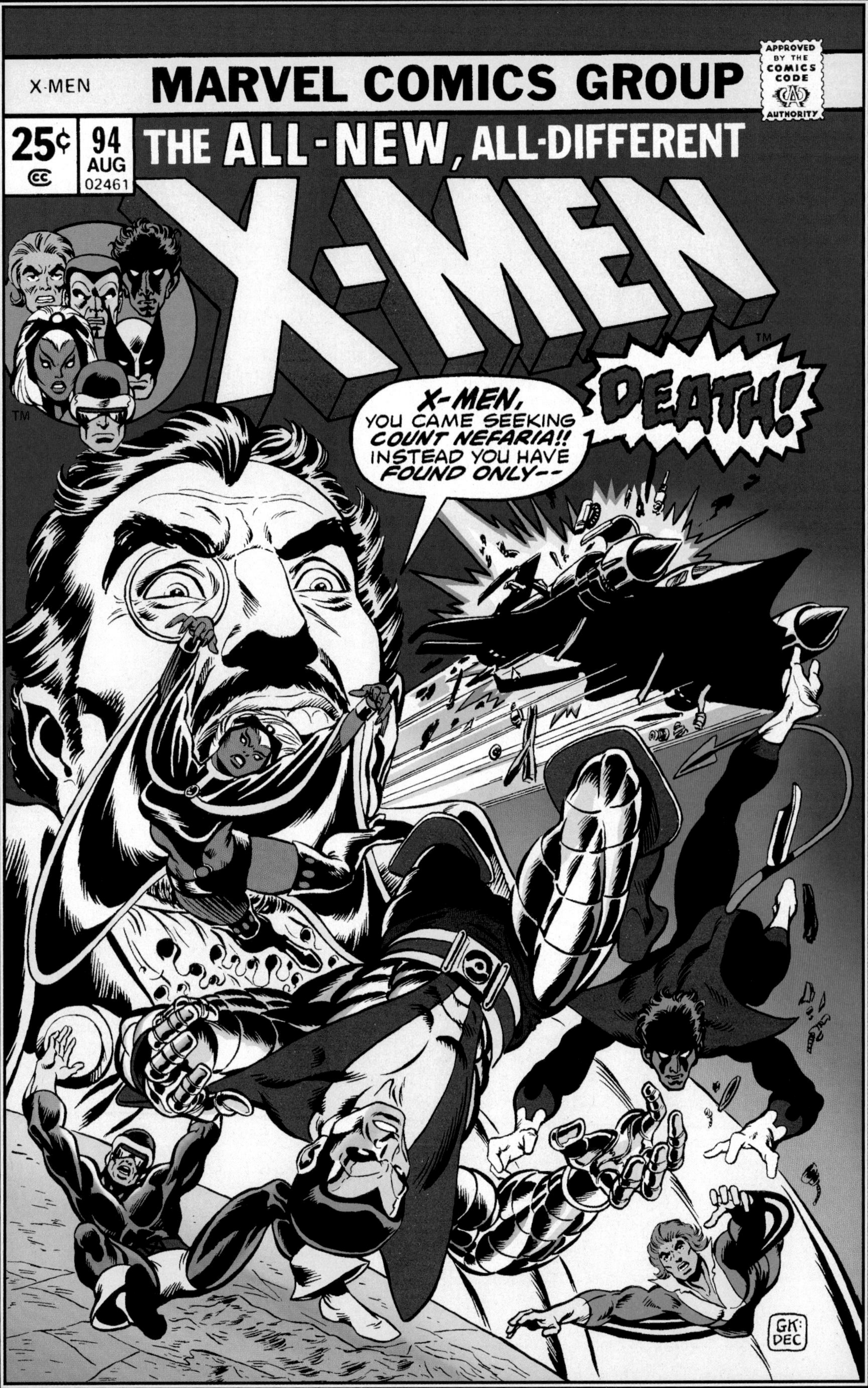

X-MEN
MARVEL COMICS GROUP
APPROVED BY THE COMICS CODE AUTHORITY
25¢
94
AUG
02461
THE ALL-NEW, ALL-DIFFERENT
X-MEN
X-MEN, YOU CAME SEEKING COUNT NEFARIA!! INSTEAD YOU HAVE FOUND ONLY--
DEATH!
GK: DEC

CHRIS CLAREMONT, WRITER
LEN WEIN, PLOTTER-EDITOR
| DAVE COCKRUM ARTIST
| BOB McCLEOD INKER
| PHIL RACHELSON, COLORIST
TOM ORZECHOWSKI, LETTERER

THE DOOMSMITH SCENARIO!

I CALLED YOU HERE, X-MEN, BECAUSE THERE'S SOMETHING I WANT TO TELL YOU ALL...

IT BEGINS... WITH AN ENDING -- AND, PERHAPS, THE BREAKING OF A MAN'S HEART. THIS MAN'S HEART...

...THE HEART OF CHARLES XAVIER.

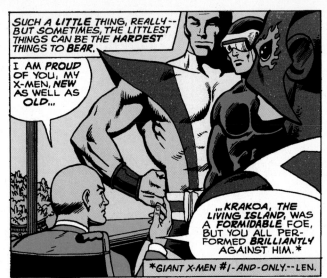

SUCH A LITTLE THING, REALLY-- BUT SOMETIMES, THE LITTLEST THINGS CAN BE THE HARDEST THINGS TO BEAR.

I AM PROUD OF YOU, MY X-MEN, NEW AS WELL AS OLD...

...KRAKOA, THE LIVING ISLAND, WAS A FORMIDABLE FOE, BUT YOU ALL PERFORMED BRILLIANTLY AGAINST HIM.*

*GIANT X-MEN #1-AND-ONLY.--LEN.

"NOW, AS TO THE FUTURE..."

AS TO THE FUTURE, PROFESSOR, IT IS A FUTURE THAT DOES NOT INCLUDE SUNFIRE.

SHIRO, I DON'T UNDERSTAND. I THOUGHT YOU'D AGREED TO JOIN US...

I AGREED TO HELP YOU, PROFESSOR. ONCE!

AND ONCE WAS QUITE ENOUGH. MY DUTY IS TO MY COUNTRY AND MY EMPEROR.

I CARE NOTHING FOR THE WORLD YOU OFFER. I WANT NONE OF IT, NONE OF YOU, AND NONE OF YOUR X-MEN!

I SEE. DO ANY OF THE REST OF YOU ECHO SUNFIRE'S THOUGHTS? NIGHTCRAWLER? THUNDERBIRD?

COLOSSUS?

I ... DO NOT KNOW, GOSPODIN XAVIER... I ...

I SAY WE HAVE BEEN TOGETHER BARELY TWO DAYS. AND TWO DAYS ARE NOTHING.

I AM INTRIGUED BY THE PROFESSOR'S OFFER. I WILL STAY.

WHAT THE HEY? IT SURE BEATS SITTIN' ROUND ALPHA BASE WAITIN' FOR A GO CALL.

THEN SUNFIRE BIDS YOU FAREWELL, PROFESSOR; YOU AND YOUR PACK OF IDEALISTIC FOOLS.

...BUT HEAR ME, XAVIER...

...SHOULD YOU NEED THIS SAMURAI'S HELP AGAIN, DO NOT SEEK ME OUT AND DO NOT ASK ...

...FOR SUNFIRE WILL REFUSE!

39

WHAT ABOUT *YOU*, BANSHEE? WILL YOU GO, OR WILL YOU *STAY*?

WELL, I WON'T *LIE* TO YE, PERFESSER. I *LIKE* IT HERE AN' THAT'S THE *TRUTH*.

BUT I WON'T LIE TO *MESELF*, EITHER. YOUR X-MEN ARE ALL *YOUNG PEOPLE*. STUDENTS. ME, I'M A *BARELY LITERATE* EX-COP, AN' LIKE IT OR NOT...

...THERE'S SOME *GREY* AMONG THE BANSHEE'S *GOLDEN HAIR*.

IT'S BEEN *GRAND*, BUT IT'S TIME I WAS *MOVIN'* ON.

RUBBISH! YOUR HAIR'S ABOUT AS GREY AS MINE. AND YOUR *BRAIN'S* A FRACTION *KEENER*.

HOWEVER, IF THESE 'YOUNG PEOPLE' ARE TOO MUCH OF A *CHALLENGE* FOR YOU...

NOW I DIDN'T SAY *THAT*, DID I? *SINCE WHEN* HAS THE BANSHEE EVER *REFUSED* A CHALLENGE? IT'S JUST...

BANSHEE, YOU WOULDN'T HAVE TO *RUN* ANYMORE. YOU'D BE WITH *FRIENDS*. YOU'D... *BELONG*.

AYE. THAT'S A *POINT*. IT'D BE... *NICE*... T' BELONG.

ALL RIGHT, PERFESSER, *I'M SOLD*. YE'VE GOT YERSELF A *NEW X-MAN*.

EXCELLENT, MY FRIEND. AND NOW THAT THAT'S ALL *SETTLED*...

I'M AFRAID IT *ISN'T*... ALL SETTLED, PROFESSOR.

WHAT DO YOU *MEAN*, WARREN?

I'M *SORRY*, PROFESSOR... THERE'S NO *EASY* WAY TO SAY THIS... ah, WE-- THE *OLD X-MEN* -- WE'RE...

...WE'RE *LEAVING*, SIR. PULLING OUT.

40

YOU'RE... **WHAT?!?**

BUT **WHY,** WARREN? JEAN? **ALL OF YOU?** **WHY!?!**

BECAUSE... WE WERE **CHILDREN** WHEN YOU TOOK US IN, PROFESSOR. **SCARED** AND **UNCERTAIN** ABOUT WHO AND **WHAT** WE WERE...

YOU **TAUGHT** US, HELPED US **REALIZE** OUR FULL POTENTIAL.

YOU HELPED US **GROW UP...** AND THAT'S JUST **IT.** WE'VE GROWN UP.

WE'RE NOT **CHILDREN** ANYMORE, PROFESSOR. WE HAVE TO LIVE OUR **OWN** LIVES NOW.

LOOK, LADY, YOU GUYS WANT **OUT** THAT BADLY, THEN **GO! SPLIT! TAKE OFF!** WHAT DO **WE** CARE?

JUST DO US ALL A **FAVOR** AND **SPARE** US THE **SOAP OPERA,** HUH?

WHY YOU...

LISTEN, MIDGET, **ONE MORE WORD** OUTTA YOU AND I'M GONNA **SLAM...**

C'MON... **TRY IT,** BUB. I NEVER CARVED UP AN **ICICLE** BEFORE.

THAT'S ENOUGH! BOTH OF YOU!

I SAID, **THAT'S ENOUGH!**

YOU'RE **OUT OF LINE,** WOLVERINE! NOW PUT YOUR **CLAWS** AWAY AND **CALM DOWN** OR YOU'LL HAVE TO DEAL WITH **ME.**

BIG TALK, **BOSS-MAN...**

ANY TIME YOU WANT TO **TRY,** MISTER, I'LL BE **READY.**

UH... **SCOTTY...** I DON'T WANT TO **PUSH** YOU, BROTHER... BUT WHAT'RE **YOU** GONNA DO?

ARE YOU **COMING** WITH **US** -- OR **STAYING?**

I... **DON'T KNOW,** ALEX, I JUST **DON'T KNOW.**

41

IT'S A LONG NIGHT FOR THE MUTANT X-MAN, SCOTT SUMMERS. HE CANNOT SLEEP AND, IN TRUTH, HE DOESN'T REALLY TRY.

INSTEAD, HE ROAMS THE MANSION THAT HAS BEEN HIS HOME FOR SO MANY YEARS... ROAMS AND THINKS. AND REMEMBERS...

...AND CURSES.

FACE IT, SUMMERS. NO MATTER WHICH WAY YOU CUT IT, YOU'RE THE ONE X-MAN WHO CAN'T HIDE WHAT HE IS...

...AND WHO DARES NOT FORGET, BECAUSE IF HE DOES, SOMEONE MIGHT GET KILLED.

KILLED BY MY EYES! MY CURSED, MUTANT, ENERGY-BLASTING EYES!

THE ANGUISHED, DESPERATE CRY RINGS HOLLOW IN THE STILLNESS. AND IF ANYONE HEARS IT, THEY GIVE NO SIGN...

...FOR THE MANSION IS QUIET, 'TIL MORNING.

WHEN OLD FRIENDS GATHER TO SAY... GOOD-BYE.

SCOTT, YOU'RE STILL WEARING YOUR COSTUME...

YEAH.

JEAN, I'VE THOUGHT THIS OVER ALL NIGHT, AND... I'VE DECIDED TO STAY.

I THOUGHT YOU WOULD... BUT... I'D HOPED...

I'M AN X-MAN, PURE AND SIMPLE. THIS IS MY HOME, MY LIFE. THIS IS WHERE I... BELONG.

WHERE YOU BELONG, SCOTT. BUT NOT ME. NOT ANYMORE!

I KNOW. A LOUSY SITUATION, ISN'T IT? I... I DON'T WANT TO LOSE YOU, JEAN. I CAN'T.

I LOVE YOU.

AND I LOVE YOU.

THEN, SHE IS GONE.

AND THE MAN CALLED CYCLOPS IS ALONE.

THE PARTING IS A QUICK ONE, BUT THE FAREWELLS ARE REAL AND HEARTFELT...

... FOR THESE PEOPLE HAVE **FOUGHT** TOGETHER -- FACED **DEATH** TOGETHER -- AND THAT HAS FORGED A SPECIAL **BOND** BETWEEN THEM...

... A BOND THAT MAKES THEM **COMRADES.** AND, IN A WAY, **FRIENDS.**

ALL RIGHT, PEOPLE! THE SHOW'S OVER AND IT'S TIME **PROFESSOR XAVIER'S SCHOOL FOR GIFTED YOUNGSTERS** WAS A GOING CONCERN AGAIN...

...TIME YOU LEARNED WHAT BEING AN X-MAN IS **ALL ABOUT.**

LESSON ONE IS HOW TO STAY **ALIVE** -- THAT'S WHAT THE **DANGER ROOM** IS FOR...

...TO GIVE YOU A **SECOND,** MAYBE TWO. **TIME** -- AND THE **SKILL** TO TAKE THAT TIME AND **USE** IT TO **DEFEAT** YOUR OPPONENT. IN A WORD, TO **SURVIVE.**

DANGER ROOM

AN ... **EMPTY ROOM** WILL DO ALL THAT?

THAT'S RIGHT, STORM. AND THE **OBJECT** OF THE EXERCISE IS TO **CROSS** THE ROOM...

... WALK IN **THIS** DOOR AND **OUT** THE OTHER...

EXIT

YOU GOTTA BE **KIDDIN',** ONE-EYE. AN' I'M GONNA **CALL** YA.

SEE YA AT THE **EXIT,** TROOPS.

PERHAPS, JOHN PROUDSTAR...

CLICK WRRRR

WHAT THE...

HEY! LEGGO!

CHAKA CHAKA CHAK!

... THEN AGAIN, PERHAPS **NOT.**

POW

...IF THE ROOM **LETS** YOU.

AND SO, IT BEGINS. THE DAYS -- THE WEEKS -- OF TRAINING, SIX HOURS A DAY, FIVE DAYS A WEEK. WEEK IN, WEEK OUT...

...UNTIL THE HALLS OF THIS OLD, VENERABLE WESTCHESTER MANSION SEEM TO ECHO AND RE-ECHO WITH THE SOUNDS OF BATTLE; UNTIL THESE NEOPHYTE X-MEN BEGIN TO WONDER IF THERE EVER WAS A TIME WHEN THEY WEREN'T FIGHTING FOR THEIR LIVES.

AND WHEN THEY FALTER, GIVE IN A LITTLE, GIVE UP, A VOICE SNAPS THEM BACK INTO LINE. A HARSH VOICE, ANGRY, BITING, MERCILESS.

THE VOICE OF THE MAN NAMED CYCLOPS, WHO DRIVES THE X-MEN HARD AND HIMSELF HARDER.

WHO TAKES SIX PROUD, UNIQUE INDIVIDUALS. SIX LONERS. SIX OUTCASTS...

...AND FORGES THEM INTO A TEAM.

BUT EVEN THE X-MEN, AFTER ALL, ARE ONLY... HUMAN. PUSHED TO THE LIMIT; PUSHED BEYOND, EXHAUSTION BEGINS TO TAKE ITS TOLL ON TEACHER AND STUDENTS BOTH.

AND PEOPLE BEGIN TO MAKE MISTAKES.

THUNDERBIRD, LOOK OUT! THE LASERS-- YOU'RE CUTTING IT TOO CLOSE--!

AAIRRRGH!!

TAKE IT EASY, LAD -- THAT'S A NASTY BURN ON YER LEG. I'LL HELP YE UP.

BACK OFF, SHAMROCK! I DON'T NEED ANY HELP.

NOT FROM YOU-- NOT FROM ANYBODY!

I'M OKAY, ONE-EYE...

THE NAME IS CYCLOPS, MISTER-- AND YOU'RE NOT 'OKAY.'

I'VE GOT NEWS FOR YOU, FELLA-- IF THIS WERE COMBAT, AND THOSE LASERS RUNNING AT FULL STRENGTH...

...YOU'D HAVE LOST YOUR LEG!

YOU'RE CARELESS, THUNDERBIRD. AND YOUR CARELESSNESS COULD GET US ALL KILLED!

MAN, YOU BEEN RIDIN' ME SINCE THE DAY I GOT HERE-- AND I HAVE HAD IT!

YOU LAY OFF ME, ONE-EYE, AND YOU DO IT NOW-- OR SO HELP ME--

-- I'LL REARRANGE YOUR FACE!!

CYCLOPS! THUNDERBIRD! CEASE THIS DISGRACEFUL DISPLAY IMMEDIATELY!

THUNDER-BIRD, REPORT TO THE INFIRMARY!

AS FOR YOU, SCOTT-- I'LL SEE YOU IN MY OFFICE.

WAY TO GO, HOTSHOT. LOOKS LIKE YOU'VE BLOWN ANOTHER CHANCE FOR YOURSELF. MAYBE THE LAST ONE...

WHAT'S'A MATTER, LADY? IT BOTHER YOU TO WORK WITH A LOSER?

I SEE NO 'LOSER', JOHN PROUDSTAR. IN THIS ROOM, I SEE ONLY A MAN.

45

CHAPTER TWO

DEATH O'ER VALHALLA HIGH!

IN THE *ROCKIES*, IN COLORADO STATE, SOME FORTY MILES WEST OF *COLORADO SPRINGS*, THERE STANDS A MOUNTAIN. LONELY, *FORBIDDING*, THRUSTING ITS ROUGH, GRANITE FACE NEARLY *TWO MILES* HIGH INTO THE CRISP, COOL *ROCKY MOUNTAIN* AIR.

THE MOUNTAIN IS CALLED VALHALLA, THE HOME OF THE GODS.

THOSE WHO KNOW IT BETTER... CALL IT *DEATH.*

AND BURIED DEEP WITHIN THE MOUNTAIN, *SAFE FROM ANY ENEMY, SECURE FROM EVEN A 100-MEGATON THERMONUCLEAR BOMB...*

...IS THE *NORAD WAR ROOM,* OPERATIONAL COMMAND OF THE MOST POWERFUL *WAR MACHINE* EVER CONCEIVED...

... A PLACE WHERE EVEN THE MOST *MUNDANE* OF EVENTS ...

... CAN ASSUME *FRIGHTENING SIGNIFICANCE.*

ONE FOR YOU, HARRIS!

FOR VALHALLA MOUNTAIN IS HEADQUARTERS OF NORAD, THE NORTH AMERICAN AIR DEFENSE COMMAND.

HEADS UP, JOY BOYS! MAIL CALL! MAIL CALL!

HUH? WHAT GIVES? I WASN'T EXPECTING ANYTHING.

LOOKS LIKE THIS IS YOUR *LUCKY DAY,* JOE.

GUESS SO. WONDER *WHAT* IT...

...IS...

IS THIS SOMEBODY'S IDEA OF A *GAG* OR SOMETHIN'? WHAT *GOES ON* HERE?

PRESS ME

MAYBE IT'S THAT *RAQUEL WELCH DOLL* YOU WANTED FOR *CHRISTMAS,* JOE!

VERY FUNNY. SO HELP ME, IF YOU CLOWNS ARE *BEHIND* THIS, I'LL...

OH... MY...

THE BOX DISAPPEARS, LEAVING IN ITS PLACE A *SHIMMERING SILVER OVAL,* A HOLE IN THE AIR, A RIP IN THE FABRIC OF TIME AND SPACE.

IN SHORT, A PORTAL.

AND THROUGH THAT PORTAL ERUPTS A NIGHTMARE. FIVE OF THEM, IN FACT. ALL OF THEM DEADLY, NONE OF THEM EVEN REMOTELY... HUMAN.

THE BATTLE IS QUICKLY JOINED...

...THE STUNNED, UN-ARMED HUMANS AS QUICKLY ROUTED.

INTRUDER ALERT IN THE WAR ROOM! GET EVERY AVAILABLE MAN DOWN HERE--AND FOR GOD'S SAKE HURRY!!

IN MINUTES, THE VAST COMPLEX IS MOBILIZED, TROOPS ON THE MOVE...

HAUL IT, YOU MEN! THIS ISN'T A DRILL-- HAUL IT!

IF IT WERE ONLY THAT EASY.

OKAY, FREAKS, THE PARTY'S OVER--

ONE WRONG MOVE 'AN YOU'RE DEAD!

YOU HUMANS THREATEN GORT--?

--YOU DARE!?

THE SECOND BATTLE IS LIKE THE FIRST, QUICKLY JOINED, QUICKLY ENDED...

...AND THE VICTORS ARE THE SAME.

WELL DONE, MY ANI-MEN. WELL DONE!

I HAD EXPECTED VICTORY, TRUE, BUT NOT SO GREAT A ROUT AS THIS, I AM PROUD OF YOU.

WHAT? WHO SSSPEAKSSS?

WHO D'YA THINK, DRAGONFLY? IT'S THE BOSS.

OUR LORD AN' MASTER.

QUITE TRUE, MY DEAR CROAKER, COUNT NEFARIA IS YOUR LORD AND MASTER.

YOU WOULD DO WELL TO REMEMBER THAT...

...IF YOU HARBOR ANY HOPES OF EVER BECOMING HUMAN AGAIN.

BUT *NO MORE* OF THAT-- NEFARIA'S PLAN GOES ACCORDING TO *SCHEDULE* AND *ALL IS WELL.*

THE WAR ROOM IS *OURS.*

FOR *HOW LONG,* BOSS? THERE'S A *WHOLE ARMY* MANNIN' THIS PLACE...

... HOW'RE THE *FIVE* OF US SUPPOSED TO *HOLD 'EM OFF?*

I DO NOT *EXPECT* YOU TO.

BY PRESSING THIS BUTTON AND *FLOODING* THE MOUNTAIN WITH *ANESTHETIC* GAS...

"... I HAVE *NEUTRALIZED* THIS ARMY YOU SEEM TO *FEAR* SO MUCH.

IN *ALL VALHALLA* BASE, MY CHILDREN, WE SIX ARE THE ONLY ONES STILL *CONSCIOUS.* AND, ONCE AGAIN, COUNT NEFARIA IS *TRIUMPHANT...*

...THIS TIME TO HOLD THE *FATE* OF A *WORLD* IN HIS HANDS.

"THESE *FOOLS* THOUGHT ME DEFEATED, *DESTROYED,* WHEN MY ASSAULT ON WASHINGTON *FAILED* THOSE MANY MONTHS AGO...*

*WAY BACK IN X-MEN #22/23. --LONG-AGO LEN.

"... ALL THOUGHT *WRONG.* I *ESCAPED* FROM PRISON AND BEGAN PLANNING ANEW, CALLING IN OLD *DEBTS* AND USING *MAGGIA SCIENCE* TO CREATE *STRONGER ALLIES...* TO MAKE YOU *LESS THAN HUMAN* ... AND *FAR, FAR MORE...*

"... SO THAT *THIS* DAY WE RANSOM NOT A MERE CITY-- BUT A *WORLD!!*"

 ...AND NOW, MY CHILDREN, THE *GAME* BEGINS IN *EARNEST.*

 GAMES. SOME LIKE 'EM; SOME *DON'T.* TAKE *SCOTT SUMMERS,* FOR INSTANCE...

...HE *GAVE UP* GAMES A LONG TIME AGO.

 ON THE *DAY* HE BECAME *LEADER* OF THE X-MEN. AND IT'S *COST* HIM OVER THE YEARS...

 ...SO THAT, *SOMETIMES,* HE WONDERS IF THE JOB IS *WORTH* THE GRIEF. WONDERS...

EXCUSE ME. I DID NOT MEAN TO *INTRUDE.*

'S'OKAY. I WAS JUST *THINKING.* COME ON *IN.*

WHAT CAN I *DO* FOR YOU, KURT?

ACTUALLY, I WAS WONDERING IF THERE WAS ANYTHING *I* COULD DO FOR *YOU.* I MEAN-- THE *ARGUMENT* WITH THUNDER... WITH *JOHN...* IT *UPSET* YOU, NO?

SURE, IT UPSET ME.

WE WERE *BOTH* CARELESS, KURT. EXCEPT THAT *I* WAS *RESPONSIBLE* AND THUNDERBIRD ENDED UP TAKING *ALL* THE *LUMPS...*

 SCOTT! KURT! PLEASE REPORT TO THE *BRIEFING ROOM...*

...SOMETHING *IMPORTANT* HAS COME UP.

ON OUR WAY, PROFESSOR.

 I THINK, MY FRIEND, THAT IF I REMAIN AN X-MAN TO MY *DYING DAY,* I WILL *NEVER* GET USED TO THAT...

WELCOME TO THE CLUB... *FRIEND.*

 ...SEIZED CONTROL OF *VALHALLA BASE,* THE *NORAD COMMAND CENTER...*

SIT DOWN, ALL OF YOU...

...AND *PAY ATTENTION.* THIS IS OF *VITAL IMPORTANCE.*

I HAVE ACTIVATED THE *DOOM-SMITH COMMAND SYSTEM* -- AND I NOW POSSESS *OPERATIONAL* CONTROL OF AMERICA'S *STRATEGIC MISSILE FORCE.*

I DEMAND A *RANSOM* FROM EACH NATION ON EARTH, THE *AMOUNT* TO BE DETERMINED BY EACH NATION'S *ABILITY* TO PAY. IF MY DEMANDS ARE *NOT* MET...

...I SHALL *LAUNCH* AMERICA'S ENTIRE INVENTORY OF *NUCLEAR MISSILES.*

NICE GUY.

WONDER WHAT HE DOES FOR AN *ENCORE?*

YOU HAVE *THREE HOURS* TO DECIDE.

KL!K!

THAT'S THE STORY, PROF -- HEY! WHAT *HAPPENED* TO THE *X-MEN?!?*

THESE *ARE* THE X-MEN, HANK. PLEASE *CONTINUE.*

UH, OKAY, PROF, IF YOU *SAY* SO. THE AIR FORCE CALLED THE *AVENGERS* FOR HELP, BUT WE CAN'T *HANDLE* IT RIGHT NOW...

...I FIGURED THE X-MEN COULD.

YOU *HEARD* THE BEAST, X-MEN -- LET'S GET *GOING.* THUNDERBIRD, YOU'RE *INJURED* -- YOU'LL HAVE TO STAY *BEHIND.*

YOU WANNA TRY SAYIN' THAT THROUGH A MOUTHFUL OF *KNUCKLES,* ONE-EYE!?! *I'M GOIN'!!*

SCOTT, THERE'S NO TIME TO *ARGUE!* THUNDERBIRD CAN GO!

"JUDGING FROM WHAT *HANK* SAID, YOU'LL NEED *EVERY* X-MAN TO *DEFEAT* NEFARIA IN TIME."

MINUTES LATER, THE X-MEN ARE *ALOFT,* SCREAMING WESTWARD AT BETTER THAN *MACH 4.*

I GOT SOME *FRIENDS* IN VALHALLA -- IF THIS NEFARIA'S *HURT* ANY OF 'EM, I THINK I'M GONNA *CUT* HIM INTO *VERY...* TINY... *PIECES...*

YER *JOSHIN'*, LAD, AREN'T YE?

AREN'T YE?

LET'S *HOPE* YOU GET YOUR *CHANCE*, WOLVERINE --

--RIGHT NOW, WE'VE GOT *TROUBLES* OF OUR *OWN:*

THE *U.S. AIR FORCE.*

UNIDENTIFIED *BLACKBIRD* FROM ALPHA LEADER, YOU ARE IN *RESTRICTED AIR-SPACE.* RESPOND OR WE WILL *OPEN FIRE.*

WE ARE RESPONDING TO *AVENGERS* CALL. OVER.

GOTCHA, HEROES. CONTACT *GENERAL FREDERICKS* ON *TAC TEN.*

TAC TEN, ROGER.

HELLO, GENERAL. IT'S BEEN A *LONG TIME.*

WHO'RE *YOU?* IRON MAN? CAP??

NO, SIR. THE AVENGERS *COULDN'T MAKE* IT. WE'RE THE *X-MEN.*

FIGURES. I MIGHTA KNOWN YOU *MUTIES'D* SHOW UP WITH NEFARIA *AROUND.*

I DON'T REALLY *TRUST* YOU, MISTER. BUT RIGHT NOW, I'VE GOT *NO CHOICE.*

NEFARIA *CONTROLS* VALHALLA AND HE'S *ARMED* THE DEFEN-SIVE SYSTEMS -- *SAM'S,* LASERS, *SONIC DISRUPTORS,* THE WORKS...

...BUT THAT'S THE *LEAST* OF YOUR WORRIES.

BECAUSE THE *FOOL* HAS ARMED THE *DOOMSMITH* SYSTEM.

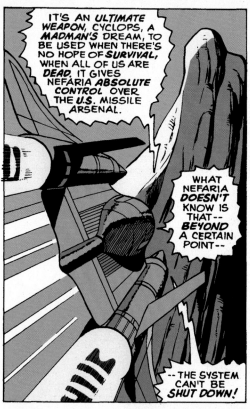

IT'S AN *ULTIMATE WEAPON*, CYCLOPS, A *MADMAN'S* DREAM, TO BE USED WHEN THERE'S NO HOPE OF *SURVIVAL*, WHEN ALL OF US ARE *DEAD*. IT GIVES NEFARIA *ABSOLUTE CONTROL* OVER THE *U.S. MISSILE ARSENAL*.

WHAT NEFARIA *DOESN'T KNOW* IS THAT-- *BEYOND A CERTAIN POINT*--

-- THE SYSTEM CAN'T BE *SHUT DOWN!*

THE MISSILES WILL FIRE *AUTOMATICALLY* AND NO POWER ON EARTH CAN *STOP THEM*.

NEFARIA'S *DEAD-LINE* IS TWO HOURS EVEN. BUT YOU PEOPLE HAVE ONLY *FIFTY-TWO MINUTES* TO CANCEL THE *DOOMSMITH*.

GOOD LUCK, SON.

"YOU'LL *NEED* IT." STARTING *RIGHT NOW*.

COUNT NEFARIA, AN *AIRCRAFT* ENTERS THE *DEFENSE PERIMETER*.

SO, THE *FOOLS* LAUNCH YET *ANOTHER FUTILE ATTACK*...

INTERESTING, THE *COMPUTER* IDENTIFIES THE AIRCRAFT AS...

... THE *X-MEN!!*

BY *HEAVEN*, THIS IS TOO *RICH A JEST!*

MY *GREATEST FOES* WALKING INTO MY *PARLOR*...

... LIKE *LAMBS* GOING TO THE *SLAUGHTER*.

"AND SLAUGHTER THEM I SHALL. WITHOUT PITY. *WITHOUT MERCY!*

"THE *FOOLS* SOUGHT COUNT NEFARIA. LET THEM *INSTEAD* FIND ONLY...

"...*DEATH!!*"

CYCLOPS! THEY'VE FIRED MISSILES!

I SEE THEM, KURT. HOLD ON, PEOPLE. BECAUSE RIGHT ABOUT NOW...

... THE GOING GETS ROUGH.

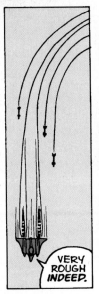

VERY ROUGH INDEED.

THROTTLE FIRE-WALLED, THE MODIFIED SR-71 BLACKBIRD SKIMS THE TREELINE AT A BARE TWENTY FEET, ITS MACH 4 SONIC BOOMS THUNDERING THROUGH THE NARROW PASSES LIKE THE THUNDER OF THOR HIMSELF...

IT'S A MAD, DESPERATE GAMBLE CYCLOPS TRIES...

... A GAMBLE THAT PAYS OFF...

SKRROOOOSH!

TRAKAM

... ALMOST.

NICE TRY, BOSS-MAN.

TOO BAD ONE OF THOSE LITTLE FUTZERS GOT AWAY.

HEADS UP, IT'S GONNA...

WHRAMM!

ITS NOT A DIRECT HIT BUT AT MACH 4, EVEN A NEAR MISS CAN KILL.

IN AN INSTANT, THE DELICATE BLACKBIRD IS TEARING HER-SELF APART.

STABILITY'S GONE! I CAN'T CONTROL HER!

OUR **ONLY** CHANCE...

EJEC

...IS FOR ME TO **PRESS**... THIS... **SWITCH**...

MADE IT!

A SWITCH IS PRESSED, AND THE DYING BLACKBIRD BECOMES A PHOENIX...

... AND IS REBORN, THE LIFTING BODY RISING SWIFTLY, SURELY, FROM THE **ASHES** OF ITS DEAD PARENT.

FHWOOM!

IF WE'RE **LUCKY**, THE CRASH **SHIELDED** THE LIFTING BODY FROM NEFARIA'S **SENSORS**. AS FAR AS **HE** KNOWS, WE'RE **DEAD**...

... AND WE STILL HAVE A **CHANCE** TO **STOP** HIM.

NO!!

BY ALL THAT'S UNHOLY, THE X-MEN STILL **LIVE!!**

HOW MANY TIMES MUST I **KILL** THEM BEFORE THOSE CURSED MUTANTS FINALLY STAY **DEAD!?!**

VERY WELL, THEN. THEY WILL FIND **COUNT NEFARIA** A MORE THAN WORTHY FOE.

LET US SEE THEM **SURVIVE VALHALLA'S SONIC DISRUPTORS.**

FIERY EMERALD CORRUSCATIONS BATHE THE LIFTING BODY FOR A **MOMENT**...

... AND WHEN THE DISRUPTOR BEAM IS GONE...

... THE LIFTING BODY IS GONE AS WELL.

NEXT ISSUE: WARHUNT!

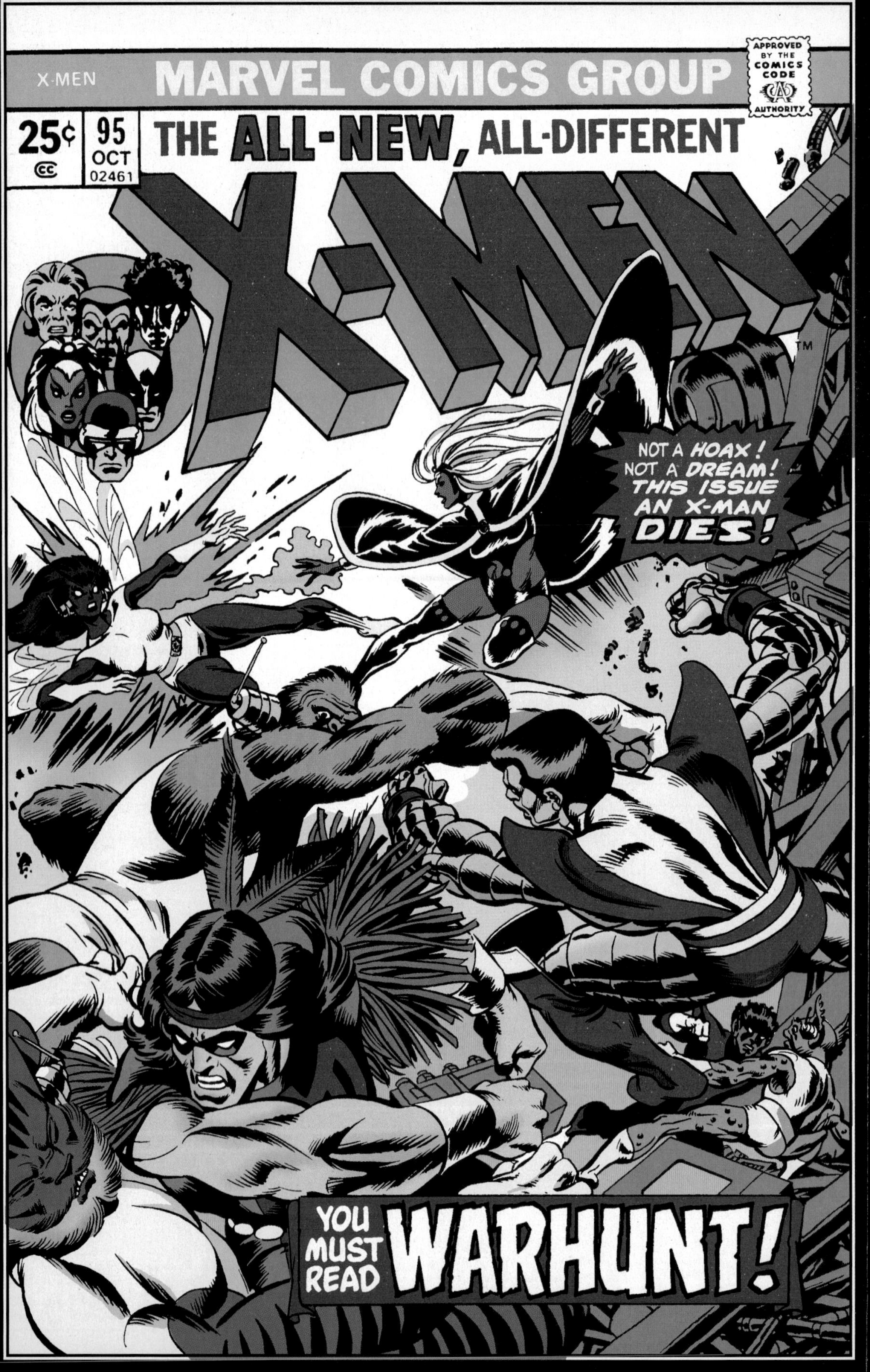
X-MEN
MARVEL COMICS GROUP
APPROVED BY THE COMICS CODE AUTHORITY
25¢
95
OCT
02461
THE ALL-NEW, ALL-DIFFERENT
X-MEN
NOT A HOAX! NOT A DREAM! THIS ISSUE AN X-MAN DIES!
YOU MUST READ WARHUNT!

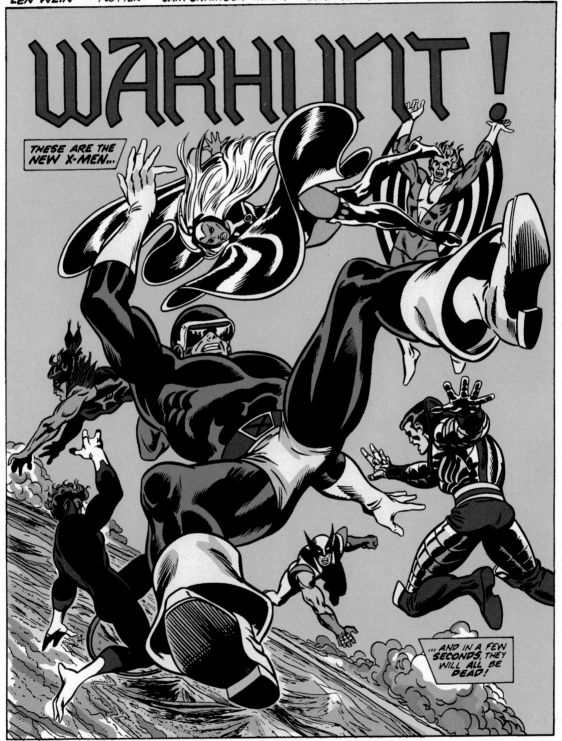

STAN LEE presents: THE UNCANNY X-MEN!™

CHRIS CLAREMONT · WRITER ★ DAVE COCKRUM · ARTIST ★ KAREN MANTLO · LETTERER ★ MARV WOLFMAN · EDITOR
LEN WEIN · PLOTTER ★ SAM GRAINGER · INKER ★ PETRA GOLDBERG · COLORIST

WARHUNT!

THESE ARE THE NEW X-MEN...

...AND IN A FEW SECONDS, THEY WILL ALL BE DEAD!

UNLESS...

IMPACT MINUS 100 SECONDS...

THINK, CYCLOPS, THINK! YOU CAN'T GIVE UP NOW!

MEMORIES, FIRST-- FLASHING INSANELY, KALEIDOSCOPICALLY ACROSS CYCLOPS' MIND AS HE FALLS...

...MEMORIES OF HOW THE BEAST HAD CONTACTED THE X-MEN...

...TO TELL THEM THAT COUNT NEFARIA AND HIS ANI-MEN HAD TAKEN OVER NORAD HEADQUARTERS AND GAINED CONTROL OVER AMERICA'S NUCLEAR ARSENAL -- THAT NEFARIA WAS HOLDING THE WORLD FOR RANSOM.

*ALL THIS TRANSPIRED LAST ISH-- M.W.

THE X-MEN HAD FLOWN TO STOP HIM. AND NEFARIA HAD SHOT THEM OUT OF THE SKY. TWICE.

NOW THE X-MEN ARE FALLING TO THEIR DEATHS, THEIR MISSION A TOTAL WASHOUT.*

IMPACT MINUS 50 SECONDS-- AND MEMORIES HAVE GIVEN WAY TO ACTION.

STORM! BANSHEE! LISTEN UP, YOU TWO!

EACH OF YOU GRAB A PAIR OF X-MEN AND HEAD FOR THE GROUND. NIGHTCRAWLER CAN TELEPORT...

BUT I CANNOT, CYCLOPS-- NOT FROM HERE!

WHA-A-AT?!

I CAN TELEPORT, YES. BUT IF I TELEPORT FROM THIS HEIGHT, THE LAW OF CONSERVATION OF ENERGY DEMANDS I MATERIALIZE WITH THE SAME VELOCITY I STARTED WITH...

I WILL BE KILLED REGARDLESS.

DO NOT WORRY, KURT. I CAN CARRY YOU AND COLOSSUS EASILY.

ORRO, *NO!* I CAN GET DOWN *ON MY OWN--!*

TAKE THAT БЕЗУМНЫЙ ЧЕЛОВЕК --THAT *WOLVERINE--*

PETER, DON'T BE A *FOOL--!*

DON'T *ARGUE,* STORM. THERE ISN'T *TIME--* SO BOTH OF YOU GET OUT *OUT OF HERE! NOW!!*

CYCLOPS, LAD, I *HAVEN'T* ENOUGH *LIFT* TO CARRY TWO *GROWN MEN...*

I'M *SORRY,* BUT I'LL HAVE TA *COME BACK* FOR YE.

WELL, I'LL *SEE YOU AROUND,* BANSHEE--

--JUST *DON'T* BE TOO *LONG,* HUH?

IMPACT MINUS 63 SECONDS. AND THE MUTANT CALLED CYCLOPS IS...ALONE.

COLOSSUS IS THE FIRST TO LAND...

...IF ONE COULD TRULY CALL THIS...

...A LANDING.

SHKOW!

FOR A MOMENT, ALL IS SOUND AND FURY, THE FORCE OF THE IMPACT WHIPCRACKING DOWN THE MOUNTAIN-- AND WHEN THE SOUND FADES AND THE FURY DIES...

...COLOSSUS IS NOWHERE TO BE SEEN.

LORD, NO-- THE LAD'S *KILLED* HIMSELF...

SHEESH-- AND THAT *NUT* HAD THE NERVE TO CALL *ME* A *CRAZY MAN.*

PETER, ARE YOU *THERE?* ARE YOU *ALL RIGHT?*

PETER?!?

WHY ARE YOU *YELLING,* ORORO? *OF COURSE,* I AM ALL RIGHT -- WHY *SHOULDN'T* I BE?

BUT WHAT *KEPT* ALL OF YOU....?

IMPACT MINUS *37 SECONDS.*

COME ON, BANSHEE, GET THE *LEAD* OUT.

IF YOU'RE NOT UP HERE *SOON,* YOU'RE GONNA BE *SCRAPING* ME OFF THE MOUNTAIN WITH A VERY *THIN* SPATULA.

IMPACT MINUS *12 SECONDS.*

LOOKS LIKE THIS IS *IT,* SUMMERS.

IMPACT MINUS *5 SECONDS.*

FUNNY, I ALWAYS FIGURED MY NUMBER'D BE UP *SOMEDAY* --

--BUT I *NEVER* THOUGHT IT'D END LIKE --

GOT YOU!!

--THIiiiSSSSS!!

YOU KNOW, YOU SURE *TOOK YOUR TIME* ABOUT PICKING ME UP, BANSHEE.

AH, LADDIE, DID YE *REALLY* THINK I'D LET A *FOINE* BROTH OF A BOY SUCH AS *YERSELF* GET SPLATTERED ALL OVER THAT *COLD, COLD MOUNTAIN...?*

THE THOUGHT *HAD* CROSSED MY MIND.

OH YE OF *LITTLE FAITH...*

CUT THE *COMEDY,* BANSHEE. WE'VE GOT *WORK* TO DO.

ALL RIGHT, X-MEN -- ACCORDING TO *GENERAL FREDERICKS,* WE'VE GOT *LESS THAN AN HOUR* TO DE-ACTIVATE THE *DOOM-SMITH* SYSTEM BEFORE IT AUTOMATICALLY *FIRES* EVERY *ICBM* IN THE *US STRATEGIC ARSENAL.*

SO OUR FIRST STEP IS TO GET INSIDE *VALHALLA BASE.*

HOW YA GONNA DO *THAT,* ONE-EYE? YOU GOT A *KEY* THAT'LL CRACK OPEN A *MOUNTAIN?*

AS A MATTER OF FACT, THUNDERBIRD, I *DO.*

AND THE NAME IS *CYCLOPS,* MISTER . NOT ONE-EYE. *UNDERSTAND?*

NIGHTCRAWLER, TELEPORT INSIDE -- THOSE *SAME* MISSILES THAT *SHOT US DOWN* CAME FROM AROUND *HERE* -- WHICH MEANS THERE'S GOT TO BE A *SURFACE ACCESS HATCH...*

IT IS AS GOOD AS *DONE,* CYCLOPS.

THERE IS A CRACK OF *FLAME* AND A GUSTING STENCH OF *BRIMSTONE...* AND NIGHT-CRAWLER IS SUDDENLY...

BAMF

...GONE.

ONLY TO *RE-APPEAR* A SPLIT-INSTANT LATER *DEEP* WITHIN THE MAN-MADE *LABYRINTH* THAT IS VALHALLA BASE.

AT LEAST, I *THINK* IT'S AS GOOD AS DONE...

I AM *INSIDE* VALHALLA, AT ANY RATE -- IN SOME SORT OF *MAINTENANCE TUNNEL...*

BUT *HOW* AM I TO FIND THIS MISSLE BAY CYCLOPS *SPOKE OF...*

I *WOULDN'T* WORRY ABOUT THAT, IF I WERE YOU, *MUTIE* --

-- I'D WORRY ABOUT *STAYIN' ALIVE!!*

WHAT THE !? YOU'RE STILL *CONSCIOUS!*

BUT I HIT YOU *HARD ENOUGH* TO FLATTEN A *DOZEN MEN!*

PERHAPS, BUT LIKE YOURSELF, *NIGHT-CRAWLER* IS NOT PRECISELY...

...A MAN.

IT DON'T MATTER *WHAT* YOU ARE, MUTIE--

--*NEFARIA* WANTS YOU *DEAD!*

THEN HIS AGENTS WILL HAVE TO DO A *FAR BETTER JOB* THAN YOU ARE DOING *HERR FROSCH.*

I DO NOT WISH TO *HURT* YOU, HERR *FROG...*

DON'T CALL ME THAT--! I AIN'T NO *FROG*-- I AIN'T NO FREAKIN' MUTANT LIKE *YOU*--

--I'M A *MAN!!*

AN' I DON'T NEED NO *HELP* STOMPIN' YOU INTO THE *GROUND...*

...NO HELP AT ALL...

BAMF

HUH?? WHERE'D HE GO??

NOWHERE, HERR FROSCH--

--*NOWHERE AT ALL!!*

KRAKK

AND *NOW,* HERR FROSCH, WE WILL GO AND FIND MY *FRIENDS...*

...AND THEN YOU WILL TELL US *ALL* WE WISH TO KNOW ABOUT YOUR *MASTER* AND HIS *PLANS...*

SPEAK OF THE DEVIL...

CROAKER, YOU UNMITIGATED IDIOT--!!

YOU HAD TO TRY AND DEFEAT THE X-MAN ON YOUR OWN-- YOU COULDN'T HAVE SUMMONED AID...

WHAT'S THE HASSLE, BOSS -- THE REST OF US CAN GO AFTER THE MUTIE AN' TAKE HIM EASY...

NO. LET HIM BE.

I HAVE...OTHER SURPRISES IN STORE FOR THE X-MEN.

DOOMSMITH MINUS 43 MINUTES-- IT DOESN'T TAKE NIGHTCRAWLER LONG TO FIND THE MISSLE BAY...

DON'T GO AWAY, HERR FROSCH--I SHOULD ONLY BE A MOMENT.

...BUT EVEN THOSE FEW MINUTES ARE MINUTES THE X-MEN CAN ILL AFFORD.

ALL I HAVE TO DO IS FIND THE MANUAL OVERRIDE CONTROL...

AH, THERE IT IS...

THE FROG-MAN -- HE'S GONE!

KTAK!

WITH BARELY A SOUND, THE HEAVY BLAST DOOR LIFTS HIGH INTO THE AFTERNOON SUNLIGHT...

NIGHTCRAWLER!

ALL RIGHT, PEOPLE, WE'VE GOT OUR DOOR...

...LET'S GET INSIDE.

WE HAVE A PROBLEM, CYCLOPS-- I HAD A PRISONER, A TALKING FROG-MAN...

...BUT...HE ESCAPED.

CAN'T BE HELPED, KURT-- WE ALL MAKE MISTAKES-- BUT THE SOONER WE'RE IN THE COMMAND POST, THE BETTER.

SO LET'S MOVE IT, X-MEN.

ALL GOES WELL, AT FIRST-- ALMOST TOO WELL.

CYCLOPS... IS IT MY IMAGINATION, LAD...

...OR IS IT GETTIN' A BIT STUFFY IN HERE...?

63

IRISH HAS A *POINT,* ONE-EYE... I FEEL KINDA *WOOZY* MYSELF... AN' I'VE FELT THIS WAY... *BEFORE...*

THERE'S YOUR ANSWER, BANSHEE-- *GAS!*

BEFORE THE X-MEN CAN *REACT,* THE GAS CLOUD IS *ON* THEM...

...CHOKING, BLISTERING, BLINDING, TEARING AT THEIR SKIN LIKE *ACID,* TEARING AT THEIR *MINDS...*

...IN A MOMENT, IT'LL BE ALL OVER.

IF THE X-MEN *LET* THAT MOMENT *HAPPEN.*

WE'VE GOT TO GET *OUT OF HERE...*

ALL OF YOU-- *SMASH* THRU THAT WALL INTO THE *NEXT TUNNEL!!*

THE *AIR FORCE* DESIGNED THIS COMPLEX TO SURVIVE *ANYTHING*--NUCLEAR WAR, BIOLOGICAL HOLOCAUST, EVEN A *METEOR STRIKE...*

...TROUBLE IS, THEY *NEVER* EXPECTED THE *X-MEN.*

DOOMSMITH MINUS 35 MINUTES

CYCLOPS, *LOOK!*

A *SQUAD* OF АМЕРИКАНСКИЙ *SOLDIERS*-- AND THEY DO NOT LOOK AT ALL *FRIENDLY.*

THAT MAY GO DOWN ON RECORD AS THE *UNDER-STATEMENT* OF THE YEAR...

GET-- THOSE MUTIES-- MEN--

--KILL --THEM-- *ALL!!*

X-MEN, *GET BEHIND ME!* I WILL SHIELD YOU FROM THE *BULLETS.*

CYCLOPS, WE *CANNOT* STAY HERE -- IF WE *DO*, THE *GAS* WILL *OVERCOME US...*

I *KNOW* THAT, STORM! BUT WE CAN'T *HURT* THOSE SOLDIERS--

THEY'RE NOT *RESPONSIBLE* FOR THEIR ATTACK. *LOOK AT THEM* -- THEY'VE BEEN *HYPNOTIZED!*

VERY WELL -- IF YOU DO NOT WANT THESE SOLDIERS *HURT*, THEY WILL *NOT* BE HURT--

--BUT THEY *WILL* BE STOPPED!

RAW ENERGY CRACKLES IN THE STILL AIR, *LIGHTNING* FLARING BRIGHT AROUND THEM...

...AS A *WIND* SPRINGS UP FROM *NOWHERE.*

...AND WITH THE WIND, A SOUND *NEVER BEFORE HEARD* WITHIN THE SAFE, SECURE CONFINES OF *VALHALLA'S BASE...*

...THE *SOUND* OF *RUNNING WATER...*

...THE SOUND OF A *FLOOD!*

IT GATHERS THE SOLDIERS IN LIKE A *LIVING THING,* GENTLY SWEEPING THEM DOWN THE LONG CORRIDORS UNTIL THEY ARE *NO LONGER A THREAT* TO THE *X-MEN...*

...AND THEN IT *SETS THEM DOWN...*

...AND FADES AWAY, AS QUICKLY, AS QUIETLY, AS IT HAD *COME.*

I THINK WE MAY *PROCEED* NOW, CYCLOPS...

...THE *SOLDIERS* WILL NOT *BOTHER* US ANYMORE.

MAYBE NOT THE SOLDIERS... BUT AIR FORCE SECURITY TROOPS AREN'T THE ONLY THREATS LURKING IN THE VAST SILENT HALLS...

THERE THEY ARE, GORT!

GORT SEES THEM, CATMAN--

...NOT BY A LONG SHOT.

--AND GORT WILL KILL!

BANSHEE, LOOK OUT -- HE'S GONNA THROW MEEEE

WOK

EEEE

THE FIGHT HAS BARELY BEGUN--AND ALREADY TWO X-MEN ARE OUT FOR THE COUNT. A BAD OMEN.

CYCLOPS-- IT'S THE MAN-FROG I TOLD YOU OF...

AND HE'S GOT THE REST OF NEFARIA'S ANI-MEN WITH HIM...

WE HAVEN'T TIME TO BE GENTLE, X-MEN --SO TAKE 'EM DOWN!

TAKE 'EM DOWN HARD!!

EASIER SAID THEN DONE, CYCLOPS.

BECAUSE--THOUGH BOTH SIDES ARE NUMERICALLY EQUAL...

...THE ANI-MEN ARE FRESH, UNGASSED, EAGER FOR THE KILL -- THE X-MEN ARE NOT.

THUS, IN THE *BEGINNING*, WEAKNESS, *FATIGUE*--THE SURPRISE AND FEROCITY OF THE *AMBUSH*--ALL TAKE THEIR *DEADLY* TOLL...

...AND THE BATTLE *QUICKLY* GOES *AGAINST* THE X-MEN.

AAAARRGKH!!

THAMM!

YOU THINK YOU'RE SOME *HOTSHOT* WITH THOSE *METAL CLAWS* HUH, MUTIE?

WELL *MY* CLAWS AIN'T FAKE-- THEY'RE *REAL*--

--AN' THEY CAN *KILL*!

NOT WHILE *COLOSSUS* LIVES!

HUH!?! WHO GRABBED MY ARM!?!

I 'GRABBED' IT-- I, *COLOSSUS*--

K-TOM!

--AND WHILE COLOSSUS *LIVES*, THE WOLVERINE WILL NOT BE *HARMED*!

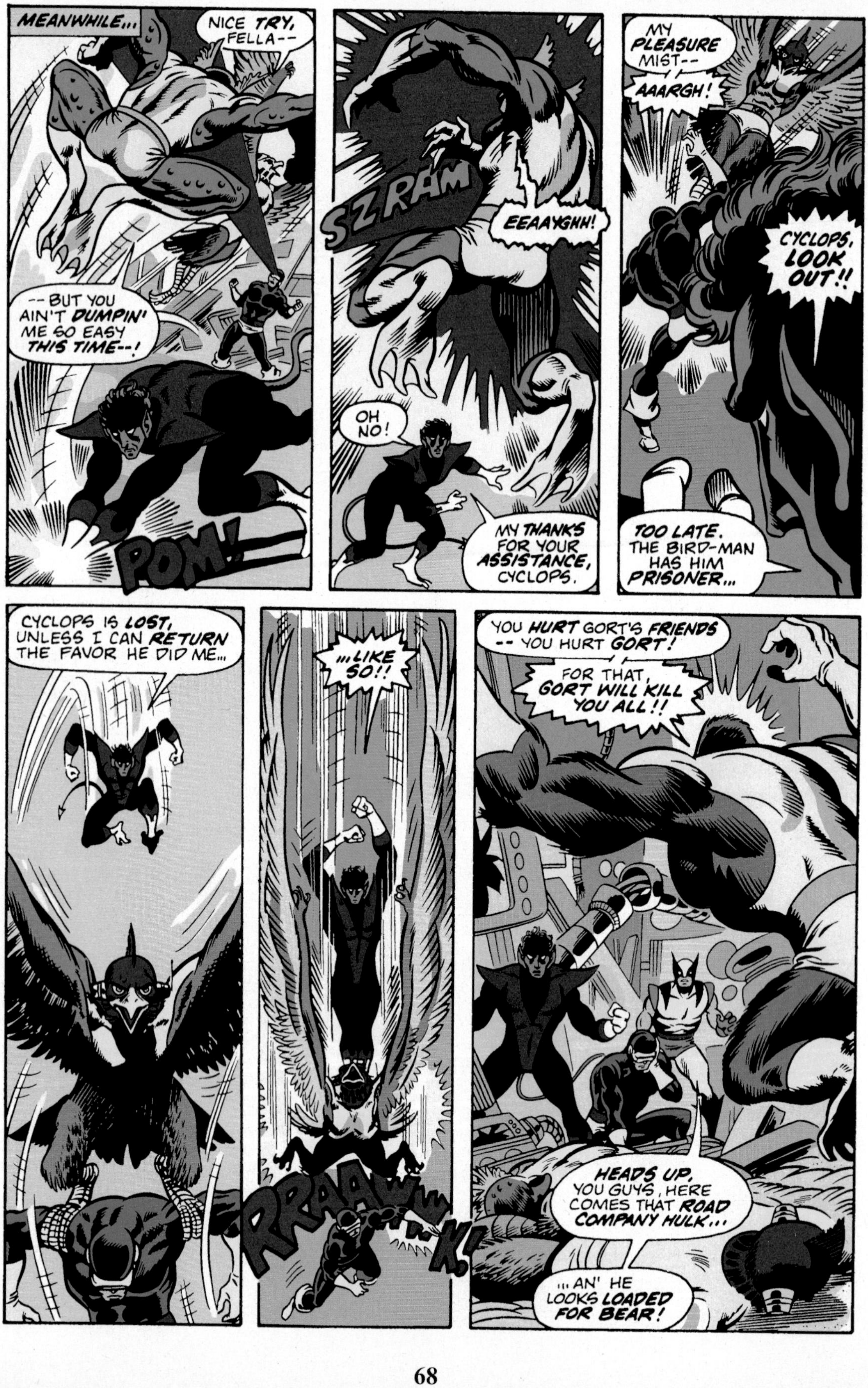
MEANWHILE...
NICE TRY, FELLA--
--BUT YOU AIN'T DUMPIN' ME SO EASY THIS TIME--!
POM!
SZRAM
EEAAYGHH!
OH NO!
MY THANKS FOR YOUR ASSISTANCE, CYCLOPS.
MY PLEASURE MIST--
AAARGH!
CYCLOPS, LOOK OUT!!
TOO LATE. THE BIRD-MAN HAS HIM PRISONER...
CYCLOPS IS LOST, UNLESS I CAN RETURN THE FAVOR HE DID ME...
...LIKE SO!!
RRAAAWWK!
YOU HURT GORT'S FRIENDS -- YOU HURT GORT!
FOR THAT, GORT WILL KILL YOU ALL!!
HEADS UP, YOU GUYS, HERE COMES THAT ROAD COMPANY HULK...
...AN' HE LOOKS LOADED FOR BEAR!

I THINK NOT!

SZKRAU!

SONUVAGUN, THE FUTZER'S STILL ON HIS *FEET*...

WHAT SAY WE...

AS YOU *WISH*, MY FRIEND...

WAMMO!

THE ANI-MEN ARE *DEFEATED*...

...I MUSSST *FLEE*, TO WARN COUNT *NEFARIA*.

HEAR ME, X-MAN! MY WILL ISSS *YOUR* WILL -- YOU CANNOT *RESISSST* MY *HYPNOTIC* POWERS.

MY *MIND*--! SHE'S IN MY *MIND* -- I CAN'T *KEEP*-- HER OUT--

IN A MOMENT, DRAGONFLY'S SPELL IS *COMPLETE*, AND BEHIND CYCLOPS' *RUBY QUARTZ VISOR*... HIS EYES SO *BLANK*...

...AND OPEN *WIDE*...

... HIS EYES MOTION AUTO- MATICALLY *RAISING* THE QUARTZ CRYSTAL SHIELD, *FREEING* HIS EYEBEAMS FROM THEIR *CAGE*.

THE *RESULTS* ARE *PREDICTABLE*.

ZZRRAP!

WE'VE BEATEN THE *MOUNTAIN* -- AND WE'VE *BEATEN* NEFARIA'S *ANI-MEN*...

...ALL THAT'S LEFT NOW IS THE *GOOD COUNT* HIM- SELF AND WE'RE *HOME FREE.*

DOOMSMITH MINUS 18 MINUTES.

WAIT A MINUTE-- WHERE ARE BANSHEE AND THUNDERBIRD?

OUT COLD-- THAT GORILLA WASTED 'EM PRETTY GOOD.

WE'LL HAVE TO LEAVE THEM HERE...

WE HAVEN'T TIME TO WAKE THEM UP-- WE'VE GOT TO GET TO NEFARIA AND THE DOOMSMITH SYSTEM.

NICE THOUGHT, CYCLOPS. BUT VALHALLA'S A HUGE COMPLEX, THREE CUBIC MILES OF CORRIDORS AND CUBICLES...

...AND BY THE TIME A BODY'S FOUND THE PLACE HE'S LOOKING FOR, IT CAN SOMETIMES BE...

...TOO LATE.

NO!!

...IT'S ARMED AND COUNTING AND THERE'S NO WAY ON EARTH WE CAN SHUT IT OFF IN TIME!

NEFARIA'S LOCKED THE DOOMSMITH SYSTEM INTO THE SELF-DESTRUCT CIRCUIT...

SELF-DESTRUCT ENGAGED T-0.09 MIN.

CUT: TO A PAIR OF VERY WEARY HEROES...

OHHH, ME ACHIN' BACK...

I'M THINKIN' I'M GETTIN' A MITE TOO OLD FOR THIS SORT OF ROUGH-HOUSE.

SPEAK FOR YOURSELF, IRISH.

LORD ABOVE... WILL YE LOOK AT THIS MESS. IT MUST HAVE BEEN A GRAND AND GLORIOUS FIGHT.

YEAH. LOOKS LIKE THEY DIDN'T NEED OUR HELP FOR ANYTHING-- IT FIGURES.

CUT AGAIN: TO ONE OF VALHALLA'S HANGER LEVELS...

THE FOOLS! THE X-MEN THINK COUNT NEFARIA IS BEATEN, THAT THEY'VE WON--

--BUT THE VERY MOMENT OF THEIR 'VICTORY' WILL BE THE MOMENT OF THEIR DEATH --THE MOMENT OF NEFARIA'S GREATEST TRIUMPH!!

THE SELF-DESTRUCT SYSTEM WILL BLOW THIS MOUNTAIN-- AND ALL IN IT-- TO THE DEEPEST PITS OF HELL...!

...AND WHEN THAT HAPPENS, COUNT NEFARIA WILL BE LONG GONE--

--EH!?

I RECOGNIZE THEM FROM THE MONITOR SCREENS -- THEY'RE TWO OF THE X-MEN!

HEY, IRISH, GET A LOAD OF THIS--

--LOOKS LIKE THAT NEFARIA'S DUDE'S BUGGIN' OUT ON HIS COMPADRES.

YOU'RE TOO LATE, MUTANTS--

--YOU'LL NEVER STOP ME NOW!!

HE'S TAKIN' OFF!!

ONCE HE GETS AIRBORNE IN THAT HARRIER, THERE'S NOT A CRATE IN THIS MOUNTAIN THAT CAN STOP HIM!

SHRREEEE

YEAH, MAYBE NOT A PLANE-- BUT A MAN CAN DO WHAT A PLANE CAN'T--

THUNDERBIRD, NO!

--AND THUNDERBIRD IS JUST THAT MAN!

DON'T GO AWAY, NEFFIE BABY-- 'CAUSE JOHN PROUDSTAR IS COMIN' TO GET YOU...

...AN' HE'S A MAN WHO DON'T GIVE UP!

SKRAK!

ARE YE CRAZY, LAD--?

GET OFF THE PLANE, THUNDERBIRD-- I CAN STOP HIM WITH A SONIC BLAST--

--BUT YE'VE GOT TA GET OFF!!

CYKE, WE'RE RUNNIN' OUTA TIME-- WE GOTTA GO!

HOW FAR D'YOU THINK WE'D GET IN FIVE MINUTES, WOLVERINE-- BECAUSE THAT'S ALL THE TIME WE'VE GOT!

OUR ONLY CHANCE-- THE WORLD'S ONLY CHANCE IS TO TRY AND SHUT THE SYSTEM DOWN--

CYCLOPS, WHAT ARE YOU DOING!?!

WHA--? PROFESSOR, THE DOOMSMITH...

IS TOTALLY OUT OF COMMISSION! I'VE MENTALLY SCANNED THE SYSTEM-- YOUR BATTLE WITH THE ANI-MEN DESTROYED THE COMMAND RELAYS AND THE BACK-UPS...

BUT ENOUGH OF THAT--

--YOU MUST GET OUTSIDE THE MOUNTAIN, AND QUICKLY -- YOU'VE AN X-MAN IN MORTAL DANGER!

YOU HEARD THE MAN, PEOPLE--

--MOVE IT!

AND THE X-MEN MOVE, AS ONLY X-MEN CAN...

...BUT EVENTS OUTSIDE ARE MOVING AS WELL, TOO FAR, TOO FAST.

YOU MADMAN--! YOU'LL KILL US BOTH!!

JOHN PROUDSTAR, GET OFF THE AIRPLANE, BEFORE IT'S TOO LATE!

BUTT OUT, BALDY -- I'M THRU TAKIN' ORDERS--!

I'VE BEEN A LONER ALL MY LIFE, XAVIER -- AN OUTCAST -- DUMPED ON BY EVERYBODY I MET--

--BUT I'M A MAN, XAVIER, A WARRIOR OF THE APACHE--

--AN' TODAY I'M GONNA PROVE IT!!

RAKT!

FOR GOD'S SAKE, LADDIE-- GET OFF THE PLANE!!

JOHN PROUDSTAR'S HANDS RIP *DEEP* INTO THE HARRIER'S *COCKPIT*, RAVAGING *CONTROL SYSTEMS*, COMPUTERS, ELECTRONIC HARDWARE...

THERE THEY ARE!

STORM, *GET AFTER THEM!* GIVE BANSHEE A *HAND!*

...RIPPING THE TECHNIC *NERVOUS SYSTEM* OUT OF THE *AIRCRAFT.*

IT'S A *POUNDING* THAT NO PLANE WAS DESIGNED TO TAKE. SOONER OR LATER *SOMETHING* HAS TO GIVE...

...SOONER OR LATER, SOMETHING *DOES.*

OH MY GOD.

WHDOOMM!

THUNDERBIRD, NO! GET OUT. BOY--

GET OUT!

CYCLOPS, THE AIRCRAFT... IT'S...

I CAN SEE IT, PETER...

YOU, CYCLOPS... AND ONE OTHER.

THUNDERBIRD--!

NNNOOOO!!

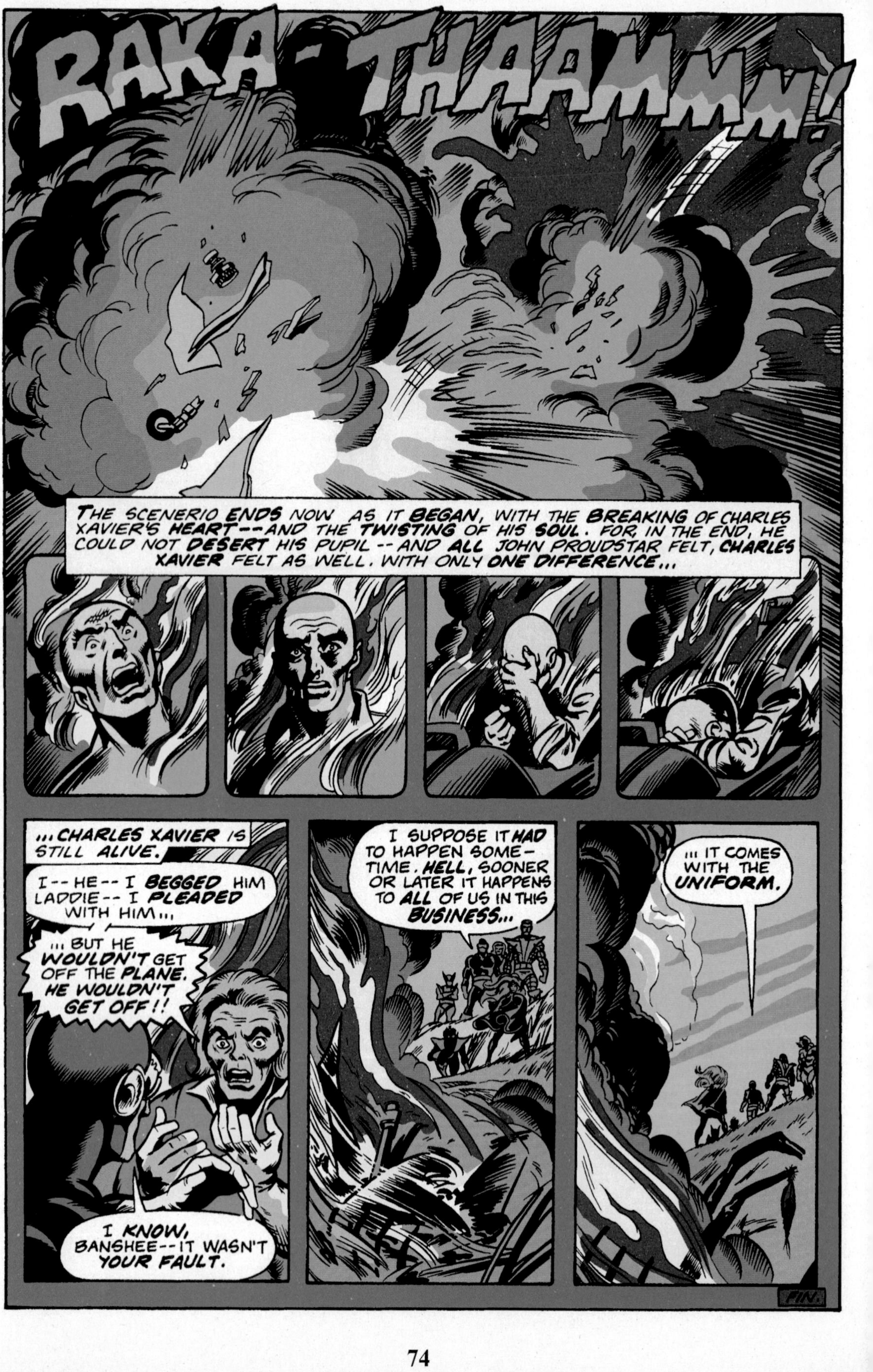
RAKA-THAAMMM!!
THE SCENERIO ENDS NOW AS IT BEGAN, WITH THE BREAKING OF CHARLES XAVIER'S HEART--AND THE TWISTING OF HIS SOUL. FOR, IN THE END, HE COULD NOT DESERT HIS PUPIL--AND ALL JOHN PROUDSTAR FELT, CHARLES XAVIER FELT AS WELL. WITH ONLY ONE DIFFERENCE...
...CHARLES XAVIER IS STILL ALIVE.
I--HE--I BEGGED HIM LADDIE--I PLEADED WITH HIM...
...BUT HE WOULDN'T GET OFF THE PLANE. HE WOULDN'T GET OFF!!
I KNOW, BANSHEE--IT WASN'T YOUR FAULT.
I SUPPOSE IT HAD TO HAPPEN SOME-TIME. HELL, SOONER OR LATER IT HAPPENS TO ALL OF US IN THIS BUSINESS...
...IT COMES WITH THE UNIFORM.
FIN.

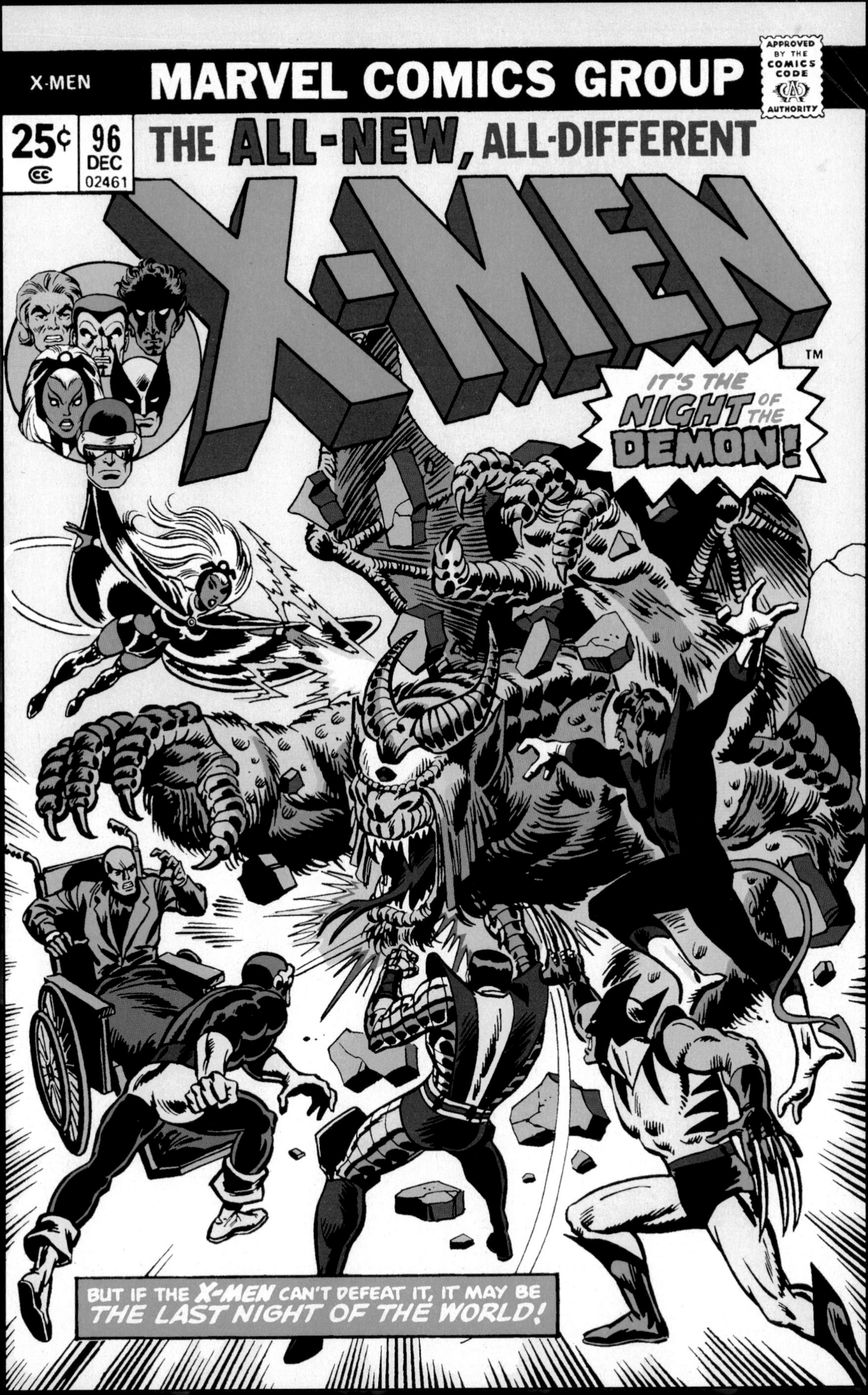
X-MEN
MARVEL COMICS GROUP
APPROVED BY THE COMICS CODE AUTHORITY
25¢
CC
96
DEC
02461
THE ALL-NEW, ALL-DIFFERENT
X-MEN
TM
IT'S THE NIGHT OF THE DEMON!
BUT IF THE X-MEN CAN'T DEFEAT IT, IT MAY BE THE LAST NIGHT OF THE WORLD!

STAN LEE PRESENTS: **THE UNCANNY X-MEN!**

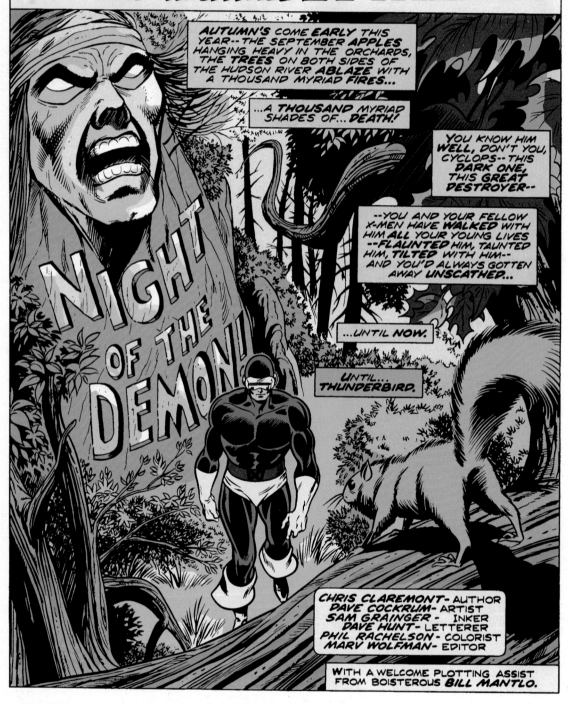

AUTUMN'S COME *EARLY THIS YEAR*-- THE *SEPTEMBER APPLES* HANGING HEAVY IN THE ORCHARDS, THE *TREES* ON BOTH SIDES OF THE HUDSON RIVER *ABLAZE* WITH A THOUSAND MYRIAD *FIRES...*

...A THOUSAND MYRIAD SHADES OF... *DEATH!*

YOU KNOW HIM *WELL,* DON'T YOU, *CYCLOPS*-- THIS *DARK ONE,* THIS *GREAT DESTROYER*--

--YOU AND YOUR FELLOW X-MEN HAVE *WALKED* WITH HIM *ALL* YOUR YOUNG LIVES --FLAUNTED HIM, *TAUNTED* HIM, *TILTED* WITH HIM-- AND YOU'D ALWAYS GOTTEN AWAY *UNSCATHED...*

...UNTIL *NOW.*

NIGHT OF THE DEMON!

UNTIL... *THUNDERBIRD.*

CHRIS CLAREMONT- AUTHOR
DAVE COCKRUM- ARTIST
SAM GRAINGER - INKER
DAVE HUNT- LETTERER
PHIL RACHELSON- COLORIST
MARV WOLFMAN- EDITOR

WITH A WELCOME PLOTTING ASSIST FROM BOISTEROUS *BILL MANTLO.*

IT'S BEEN WEEKS NOW SINCE THUNDERBIRD *DIED,* AND THE MEMORY *STILL* HURTS, DOESN'T IT, CYCLOPS...

...THE NAGGING FEELING--THE *FEAR*--THAT IF YOU'D ACTED *DIFFERENTLY,* THUNDERBIRD WOULD BE ALIVE *TODAY.*

*LAST ISH-- MARV.

AWAKE OR ASLEEP, YOU *CAN'T* ESCAPE THE IMAGES *SEARED* INTO YOUR MIND'S EYE:

YOU *MADMAN* --YOU'LL *KILL* US *BOTH!!*

IMAGES OF COUNT NEFARIA MAKING A LAST, DESPERATE ATTEMPT TO FLEE VALHALLA BASE... OF THUNDERBIRD TRYING TO STOP HIM...

FOR *GOD'S* SAKE, LADDIE-- GET *OFF* THE PLANE.!!

...OF THUNDERBIRD'S FINAL, DEFIANT CRY.

...I'M A *MAN,* XAVIER, A *WARRIOR* OF THE APACHE--

--AND *TODAY* I'M GONNA *PROVE* IT.!!

YOU *REMEMBER* WHAT HAPPENED NEXT, DON'T YOU, CYCLOPS?

WHOOM!

AND WHAT HAPPENED *AFTER* THAT?

CYCLOPS, THE *AIRCRAFT* ...IT'S...

I CAN *SEE* IT, PETER...

RAKA-THAAMMM!!

THUNDERBIRD *HADN'T* GOTTEN OUT.

THAT'S THE REAL *HELL* OF HIS DEATH, ISN'T IT, CYCLOPS-- BECAUSE YOU *KNOW* HE HADN'T EVEN *TRIED* TO GET OUT.

YOU AND THE X-MEN HAD SAVED THE WORLD FROM A NUCLEAR HOLOCAUST-- BUT YOU'D LOST A MAN TO DO IT...

... AND *TRY* AS YOU MIGHT, YOU CAN'T *BALANCE* THOSE SCALES, IN YOUR MIND *OR* IN YOUR *HEART*...

...CAN YOU, CYCLOPS?

NO.

CAN YOU?

NO!

CAN YOU?!

NO!!

NNNNOOOOOO.!!!

ZZZRRRAAMM!!

HE'S *NEVER* CUT LOOSE LIKE THIS BEFORE-- *WITHOUT* THOUGHT OR CARE OR *RESTRAINT*...

ZZRRAAUU!!

...THE *POWER* FLOWS THRU HIM LIKE A THING ALIVE--

--AND FOR THOSE *FEW* MOMENTS THERE IS *HATRED* IN HIM, YES, BUT THERE IS *GLORY* TOO--AN UNHOLY GLORY, A NEED, A ...*HUNGER*...

...BUT THEN THE MOMENTS *PASS*...

...AND *SCOTT SUMMERS* IS *HIMSELF* AGAIN.

OH MY LORD--

WHAT HAVE I DONE ??

WAY TO **GO**, HERO.

I GOT TO **HAND** IT TO YOU, SUMMERS --WHEN THEY WERE GIVING OUT **BRAINS** AND **COMMON SENSE**...

...YOU MUST **NOT** HAVE EVEN BOTHERED TO **STAND ON LINE**-- YOU **KNOW** HOW DANGEROUS YOUR **EYE BEAMS** ARE!

YOU KNEW THE **RULES**-- AND THE **RISKS**-- WHEN YOU GOT **INTO** THIS GAME...

...ALL THE X-MEN DID, THUNDERBIRD INCLUDED.

AND **YOU'RE** TOP MAN IN THIS OUTFIT, CYCLOPS--YOU **WANTED** THE JOB AND YOU'RE **GOOD** AT IT-- AND NOW YOU'VE GOT TO **PAY** THE PRICE...

...BECAUSE THIS JOB MEANS TAK-ING **BAD** AS WELL AS GOOD. IT MEANS WATCH-ING YOUR FRIENDS **LIVE**-- AND WATCHING THEM **DIE**...

...AND **THUNDERBIRD** IS **DEAD**, MISTER-- ALL THE **WISHING** IN THE WORLD WON'T **BRING HIM BACK**.

HE'S **DEAD** AND YOU'RE **ALIVE**-- AND THAT'S **IT!** LIKE IT OR NOT --NO MATTER **HOW** MUCH IT **HURTS**-- THE **REST** OF US HAVE TO GO ON **LIVING**.

REST IN **PEACE**, JOHN PROUDSTAR...

YOU'VE EARNED **THAT** MUCH, AT LEAST.

SO HAVE **YOU**, CYCLOPS...

...AND IF YOU'RE NOT **CAREFUL**...

...YOU MAY SOON BE **REST**-ING AS PEACEFULLY-- AND AS **PERMANENTLY** --AS YOUR **FRIEND**.

CUT NOW: ACROSS THE WOODLAND MILES TO AN AFTERNOON SESSION OF...

WOLVERINE, NO! YOU CAUGHT ME BY SURPRISE--

--I HIT YOU FULL STRENGTH!!

SWOT!

...FUN AND GAMES, ...X-MEN STYLE!

ARE YOU HURT, MY FRIEND?

NAW-- YOU ONLY MADE ME MAD--

--AND, BABY, THE WOLVERINE JUST LOVES TO GET MAD.

SNICKT

GANGWAY, COLOSSUS --THIS ISN'T GONNA HURT YOU-- MUCH--

--HEY!!

CORRECTION, WOLVERINE-- IT WILL NOT HURT PETER AT ALL--

--MY WIND BLASTS HAVE SEEN TO THAT.

HA HA

HEY, ELF--WHAT'S SO FUNNY--?!

YOU DON'T LAUGH AT ME, NIGHTCRAWLER --GOT THAT?!

HA

HA

HA

NOBODY LAUGHS AT THE WOLVERINE, MISTER--

KURT-- WATCH OUT!!

EH--??

--NOBODY!!

BAMF!

WOLVERINE!!

LADDIE-- TAKE IT EASY. YE COULD HAVE KILLED NIGHT- CRAWLER THEN, Y'KNOW...

BANSHEE-- COULD I HAVE A WORD WITH YOU, PLEASE?

YEAH-- I KNOW.

YE'RE LOOKING *TIRED*, CHARLES...

I *AM* TIRED. THESE LAST FEW *WEEKS* HAVE NOT BEEN ...*PLEASANT* ONES...

I KNOW-- THUNDERBIRD'S DEATH HAS GOT US *ALL* A BIT *DOWN*.

IT'S *SCOTT* I'M WORRIED ABOUT...

HE'S TRYING *NOT* TO SHOW IT, BUT THUNDERBIRD'S DEATH HAS *AFFECTED* HIM DEEPLY--

--HE'S STARTING TO *BROOD*--MAKE MISTAKES...

...IF HE DOESN'T *EASE UP* ON HIMSELF AND *RELAX*... I DON'T KNOW, BANSHEE ...I JUST *DON'T KNOW*...

BLAST! IS IT FOUR ALREADY--?

I'M EXPECTING OUR NEW *HOUSEKEEPER*--SHE'S TO *LOOK AFTER* THE HOUSE AND... *THINGS* WHILE I'M *GONE*...

GONE? GONE *WHERE*?

BING BONG

IN FACT, *THAT* SHOULD BE HER NOW.

"HOUSEKEEPER," HE SAYS-- "A NICE *WIDDER-WOMAN*, NAME OF *MOIRA MACTAGGERT*..."

...PROBABLY *80 YEARS* OLD, UGLY AS *SIN*--WITH FORTY YEARS SERVICE IN THE *SCOTS GUARDS*...

BING BONG

ALL RIGHT. ALL RIGHT--I'M *COMIN'!!*

I *SAID* I WAS COMIN' --THERE'S *NO NEED* FOR YE TA LEAN ON THE *BLOODY DOOR*... BELL...

WHO THE BLAZES ARE YE??

AH *BEG* YUIR *PARDON*--!

MAH NAME IS *MOIRA MACTAGGERT* --AN' AH'VE BEEN ENGAGED AS *HOUSEKEEPER* HERE BY *PROFESSOR CHARLES XAVIER*...

D'YOU WANT TO MAKE *SOMETHIN'* OF IT, THEN?!

81

CUT AGAIN: TO A ONCE-SECRET INSTALLATION SHROUDED DEEP WITHIN THE ADIRONDACK MOUNTAIN PRESERVE OF NORTHERN NEW YORK --AND TO WHAT MAY WELL BE...

THERE'S THE WASHINGTON COURIER, DR. LANG --RIGHT ON SCHEDULE...

ABOUT TIME, TOO.

PROJECT ARMAGEDDON

...A RENDEZVOUS WITH DESTINY.

STRANGE --I'VE BEEN WORKING ON THIS PROJECT OVER SIX YEARS-- AND NOW THAT IT'S NEARING FRUITION...

...I'M AS NERVOUS AS A FRESHMAN AT FINALS.

MICHAEL! COLONEL ROSSI! IT'S GOOD TO SEE YOU!

AM I RIGHT IN ASSUMING YOU'VE SOME GOOD NEWS FOR ME?

I HAVE SOME... NEWS, DR. LANG. FOR YOUR EARS ALONE.

THEY'VE AGREED THEN--I'VE GOT THE GREEN LIGHT.

NO. NOT YET. THE COUNCIL WANTS A FINAL REPORT --YEA OR NAY --GO OR NO GO--

--AND THEY WANT ME TO GIVE IT TO THEM.

AND YOU'RE AGAINST IT. WE USED TO BE FRIENDS, MICHAEL--WHAT HAPPENED?

THIS HAPPENED-- THIS PROJECT OF YOURS, SIX YEARS OF YOUR LIFE, A BILLION DOLLARS IN ILLEGAL APROPRIATIONS-- AND FOR WHAT--?

JUST SO YOU CAN KIDNAP A FEW LOUSY MUTANTS?!?

YES!! KIDNAP THEM --SECURE THESE MUTANT SPECIMENS FOR IN-DEPTH EXAMINATION-- SO THAT MANKIND WILL AT LAST KNOW ITS TRUE ENEMY--!

THAT'S WHAT MY WORK IS ALL ABOUT, MICHAEL--

--PROJECT ARMAGEDDON!!

THE FINAL ULTIMATE CONFLICT BETWEEN HOMO SAPIENS AND HOMO SUPERIOR-- BETWEEN MAN... AND MUTANT!

BOLIVAR TRASK KNEW-- HE UNDERSTOOD THE DANGER-- HE POINTED THE WAY--

--HE TRIED TO STOP THE MUTANTS, MICHAEL, AND THEY KILLED HIM FOR IT, HIM AND HIS SON.

YOU THINK I'M EXAGGERATING THE THREAT?

I THINK THERE IS NO THREAT.

WHY? BECAUSE THE ONLY MUTANTS ANYONE KNOWS OF FOR SURE ARE THE X-MEN? NOW WHO'S PLAYING THE FOOL?

THE BEAST

BUT THEY WON'T DESTROY ME.

EVERY CONTINGENCY HAS BEEN PREPARED FOR-- NO DETAIL HAS BEEN SPARED, MICHAEL, NOTHING LEFT TO CHANCE.

THE MUTANTS CANNOT STOP ME-- NO ONE CAN STOP ME NOW!

I CAN STOP YOU.

YOU'RE WRONG, STEVE--ALL THE WAY DOWN THE LINE...

NO, MY FRIEND, YOU ARE WRONG. BECAUSE WE ARE THE ANCIENT NEANDERTHALS FACING THE MUTANT CRO-MAGNON--

--IT IS US OR THEM, KILL OR BE KILLED--THERE IS NO OTHER WAY!

EVEN IF THAT WERE TRUE, YOUR PROJECT ISN'T THE ANSWER, NOT THESE DAYS --THE COUNTRY COULDN'T SURVIVE YOUR KIND OF MUTANT WITCH HUNT.

PROJECT ARMAGEDDON IS OVER, STEVE; IT'S FINISHED AS SOON AS I GET BACK TO WASHINGTON...I'M JUST SORRY IT HAD TO END LIKE THIS...

SO AM I, COLONEL ROSSI. BECAUSE THAT MEANS YOU MUST NEVER REACH WASHINGTON...

...ALIVE.

IT'S NIGHT NOW, THE QUIET END TO A LONG, STRENUOUS DAY...

...A TIME TO RELAX OVER A GOOD MEAL...A TIME FOR THE X-MEN TO BE FORMALLY INTRODUCED TO THEIR NEW HOUSEKEEPER...

...MRS. MOIRA MacTAGGERT.

SHE'S TO LOOK AFTER THE HOUSE--AND ALL OF YOU-- WHILE I'M AWAY.

YOU CUTTIN' OUT ON US, BOSS?

FOR A WHILE, WOLVERINE. EVERY MAN NEEDS A VACATION AT SOME POINT IN HIS LIFE...

...I'VE DECIDED THE TIME HAS COME FOR MINE.

MISTRESS MacTAGGERT-- I JUST WANTED TO APOLOGISE FOR ME BRUSQUE MANNER THIS AFTERNOON...

CASSIDY, MA'AM. SEAN CASSIDY. AN' I'D CONSIDER IT AN HONOR, INDEED IF YE'D JOIN' ME FER A CUP O' COFFEE...

IT'S NA NECESSARY, MR.... AH...

BANSHEE SEEMS QUITE TAKEN WITH MRS. MacTAGGERT--

WE ALL ARE, ONE WAY OR ANOTHER-- BUT, PROFESSOR, IF YOU ARE SO INTENT ON KEEPING OUR EXISTENCE SECRET FROM THE WORLD...

...WHY REVEAL OUR TRUE NATURE TO THIS ....HOUSEKEEPER?

THAT IS MY AFFAIR, ORORO.

BUT REST ASSURED-- OUR SECRET IS SAFE WITH MOIRA MacTAGGERT, SAFE UNTO DEATH.

BY THE WAY, HAVE YOU SEEN SCOTT ANYWHERE?

ZZR RAM MM

GOOD LORD-- THOSE ARE SCOTT'S EYE- BEAMS, BLASTING FULL POWER--

--AND THEY'RE RIGHT OUTSIDE!!

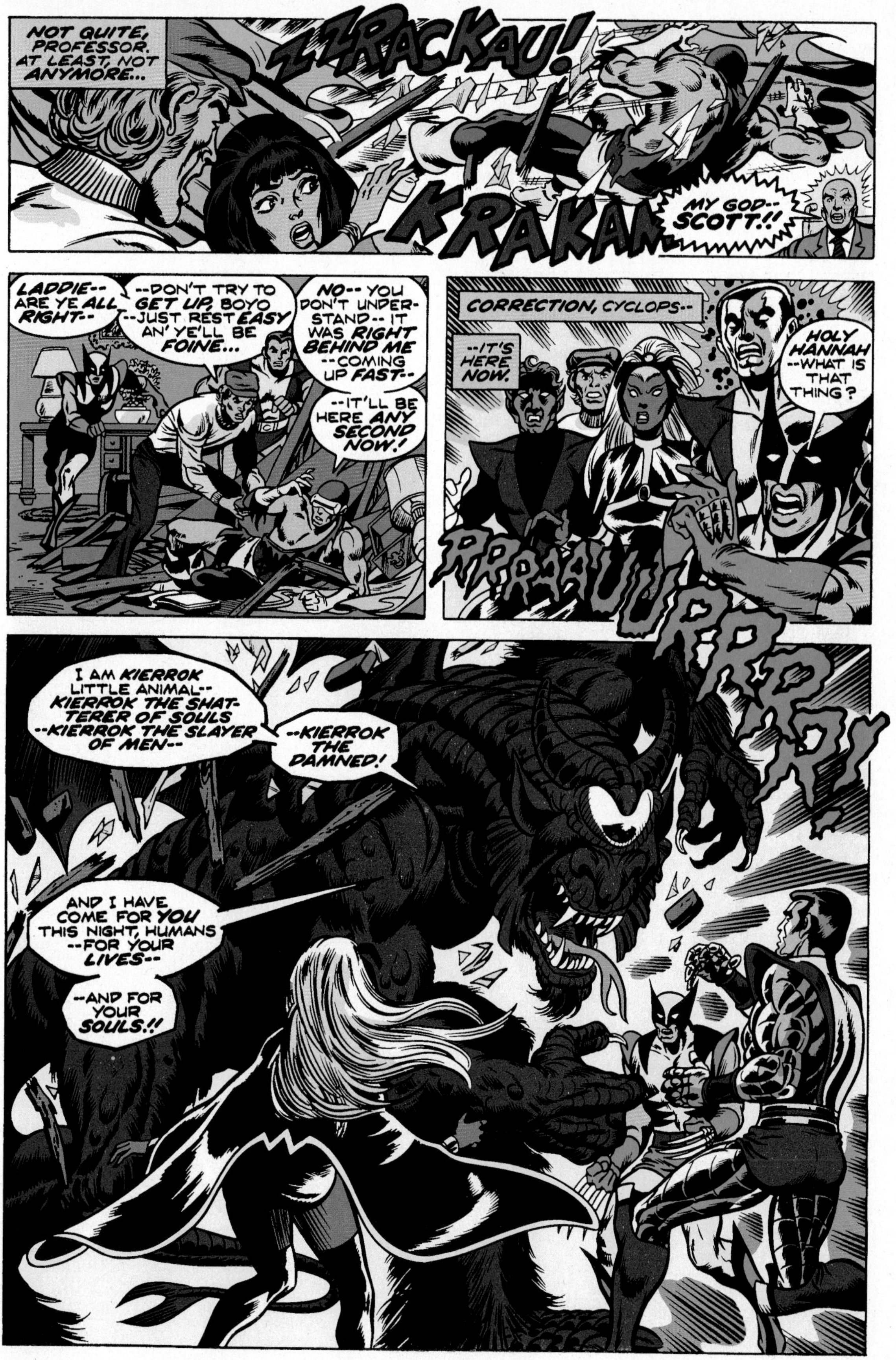
NOT QUITE, PROFESSOR. AT LEAST, NOT ANYMORE...
ZZRACKAU!
KRAKAM
MY GOD-- SCOTT!!
LADDIE-- ARE YE ALL RIGHT--
--DON'T TRY TO GET UP, BOYO --JUST REST EASY AN' YE'LL BE FOINE...
NO-- YOU DON'T UNDERSTAND-- IT WAS RIGHT BEHIND ME --COMING UP FAST--
--IT'LL BE HERE ANY SECOND NOW!
CORRECTION, CYCLOPS--
--IT'S HERE NOW.
HOLY HANNAH --WHAT IS THAT THING?
RRRAAUURRRR!
I AM KIERROK LITTLE ANIMAL-- KIERROK THE SHATTERER OF SOULS --KIERROK THE SLAYER OF MEN--
--KIERROK THE DAMNED!
AND I HAVE COME FOR YOU THIS NIGHT, HUMANS --FOR YOUR LIVES--
--AND FOR YOUR SOULS!!

I HAVE COME FOR YOU, *EYELESS ONE*, WHO AWAKENED ME *BEFORE MY TIME*--!

KRAUU!

X-MEN, *SCATTER*--ATTACK THE DEMON AS A *TEAM* --AS SCOTT AND I *TAUGHT YOU*--THAT'S OUR *ONLY HOPE*--

YOU SPEAK AS THE *LEADER*, OLD ONE--FOR THAT, MY CLAWS WILL TASTE *YOUR BLOOD* FIRST...

NOT WHILE *STORM* IS ALIVE TO *STOP YOU,* DEMON!

STORM, *NO.!!*

DON'T BOTHER ABOUT *ME*--MY *MENTAL POWERS* WILL PROTECT ME! I AM IN *NO DANGER*--BUT YOU *ARE*--!

GET OUT OF *HERE,* STORM--YOU'RE *NO MATCH* FOR KIERROK ON YOUR *OWN* --GET *OUT*-- *NOW!!*

AAAAAA!

YOU ARE *TOO SLOW,* FEMALE--AND KIERROK'S *CLAWS* ARE *TOO SHARP*--

YOUR *DEATH* WILL BE *QUICK,* WINGED ONE--

--YOU *MAY* *THANK* KIERROK FOR HIS *KIND- NESS.*

STORM WILL THANK YOU FOR *NOTHING,* MONSTER!

HE *THREATENED* YOU, ORORO--HE TRIED TO *KILL YOU*--!

BRUHMM!

PETER --BE *CAREFUL.!!*

KTAKOOOM!

AND *THAT* COLOSSUS *WILL NOT ALLOW!!*

DO YOU *ANIMALS* THINK KIERROK IS SO *EASILY DEFEATED*--ARE YOU SUCH *FOOLS*--!?!

I AM A *CHILD* OF THE *N'GARAI*--A CHILD OF THE *ELDER GODS,* WE WHO ONCE *RULED* THIS *EARTH* OF YOURS--!

I AM YOUR *MASTER,* HUMANS--

RRRRAAKK

--YOU CAN NEVER *DEFEAT* ME! *NEVER.!!*

KRUMF!

COLOSSUS, *LOOK OUT!!*

PERHAPS *NOT,* GARGOYLE--

--BUT WE CAN ALL *DIE TRYING!*

BRAP!

SO *FALL,* MONSTROUS ABOMINATION --*FALL!*

WHY DON'T YOU *FALL?!?*

KRAK!

KIERROK DOES NOT *FALL* TO SUCH AS *YOU,* CHANGELING.

TRAMM!

87

YYRRRRA!!.!!

FELLA, YOU JUST SAID THE WRONG THING--

--'CAUSE THE MISFIT MAY BE A MISFIT, BUT HE'S WOLVERINE'S BUDDY--

--AN' NOBODY BEATS ON WOLVERINE'S BUDDIES!

YOU-- HURT-- ME.!!

FOR THE FIRST TIME IN COUNTLESS AEONS A HUMAN HAS HURT ME!

HURT YOU?

BABY, YOU AIN'T SEEN NOTHIN' YET.

THERE'S A SAYING ABOUT WOLVERINES-- THE FOUR-LEGGED KIND-- YOU CAN PUSH THEM JUST SO FAR... AND THEN THEY'LL GO FOR YOUR THROAT!

HAAA!!!!!!--

AND THEY WON'T BACK OFF UNTIL YOU'RE DEAD --OR THEY ARE!

THE SAME GOES FOR THE MUTANT KNOWN ONLY AS... WOLVERINE.

--YAAAHHH!!

PUSH HIM TOO FAR AND HE GOES MAD-- AND WHEN HE DOES, HE KILLS.

CASE IN POINT:

TEN YEARS O' PSYCHO-TRAINING. O' HYPNOTISM. O' DRUG THERAPY. TEN YEARS O' PRAYIN'...

...AN' I CUT HIM TO PIECES WITHOUT A THOUGHT.

NOTHING CHANGES, PROF-- I THOUGHT I'D LEARNED TO CONTROL MYSELF--I GUESS I WAS WRONG-- AN' YA WANNA KNOW SOMETHIN' FUNNY--

--I'M GLAD!

YOU WANT TO KNOW SOMETHING EVEN *FUNNIER*--?

KIERROK'S *NOT DEAD.*

HUH--? BUT I--?

HEY, MAN-- THIS IS *CRAZY.*

I *BLASTED* HIM A *DOZEN* TIMES-- *FULL STRENGTH*-- AND EACH TIME HE *REFORMED,* STRONGER THAN BEFORE...

...WHILE *EACH* TIME, I FELT *WEAKER.*

YOU *ALL* LOOK...WEAKER. AS IF OUR *STRENGTH*-- OUR *LIFE FORCES* WERE SOMEHOW BEING *LEECHED AWAY* FROM US...

...BY *HIM!* KIERROK!

HE'S THE KEY TO THIS BATTLE AND POSSIBLY THE *KEY* TO OUR *SALVATION* AS WELL.

I MUST TRY A *MINDPROBE* BEFORE HE'S FULLY *RECOVERED.*

PROFESSOR, *NO!* IT'S TOO *DANGEROUS!!*

THE CRY COMES *TOO LATE*-- FOR ALREADY, CHARLES XAVIER'S PROBE IS *DEEP INSIDE* THE MIND OF KIERROK, THE *SHATTERER OF SOULS...*

...DEEP INSIDE... *HELL.*

HE IS *SWEPT* ALONG LIKE A WOOD CHIP IN A FLOOD OF ALIEN IMAGES ...UNTIL, FOR THE *BRIEFEST* OF MOMENTS, HE ACTUALLY *BECOMES* KIERROK

...AND IN THAT MOMENT, CHARLES XAVIER... SCREAMS!

89

LOOK OUT, ALL O' YE'S-- THE BEASTIE'S *LOOSE* AGAIN--!

GET THE PROFESSOR T' *SAFETY*-- MY *SONIC* BLASTS AREN'T GONNA HOLD THE DEMON *LONG!*

LORD IN HEAVEN, MY MIND... MY MIND...

WELL, IF SONIC BLASTS'LL DO *NAE GUID*, LET'S SEE HOW YON *KELPIE* FARES--

--AGAINST CLOSE-RANGE MACHINE-GUN FIRE!

MOIRA, ME DARLIN'--YE'RE A *FOINE* FIGURE OF A WO-MAN--AN' A *BRAVE* ONE T' BOOT--AN' I'M THINKIN' I LIKE YE A *LOT*--

--BUT *HERE* AN' *NOW*, LASSIE--YE'RE PLAYIN' WAY OUTA YER LEAGUE.

SO STAY *UNDER COVER*, STAY OUTA *TROUBLE*--

--AN' *STAY ALIVE!*

CYCLOPS, THE PROFESSOR'S *COMING AROUND.*

LORD... WHAT I SAW ...WHAT I SAW... NO MAN SHOULD SEE...

SCOTT? HOW ARE WE... DOING...

NOT WELL, SIR. HOLDING OUR OWN...

WE... *CANNOT* DEFEAT KIERROK FIGHTING *HAND-TO-HAND*... MUST DESTROY HIM AT... *SOURCE.*

THE *CAIRN*, STORM... YOU MUST... *SEAL* THE CAIRN...

GO, CHILD... I WILL... *DIRECT* YOU...

BUT *HURRY*, STORM... *HURRY!* OR WE ARE ALL... *DOOMED*...

90

THE *NIGHTWIND* IS A WELCOME *CARESS* ON HER BARE SKIN AS SHE SOARS *HIGH AND AWAY* INTO THE MIDNIGHT SKY...

...SHE IS *FREE* NOW-- OF *HOUSES, WALLS, PEOPLE* --OF THE *CAGES* MANKIND BUILDS TO LOCK HIMSELF INTO ...*FREE AND HAPPY AND ALIVE*...

...FOR THE MOMENT.

THERE IS THE *CAIRN* THE PROFESSOR SPOKE OF-- AND HE WAS *RIGHT*. THERE IS *EVIL* HERE...ANCIENT, *MONSTROUS* EVIL...

...AN EVIL THAT *HUNGERS* FOR *PREY*.

IT WILL BE A *PLEASURE* TO DESTROY IT--

AAARRRGH!

THERE IS NO *WARNING*-- ONLY A LASH OF BLINDING *AGONY* DOWN STORM'S BACK AS THE PHANTOM SPEAR STRIKES HOME...

GODS-- THE COLD --THE *COLD*!

CAN'T LET THEM HIT ME *AGAIN*-- IF THEY DO, I'M *DEAD*--!

BUT WHAT *ARE* THEY--? THEY'RE NOT *REAL*--THEY'RE JUST THINGS OF *SMOKE* AND *LIGHT*--

--THINGS CREATED BY THE *CAIRN*!

DEMONSPAWN, THEN--CREATIONS OF THE *N'GARAI*!

WELL-- *WHATEVER* THEY ARE, FROM WHAT- EVER *HELL* THAT SPAWNED THEM--THEY'LL FIND *STORM* NO EASY *PREY*!

PERHAPS NOT, BUT THE *N'GARAI*--EVEN MINOR DE- MONS--ARE NO MEAN FOES EITHER.

THAT BOLT OF ENERGY FROM THE *CAIRN*-- THERE'S NO TIME TO *AVOID* IT--

ZZZRAMM!

MY MIND... *FUZZY*... NOTHING FITS TOGETHER ...I CAN'T *CONCENTRATE* ...I...

OH NO. OH DEAR GOD, *NO*-- THE *CAIRN!* I'M BEING PULLED INTO THE CAIRN-- INTO THE *DARK*--!

I'M BEING *PULLED IN* AND NO MATTER HOW HARD I *TRY,* I CAN'T *BREAK FREE*--

--BUT I *MUST!*

I *MUST BE FREE*--

--AND I *SHALL BE FREE!!*

BRRRRBBMMMK!!

92

SIMULTANEITY: IN ONE INSTANT A *CAIRN* IS RIVEN WITH *FIRE* AND *SACRED WORDS REFORMED*--A CAGE DOOR SLAMMED SHUT FOREVER...

...AND IN THAT *SAME* INSTANT, THIRTY MILES AWAY, A DEMON SIMPLY...

A-1AAAAAAAAAAAAAA

...CEASES TO EXIST.

KIERROK --HE'S...*GONE*.

YES, SCOTT. I THINK THAT *STORM* HAS DONE HER WORK *WELL* THIS NIGHT.

BUT WHAT *WAS* HE, PROFESSOR? *WHERE* DID HE *COME FROM*? *WHY'D* HE *ATTACK* US?

I *DON'T KNOW*, SCOTT --I *DON'T THINK* WE'LL *EVER* KNOW FOR SURE.

BUT *WHATEVER* KIERROK AND HIS KIND WERE--THEY ONCE *RULED* MANKIND, AND THEY WANT *VERY MUCH* TO RULE MANKIND *AGAIN*.

WE HAVE NOT SEEN THE *LAST* OF KIERROK, SCOTT-- OR OF HIS *N'GARAI* KIND.

GOD HELP US *ALL*.

EPILOGUE: A MINOR THREAD, REALLY --COME TO REST IN AN *APPLE OR-CHARD* OUTSIDE RED HOOK, NEW YORK.

COLONEL ROSSI! MICKEY! *MICKEY!!*

IT'S *NO USE*, SIR --THEY'RE ALL *DEAD* --EVERY MAN ABOARD, INCLUDING THE COLONEL!

FOR *PITY'S SAKE*, MAJOR--THERE'S *NOTHING* YOU CAN DO!

AND MILES AWAY, A MAN WHO HAS DONE *ENOUGH* THIS NIGHT, WATCHES THIS SCENE ON HIS COMMAND CONSOLE... AND *LAUGHS!*

NEXT ISSUE: SOME OLD FRIENDS RETURN AND THE X-MEN SUDDENLY FIND THEMSELVES LOCKED IN A BATTLE TO THE *DEATH* IN THE SHOCKER WE CALL--

MY BROTHER, MY ENEMY!

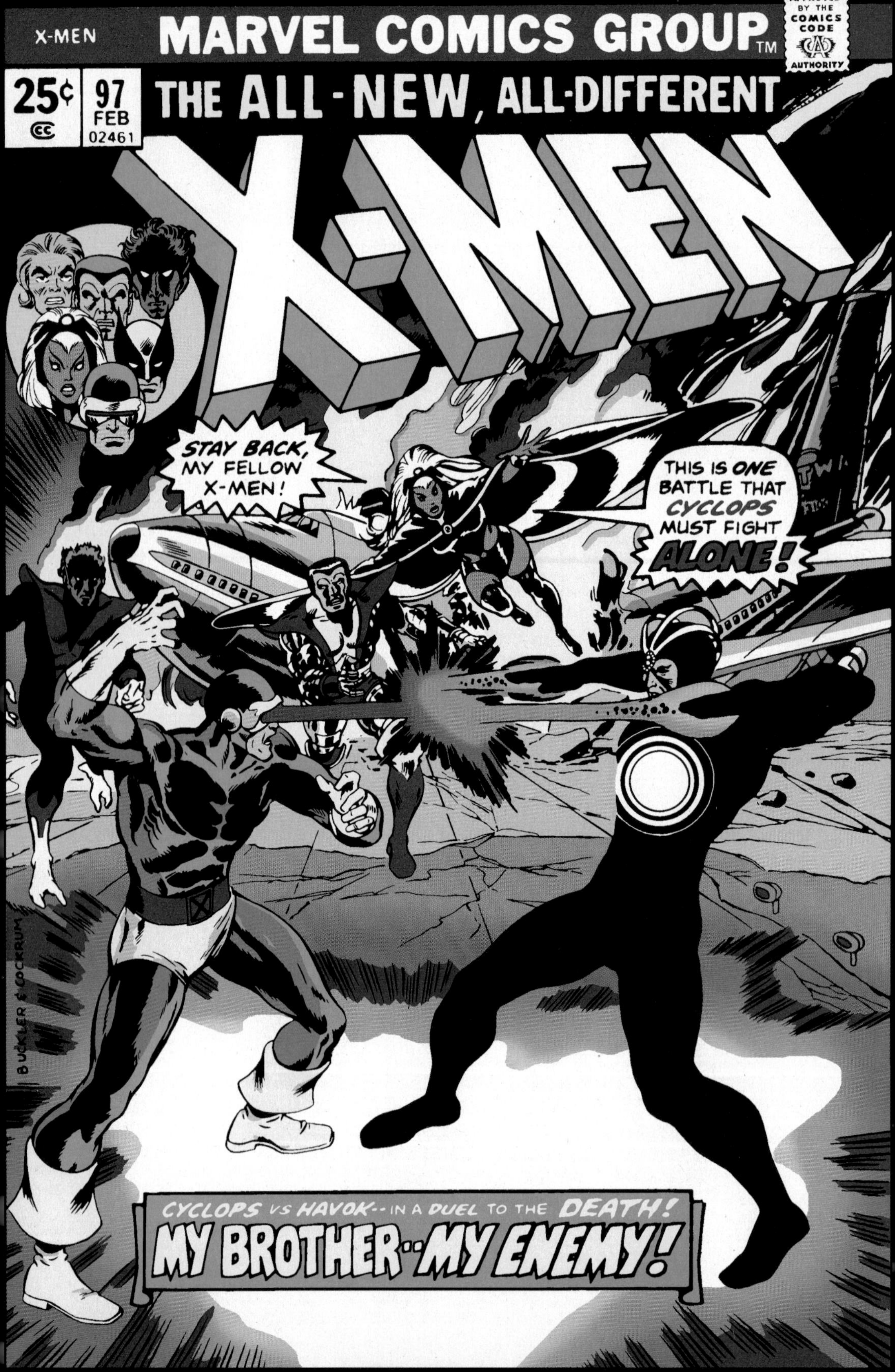

X-MEN
MARVEL COMICS GROUP™
APPROVED BY THE COMICS CODE AUTHORITY
25¢ CC
97 FEB 02461
THE ALL-NEW, ALL-DIFFERENT
X-MEN
STAY BACK, MY FELLOW X-MEN!
THIS IS ONE BATTLE THAT CYCLOPS MUST FIGHT ALONE!
BUCKLER & COCKRUM
CYCLOPS VS HAVOK-- IN A DUEL TO THE DEATH!
MY BROTHER--MY ENEMY!

Cyclops. Storm. Banshee. Nightcrawler. Wolverine. Colossus. Children of the atom, students of Charles Xavier, MUTANTS——feared and hated by the world they have sworn to protect. These are the STRANGEST heroes of all!

STAN LEE PRESENTS: THE UNCANNY X-MEN!

MY BROTHER, MY ENEMY!

THE BARD OF AVON SAID IT BEST: "TO SLEEP, PERCHANCE TO DREAM...

"... AYE, THERE'S THE RUB! FOR IN THAT SLEEP OF DEATH, WHAT DREAMS MAY COME WHEN WE HAVE SHUFFLED OFF THIS MORTAL COIL, MUST GIVE US PAUSE..."

AND IF THE DREAMS OF THE DEAD MUST GIVE US PAUSE...

...WHAT THEN OF THE DREAMS OF THE LIVING?

FOR EXAMPLE, THE DREAMS OF CHARLES XAVIER?

NO, PLEASE, NO--LET ME BE, I BEG OF YOU--GET OUT OF MY MIND AND LET ME BE--!

IN THE NAME OF ALL THAT'S HOLY--

--GET OUT OF MY MIND!!

CHRIS CLAREMONT WRITER * DAVE COCKRUM ARTIST

SAM GRAINGER, INKER
ANNETTE KAYE, LETTERER
DON WARFIELD, COLORIST

MARV WOLFMAN EDITOR

95

BUT THE DREAM DOESN'T *HEAR* XAVIER'S ANGUISHED, SOUL-TORN *CRY*--OR, IF IT *DOES*, IT DOESN'T CARE TO *ANSWER*.

AND, *ONCE AGAIN*, CHARLES XAVIER FINDS HIMSELF DRAWN OUT ACROSS THE *INFINITE*, DRAWN INTO *NIGHTMARE*...

...*DRAWN INTO HELL!*

THEN, AS *SUDDENLY*, AS SILENTLY, AS THE BATTLE BEGAN, IT *ENDS*...

HE HAS SEEN THIS BATTLE A HUNDRED TIMES BEFORE, ON A HUNDRED SLEEPLESS NIGHTS--

--TWO MIGHTY STARFLEETS CREATING THEIR OWN PRIVATE ARMAGEDDON IN THE DESOLATE SPACE AROUND A GIANT BINARY SUN.

AGAIN, HE WATCHES HELPLESSLY AS TEN-METER ENERGY BEAMS TURN TRICARDIAN STEEL TO PUDDLED SLAG, AS RUPTURED HULLS VOID PRECIOUS ATMOSPHERE INTO SPACE AND MEN DIE, QUICKLY, BRUTALLY, MERCILESSLY...

AGAIN, HE FEELS THE TERRIBLE COLD OF THIS...ALIEN SPACE, THE TERRIBLE PAIN OF THESE ALIEN DEATHS...

AND AGAIN, FOR THE HUNDREDTH TIME IN A HUNDRED NIGHTS, CHARLES XAVIER WONDERS IF HE ISN'T GOING MAD.

DRAWS HIM CLOSER, EVER CLOSER,

STRANGE, THAT SO MUCH DEATH SHOULD OCCUR IN SO MUCH SILENCE--SOMEHOW, IT DOESN'T SEEM RIGHT.

...SURVIVES TO RUN AND HIDE AND, PERHAPS, LIVE TO FIGHT ANOTHER DAY...

...TANTALIZINGLY CLOSE...

STILL, ONE SMALL SCOUT-CRAFT SURVIVES THE HOLOCAUST...

...AND, AS IT RUNS, IT DRAWS HIM IN, A MOTH DRAWN UNWILLINGLY INTO THE FLAME.

...AND TRY AS HE MIGHT, XAVIER CANNOT RESIST-- THE DREAM HAS HIM BODY AND SOUL, AND IT WILL RELEASE HIM WHEN IT WANTS, NOT BEFORE...

SO CLOSE, THIS TIME, *CLOSER* THAN HE'S EVER COME BEFORE...

...CLOSE ENOUGH TO SEE... A *FACE*...

...AND XAVIER'S DREAM... *ENDS!*

NNOOOO!

HE SITS THERE A LONG TIME, THE ECHO OF HIS *SCREAM* RINGING IN HIS EARS, HIS BODY *CLAMMY-COLD* WITH SWEAT... HIS MIND IN *TURMOIL*...

IRONIC, ISN'T IT, XAVIER-- YOU PRIDE YOURSELF ON POSSESSING THE *STRONGEST MUTANT BRAIN* ON EARTH...

...YET THIS *DREAM* TEARS YOUR MIND APART *AT WILL*.

LIKE IT OR NOT, XAVIER, IT'S TIME YOU FACED THE *TRUTH*...

...YOUR *MIND* IS NO LONGER *YOUR OWN*.

HEY, CHARLES, I HEARD YE *CRY OUT*-- DID YE HAVE A *NIGHTMARE*, THEN?

LORD ABOVE, YE'RE *SHAKIN'* LIKE A LEAF--WHAT'S *WRONG*, MAN?

HERE, GIVE ME THA' *COFFEE POT* AFORE YE *BURN* YERSEL'.

THANK YOU, MOIRA.

I... I HAD THE DREAM AGAIN, *STRONGER* THAN EVER...

THERE'S SUCH *POWER* BEHIND IT, MOIRA, SUCH *INCREDIBLE* POWER,

CHARLES, YE'RE TAKIN' *TOO MUCH* O' THIS ON YERSEL'--YE'VE GOT TO *OPEN UP* TO SCOTT AN' THE OTHERS AFORE YE...

HOW?

HOW DO I *TELL* THEM THAT...

...THAT I THINK I'M GOING *MAD?*

HEY, IT'S NA' AS *BAD* AS ALL THAT-- YE CALLED FOR *HELP*, AN' I CAME...

...AS I *SAID* I WOULD.

I HAD NO *RIGHT* TO ASK YOU, NOT AFTER...

DON'T BE *SILLY* --WHA' ELSE ARE *FRIENDS* FOR?

XAVIER SMILES THEN, FOR THE FIRST TIME IN MANY WEEKS-- AND SLOWLY SIPS HIS COFFEE...

BUT COME IT DOES-- AND TWO HOURS AFTER IT RISES OVER WESTCHESTER, THE MORNING SUN LIFTS HIGH OVER THE RIO DIABLO...

...OVER LAND THAT'S A HELL-ON-EARTH TO MOST...

HE SEEMS RELAXED, BUT HIS EYES BETRAY HIM, HUNTED EYES, EVER-SHIFTING, NEVER-STILL, WAITING DESPERATELY FOR A DAWN THAT CANNOT COME TOO SOON.

...AND YET, TO DOCTORAL CANDIDATES ALEX SUMMERS AND LORNA DANE...

...IT'S A KIND OF PARADISE.

SIX MONTHS THEY'VE BEEN HERE, WORKING THE JAGGED DIABLO RANGE--AND IN THOSE MONTHS, WHAT BEGAN AS FRIENDSHIP HAS BECOME SOMETHING...MORE.

FACE IT, LITTLE LORNA, AFTER ALL THE HASSLES, ALL THE GRIEF, YOU'VE STRUCK GOLD WITH THIS MAN...

...PURE GOLD.

I MEAN, IF THIS ISN'T LOVE, WHO NEEDS THE REAL THING...?

WHEN I'M WITH ALEX, I FEEL WHOLE... COMPLETE ...FUL-FILLED...

...I FEEL LIKE A WOMAN.

AND THAT FEELS JUST FINE.

WHAT THE--? SOMEONE AT THE DOOR? BUT WHO--? WE'RE THE ONLY PEOPLE FOR MILES.

NOK NOK

OKAY, LORNA, PLAY IT COOL--IF IT'S TROUBLE, YOUR MAGNETIC POWERS CAN HANDLE IT.

DON'T BET ON THAT, MS. DANE.

WHA-- YOU!!

ZZZAMM! ZAMM!

DON'T BET ON THAT AT ALL!

BUT IT'S IMPOSSIBLE-- IT CAN'T BE--!!

AAARRGH!

THAT *SCREAM* -- IT SOUNDED LIKE IT CAME FROM THE *HOUSE*...

AAAH

LORD, *NO!* THAT WAS *LORNA'S* VOICE--!

LORNA, YOU OKAY--?!

LORNA!!

THERE IS NO NEED TO *SHOUT*, ALEX-- I AM *WELL*.

I CAN *SEE* THAT.

WHAT *GIVES*, LADY-- I RAN ALL THE WAY FROM THE *UPPER* CANYON.

AN' WHAT'S WITH THE *NEW* COSTUME?

THE COSTUME IS *MINE*, ALEX SUMMERS -- AS THE *POWER* IS MINE--

--THE POWER OF *POLARIS, MISTRESS OF MAGNETISM*--

--THE POWER OF... *DEATH!!*

LORNA, *NO!!*

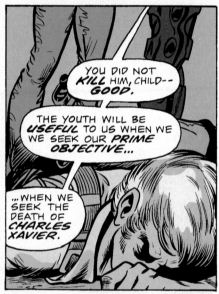

YOU DID NOT *KILL* HIM, CHILD-- *GOOD*.

THE YOUTH WILL BE *USEFUL* TO US WHEN WE WE SEEK OUR *PRIME OBJECTIVE*...

...WHEN WE SEEK THE DEATH OF *CHARLES XAVIER*.

THREE DAYS PASS, AND OUR SCENE SHIFTS TO KENNEDY INTERNATIONAL AIRPORT...

...AND A *GOOD-BYE* OF SORTS...

...AS FIVE FRIENDS GATHER TO SEE THEIR PROFESSOR OFF ON A WELL-EARNED... 'VACATION'...

...AND REMEMBER NOT TO STAY OUT IN THE *SUN* TOO LONG-- YOU *BURN EASILY*.

YES, JEAN, I'LL ALSO EAT PROPERLY, WRITE REGULARLY, AND *AL-WAYS* BE ON THE LOOKOUT FOR *GREAT WHITE SHARKS*.

IS THERE ANYTHING *ELSE*?

AH, NO SIR-- I THINK I GET THE *MESSAGE*.

BUT WHAT HAPPENED TO *BANSHEE* AND *WOLVERINE* -- I THOUGHT...

AH WELL, I GUESS IT TAKES *ALL KINDS*.

BANSHEE AND MOIRA MacTAGGERT, HM? *INTERESTING*...

HAVE A GOOD *TRIP*, SIR.

THANK YOU, SCOTT, KURT, I'LL CERTAINLY *TRY*.

BANSHEE IS SPENDING THE AFTERNOON WITH *MRS. MacTAGGERT*, I BELIEVE -- WOLVERINE WAS FEELING... *UNSOCIABLE*...

OH, JEAN, SOMETHING I *FORGOT*-- PLEASE TELL NIGHTCRAWLER THAT TONY STARK'S *IMAGE INDUCER* IS NOT A *TOY*.

IT'S TO MAKE HIM LOOK *UNOBTRUSIVE*...

...NOT LIKE SOME *1930'S MOVIE STAR*.

SPEAKING OF WHICH...

LOOK THERE, MY FRIEND, ARE THOSE NOT *MAGNIFICENT LEGS*?

I... DO NOT *KNOW*.

THE GIRLS ON THE *UST-ORDYNSKI COLLECTIVE* DID NOT WEAR SUCH...*SHORT* SKIRTS.

PHILISTINE...

PETER, WHAT *IS* IT--?

I AM NOT *SURE*, KURT-- IT MAY BE *NOTHING*...

BUT ON THE OTHER HAND...

HAVOC--!

WHAT'S GOING *ON*? WHY ARE YOU AND LORNA IN *COSTUME*?

SPEAK UP, MAN!

SCOTT, WAIT A MINUTE...SOMETHING'S *WRONG*...

I'M GETTING... IMAGES... *SENSATIONS*...

SCOTT, IT'S A *TRAP*--!!

FOOL, YOU'VE JUST SIGNED YOUR OWN *DEATH WARRANT*!

ZZZRAK!

JEAN!! HAVE YOU GONE *CRAZY,* LORNA?! WHAT D'YOU THINK YOU'RE *DOING!?!*

WE'RE DOING WHAT WE *HAVE* TO, SCOTT,

NOW GET *OUT* OF OUR WAY-- IT'S *XAVIER* WE WANT.

OVER MY *DEAD BODY.*

OKAY, IF *THAT'S* THE WAY YOU *WANT IT...*

HEY, REESE, TAKE A *LOOK*--THESE CLOWNS ARE TRYIN' TA *KILL* EACH OTHER...

Y'KNOW, I'M THINKIN WE OUGHTTA GET *OUTTA* HERE WHILE WE STILL GOT THE *CHANCE.*

I'M *WAY* AHEAD O' YA, CLANCY, *AS USUAL.*

WE'RE *ROLLIN',* BABY.

AND NOT A MOMENT TOO SOON.

KRAK OW!

LORD ABOVE--! WHAT'RE THEY TRYIN' TA' DO IN THERE-- START *WORLD WAR III?*

SURE LOOKS LIKE IT.

WELL THEN, YOU BETTER *STEP ON IT,* REESE...

...'CAUSE I THINK WORLD WAR III'S COMIN' *AFTER US--!*

THEY'RE GOING FOR THE *PROFESSOR'S* PLANE--

--GET AFTER THEM, X-MEN--STOP THEM *ANY WAY* YOU CAN--!

DON'T JUST *STAND* THERE, PEOPLE-- MOVE IT!!

AND MOVE IT THEY DO, *EACH* IN THEIR OWN *UNIQUE* STYLE.

QUICKLY, MY FRIEND--WE'VE NOT A *MOMENT TO LOSE!*

YET, FOR ALL THEIR STYLE AND ALL THEIR SPEED, THE X-MEN MAY HAVE MOVED...

...TOO LATE...

MOVE THIS CRATE, REESE--THAT FREAK'S GOT A CLEAR SHOT AT US-- AN' AT THIS RANGE--

--NO WAY IS HE GONNA MISS!!

NIGHTCRAWLER, LOOK --HAVOC IS ABOUT TO FIRE--!

NO, MY FRIEND--HE'LL NOT FIRE--

--NOT SO LONG AS NIGHTCRAWLER IS ALIVE TO STOP HIM!

WHOK!

YOU FOOL-- YOU DON'T KNOW WHAT YOU'VE DONE--!

YOU'VE MADE MY POWER BLAST GO WILD!

'WILD', IS SOMETHING OF AN...UNDERSTATEMENT.

GOOD LORD.

REESE... THAT COULD'A BEEN...US.

JUST BE THANK- FUL IT WASN'T, MR. CLANCY.

BLA-WHROOM!

JUST AS THE X-MEN ARE **THANKFUL** THAT THE 747 WAS UNDERGOING **ROUTINE MAINTENANCE**...

...THAT IT WAS **EMPTY** OF PASSENGERS AND CREW...

ALEX SUMMERS, HAVE YOU COMPLETELY **LOST YOUR MIND**--?!

WHAT IN HEAVEN'S NAME D'YOU THINK YOU'RE **DOING**!?!

SCOTT, I... I...

HE IS FOLLOWING **ORDERS**, CYCLOPS,

MY ORDERS.

AND **WHO** THE-- **HUH**!?!

YOU?!?

YOU'RE ERIC THE RED!

BUT YOU **CAN'T** BE ERIC THE RED--

--I WAS ERIC THE RED!*

IT MATTERS NOT **WHO** I AM, MUTANT.

I AM **POWER INCARNATE** -- AND NOTHING THAT LIVES CAN **STAND AGAINST ME!**

* ANYONE REMEMBER CYKE'S EPIC PORTRAYAL FROM **X-MEN** #'S 51 & 52 ? --MARV.

MISTER, I DON'T KNOW WHAT THIS **MASQUERADE** IS ALL ABOUT, BUT IF YOU THINK **YOU** CAN BEAT THE **X-MEN**--

--YOU'VE GOT ANOTHER THINK **COMING!**

TAKE HIM!

NO, CYCLOPS, YOU WILL **NOT** TAKE ME.

ALL YOU WILL DO...

...IS **DIE!**

104

THE BATTLE IS GOING *AGAINST* US...

I MUST GET *JEAN GREY* OUT OF *HARM'S WAY* AND RETURN TO THE X-MEN-- *QUICKLY*--

--BEFORE THERE'S *NO ONE* LEFT ALIVE TO *HELP!*

THE *GODS BE PRAISED* THAT NEITHER HAVOC NOR LORNA DANE CAN *FLY*...

SO, THE EBON WITCH THINKS HERSELF *SAFE* UP IN THE *SKY.*

TRUE, SHE MAY BE SAFE FROM *LORNA DANE*--

--BUT NOT FROM *POLARIS!!*

YOU CANNOT *ESCAPE* ME, STORM!

MY MAGNETIC POWERS CAN NEGATE THE *GRAVIMETRIC LINES OF FORCE* AS EASILY FOR ME AS THEY DID FOR *KRAKOA*--!

IN OTHER WORDS, THE LADY *CAN* FLY!

SHAKOW!

AARRGH!!

AND BY THE TIME STORM REALIZES WHAT'S *HAPPENED*--IT'S *TOO LATE.*

FAR TOO LATE.

MY MIND... *GROGGY* FROM THE BLAST... CAN'T *CONCENTRATE* ENOUGH TO GET TO JEAN, AND THE *GROUND'S* SO CLOSE... *TOO CLOSE*...

BUT I *MUST* GET TO HER-- IF I DON'T, SHE'LL *DIE*--!

I'LL ONLY HAVE *ONE CHANCE*...

I'VE *GOT* TO MAKE IT--

--*GOT TO*--!

MADE IT!!

JEAN SHOULD BE SAFE ENOUGH HERE ON THIS *ROOF-TOP*...

...WHICH LEAVES ME *FREE* TO DEAL WITH *POLARIS*.

AND *DEAL* WITH HER I *SHALL*.

ONLY *THIS TIME*, SHE'LL NOT BE FACING *ORORO*--

--THIS TIME SHE FACES *STORM!!*

SO IT GOES--ONE BATTLE BEGINS *ANEW*, ANOTHER PAUSES FOR *BREATH*.

LET US *GO*, SCOTT. *PLEASE*-- BEFORE SOMETHING HAPPENS WE'LL ALL *REGRET*...

NO WAY, ALEX-- NOT 'TIL I GET SOME *ANSWERS*, NOT 'TIL I FIND OUT *WHY*.

YOU *TURNED* ON US, BROTHER--YOU TRIED TO *KILL* US-- *WHY!?*

BE-CAUSE I...*HAD* TO...

IT WAS *ERIC*...HE... MY MIND...

SCOTTY, HE DID SOMETHING TO MY *MIND*--!

FIGHT IT, ALEX--!

BREAK FREE-- YOU CAN *DO* IT!

I'M... *TRYING*, SCOTT...BUT I...I...

I *CAN'T!!*

IT'S *NO GOOD*-- ALEX CAN'T BREAK FREE OF ERIC'S *CONTROL*...

...GOT TO HIT HIM *HARD*, KEEP HIM *OFF-BALANCE*...

I DON'T WANT TO *HURT* HIM, BUT IF HE CUTS LOOSE AT ME *FULL STRENGTH*, I'VE *HAD IT!*

RRAK!

THE PROBLEM, CYCLOPS, IS THAT **HAVOC** HAS NO SUCH **QUALMS** ABOUT HURTING YOU.

THRAMM!

MY GOD--THAT **WALL**--IT'S FALLING **RIGHT FOR ME**--!

SCOTT!

I'M **SORRY**--I DIDN'T MEAN TO--I DIDN'T **WANT** TO...

DEAR LORD IN HEAVEN, IF I'VE **KILLED** HIM--!

THANK GOD--HE'S **ALIVE**--!

HOLD ON, SCOTTY--I'LL GET YOU **OUT** OF HERE...

JUST TAKE IT EASY--YOU'RE GONNA BE **ALL RIGHT**...

I'M ALL RIGHT **NOW**, LITTLE BROTHER!

BOW!

I **HATE** TO DO THIS, ALEX--BUT, AS THE **SAYING** GOES, IT'S FOR YOUR OWN **GOOD**.

ONE FIGHT WINDS DOWN --ANOTHER SHIFTS INTO **HIGH GEAR**.

MUTANT **VERMIN**--YOU CAN- NOT HOPE TO **DEFEAT** ME!

PERHAPS **NOT**--BUT YOU'LL FOR- GIVE US IF WE **TRY**.

YOU'LL TRY **NOTHING**, ELF!

NOT WHEN YOU'RE **SMASHED** TO A PULP AGAINST THE **STEEL BODY** OF YOUR FRIEND!

FOR A MOMENT, ALL SEEMS **LOST**...

BAMF

THEN, IN THE INSTANT BEFORE **IMPACT**, THERE IS A **CRACK** OF FLAME, AND THE **GUSTING STENCH** OF BRIM- STONE...

107

AND THE MUTANT NAMED NIGHT-CRAWLER IS SUDDENLY...

...SOMEWHERE ELSE.

NOT TO WORRY, MY FRIEND, I AM ALL RIGHT...

...WHICH IS MORE THAN I CAN SAY FOR OUR FRIEND HERE.

HIT HIM HIGH, COLOSSUS--

--WHILE NIGHTCRAWLER HITS HIM LOW!!

WILL YOU NEVER LEARN, CHANGELING--? YOUR STRONGEST BLOWS ARE AS NOTHING TO ME!

WHAT ABOUT MY BLOWS, HORNED ONE--?

IS COLOSSUS NOTHING, TOO?!

YES!!

SKAK!

DÉJÀ VU--A FEELING THAT SOMETHING LIKE THIS HAS HAPPENED BEFORE...

THOOOMM!

EASTERN

COLOSSUS!!

108

PETER, ARE YOU **ALL RIGHT**--?! PETER--!!

BY ALL THAT'S **HOLY,** HORNED ONE, IF YOU'VE **KILLED** HIM--

DO NOT **WORRY** YOURSELF, FRIEND KURT--

--COLOSSUS IS **FAR** FROM DEAD!

PTHAMM!

AND WHEN I **DIE,** IT WILL TAKE FAR MORE THAN **ERIC THE RED** TO KILL ME--!

FOOM

HERE, VILLAIN-- COLOSSUS HAS BROUGHT YOU A **PRESENT--**

--CATCH!

IMAGES--COMING FAST NOW, ALMOST **TOO FAST**...

...**ERIC THE RED** SMASH- ING THRU A PILE OF FUEL DRUMS, LYING BROKEN AND **STILL**...

...AS THE SKY ABOVE KENNEDY AIRPORT GOES SUDDENLY **DARK**--AND TWO MUTANT ELEMENTALS COME TOGETHER IN A **DEATH-DUEL** THAT ALL-TOO-SOON BECOMES...

...A **STALEMATE.**

WE'RE TOO **EVENLY** MATCHED, STORM--

--I GUESS WE'LL JUST HAVE TO CALL THIS GAME A **DRAW**...

A.... **GAME?**

IS THAT **ALL** THIS IS TO YOU, POLARIS--A **GAME?!**

YOU **ATTACKED** US WITHOUT WARNING, WITHOUT **PROVOCATION**--

...YOU **SOUGHT** OUR DEATHS WITHOUT A THOUGHT FOR THE **INNOCENTS** WHO MIGHT BE ENDANGERED-- EVEN **SLAIN**-- BY YOUR ATTACK--!

AND YOU **DARE** CALL THIS.... A **GAME!?!**

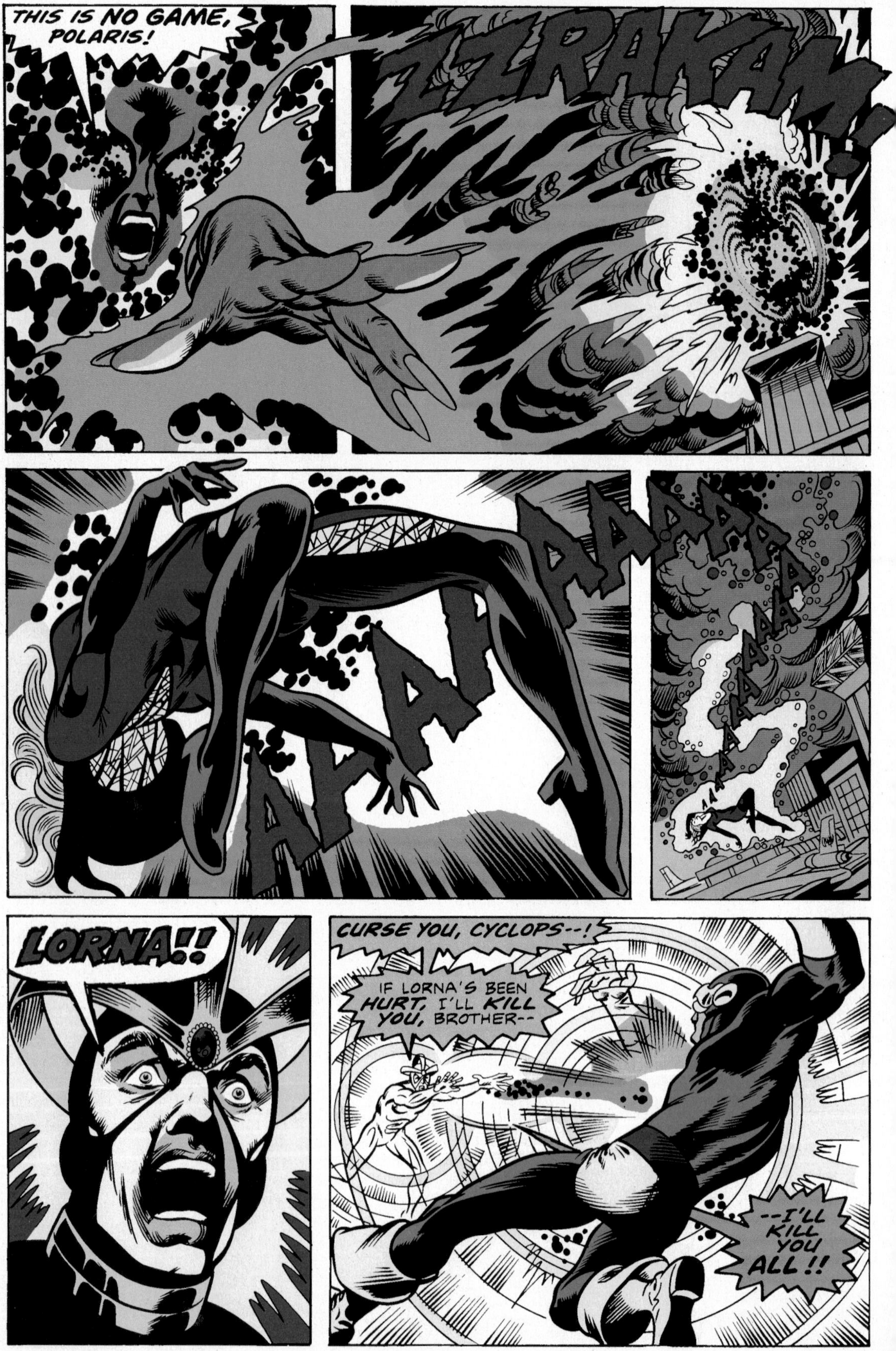
THIS IS NO GAME, POLARIS!
ZZRAKAM!
AAAAAAAAAAAAAA
LORNA!!
CURSE YOU, CYCLOPS--!
IF LORNA'S BEEN HURT, I'LL KILL YOU, BROTHER--
--I'LL KILL YOU ALL!!

THERE IS *FEAR* IN ALEX SUMMERS, A FEAR--AND A *NEED*--THAT CLAWS DEEP INTO HIS HEART AND GOADS HIM TO *STRIKE OUT* AGAINST HIS BROTHER AND HIS *FRIENDS*...

...SUCH A *SIMPLE* THING, REALLY.

HE *LOVES* LORNA DANE, AND FOR THAT LOVE, HE WOULD LIE, CHEAT, STEAL ...EVEN *KILL*.

AND IN A FEW MINUTES, HE MIGHT GET A *CHANCE* TO DO *JUST THAT.*

WHA--?! *REINFORCE-MENTS*--!

XAVIER MUST HAVE *SUMMONED* THEM WITH HIS CURSED *MENTAL POWERS.*

HAVOC, POLARIS--! TO ME, MY CHILDREN-- *QUICKLY!*

THE DAY HAS TURNED *AGAINST* US-- AND ONLY A *FOOL* STANDS TO FIGHT AGAINST *HOPELESS ODDS*--

--AND *ERIC THE RED* IS ANYTHING BUT A FOOL!

HAVOC, STOP!

STOP OR I'LL FIRE--!

I MEAN IT, ALEX--I'LL *CUT YOU DOWN* IF I HAVE TO...

I'LL...

I'LL...

DO WHAT, CYCLOPS? KILL YOUR OWN *BROTHER*--?

WHAT'RE YA *DOIN'*, BOSS-MAN--YOU GOTTA *CLEAR SHOT* AT 'EM--!

BLAST 'EM, MAN--! THEY'RE *GETTIN' AWAY-- BLAST 'EM!!*

THAT *CUTS* IT, BUB-- THOSE CLOWNS TRY TO *STOMP US* AN' YOU JUST STAND THERE AN' WATCH 'EM *FLY AWAY*...

WHAT'S'A *MATTER,* HOTSHOT-- YOU *GUT-LESS* OR SOMETHIN'...?

WOLVERINE...

SHUT UP!!

KRAK!

WHY YOU *ONE-EYED SONUVA*--!

I'M GONNA CUT YOU *WIDE OPEN* FOR THAT!!

NO!

HUH?!

YOU WILL DO *NOTHING,* WOLVERINE--NOT NOW, NOT *EVER*...

...OR YOU WILL *ANSWER* TO *ME.*

HE WALKS *ALONE* NOW-- HIS MIND *TORN* BY QUESTIONS HE *CAN'T* ANSWER, FEELINGS HE CAN'T *EXPLAIN*...

HIS BROTHER TRIED TO *KILL* HIM TODAY--AND HE KNOWS, DEEP DOWN, THAT WHEN *NEXT* THEY MEET, THERE'LL BE *NO* HOLDING BACK. BROTHER *WILL* KILL BROTHER.

AND THE *HORROR* OF THAT DAY WILL BE THAT THEY'LL KILL WITHOUT EVER KNOWING THE REASON ...*WHY.*

THAT THEY WON'T BE *MEN* AT ALL--MERELY *PUPPETS* DANCING ON A STRING.

NEXT ISSUE: THE **SENTINELS** *RETURN!*

'NUFF SAID.

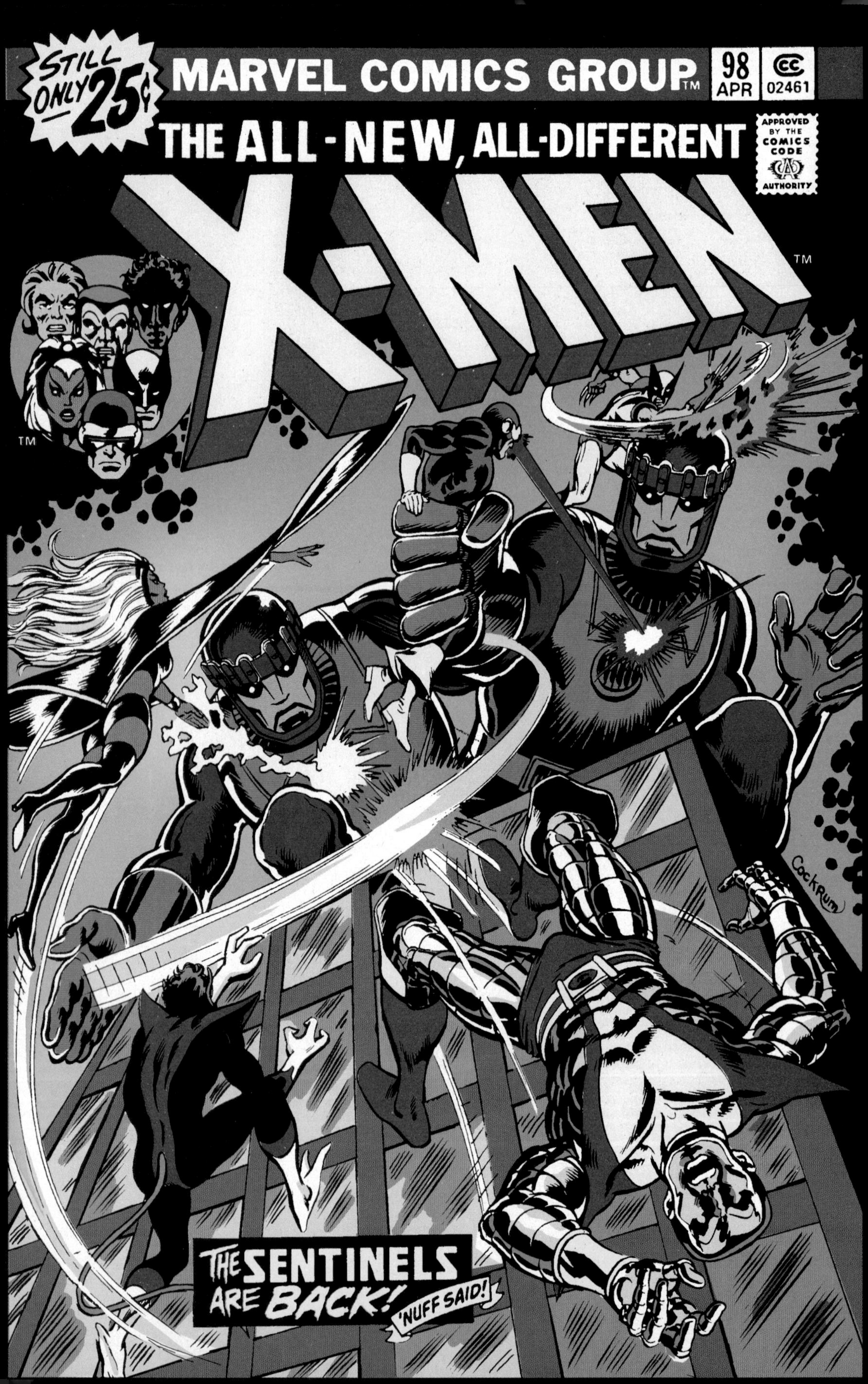
STILL ONLY 25¢
MARVEL COMICS GROUP
98 APR
CC 02461
THE ALL-NEW, ALL-DIFFERENT
APPROVED BY THE COMICS CODE AUTHORITY
X-MEN
COCKRUM
THE SENTINELS ARE BACK!
'NUFF SAID!

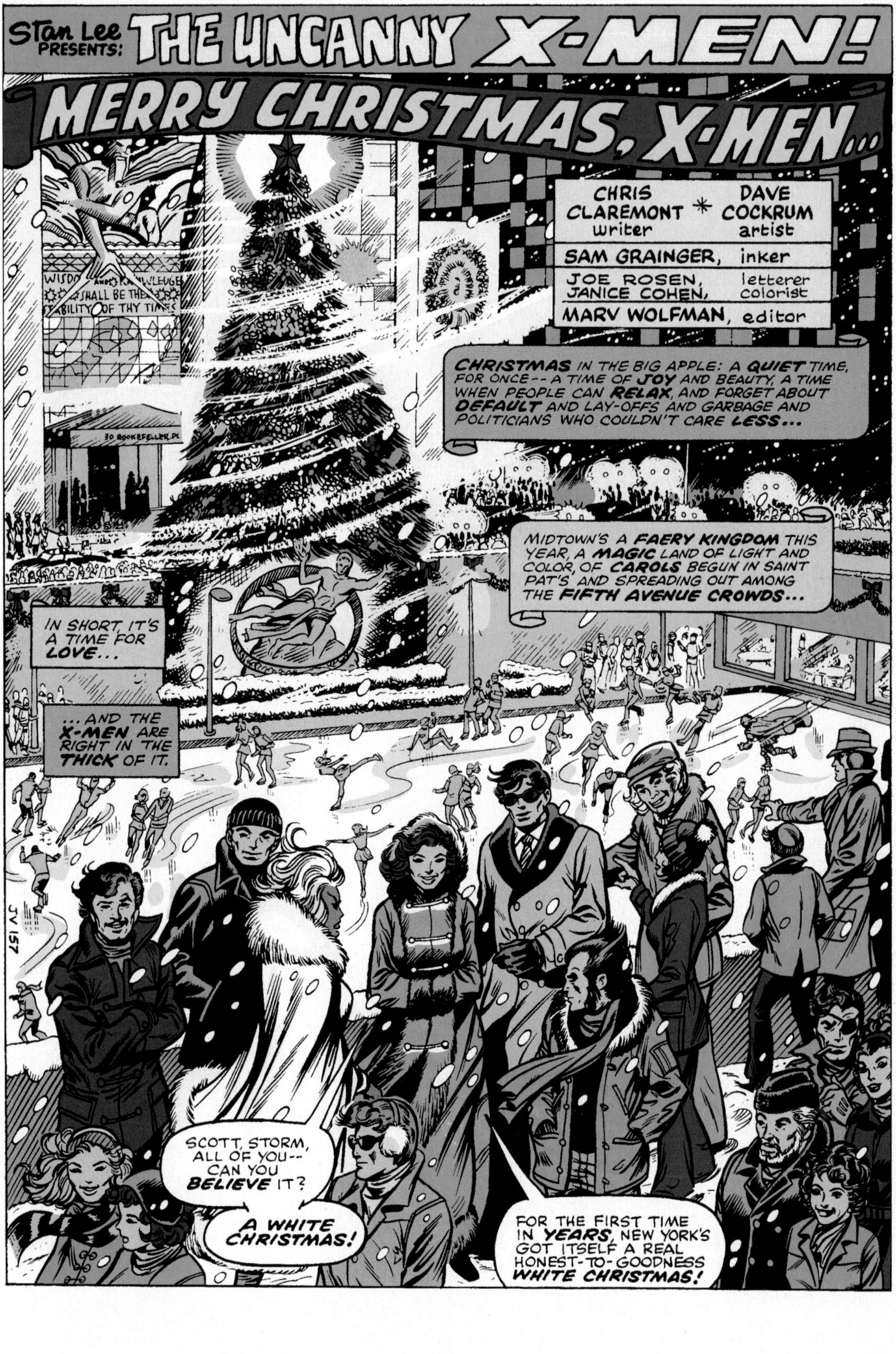
Stan Lee PRESENTS: THE UNCANNY X-MEN!
MERRY CHRISTMAS, X-MEN...
CHRIS CLAREMONT writer * DAVE COCKRUM artist
SAM GRAINGER, inker
JOE ROSEN, letterer
JANICE COHEN, colorist
MARV WOLFMAN, editor
CHRISTMAS IN THE BIG APPLE: A QUIET TIME, FOR ONCE-- A TIME OF JOY AND BEAUTY, A TIME WHEN PEOPLE CAN RELAX, AND FORGET ABOUT DEFAULT AND LAY-OFFS AND GARBAGE AND POLITICIANS WHO COULDN'T CARE LESS...
MIDTOWN'S A FAERY KINGDOM THIS YEAR, A MAGIC LAND OF LIGHT AND COLOR, OF CAROLS BEGUN IN SAINT PAT'S AND SPREADING OUT AMONG THE FIFTH AVENUE CROWDS...
IN SHORT, IT'S A TIME FOR LOVE...
...AND THE X-MEN ARE RIGHT IN THE THICK OF IT.
SCOTT, STORM, ALL OF YOU-- CAN YOU BELIEVE IT?
A WHITE CHRISTMAS!
FOR THE FIRST TIME IN YEARS, NEW YORK'S GOT ITSELF A REAL HONEST-TO-GOODNESS WHITE CHRISTMAS!

ISN'T THE SNOW *BEAUTIFUL,* ORORO?

IN ITS *WAY,* JEAN...

...BUT I CAN'T HELP *REMEMBERING* THAT ON THE SLOPES OF *KILIMANJARO,* THE SNOW IS... *WHITE.*

OH, BROTHER-- IT'S *CHRISTMAS* --!

YOU KNOW, ORORO, THERE ARE *TIMES* WHEN I THINK YOU'RE AS BAD AS *SCOTT...*

...AND YOU SHOULD *SEE* WHAT I HAVE TO GO THRU TO GET *HIM* TO LET HIS HAIR DOWN ONCE IN AWHILE.

VERY FUNNY, LITTLE LADY. I THOUGHT ALL YOU HAD TO DO WAS *SMILE.*

ANYWAY, KURT AND PETER SEEM TO BE *ENJOYING THEMSELVES.*

MR. SUMMERS, YOUR GIFT FOR *UNDER-STATEMENT* BOGGLES THE MIND.

UH, AMANDA-- I THINK WE'RE BEING *FOLLOWED.*

BETSY DEAR, DO YOU HEAR *ME* SCREAMING FOR A *COP?*

AUF WIEDERSEHEN, MEINE FREUNDE... IF YOU DON'T HEAR FROM US AGAIN...

...DON'T WORRY. MERRY CHRISTMAS, ALL.

AN' ON *THAT* NOTE, ME BOYOS, MOIRA 'N' I'LL BE *MOVIN'* ON OUR-SELVES...

...WE'RE T'BE SHOWIN' EACH OTHER THE *SIGHTS* O' NEW YORK.

WHAT ABOUT *YOU,* WOLVERINE?

WHAT *ABOUT* ME, MISS GREY--? I GOT NO USE FOR *CHRISTMAS.*

OH, WELL... HAVE A *NICE TIME,* ANYWAY.

STRANGE MAN, WOLVERINE... WE'VE BEEN TOGETHER ALMOST A *YEAR...* AND I'M *STILL* NOT SURE HE'LL *WORK OUT.*

BUT THEN... I *WAS* SURE ABOUT ALEX AND LORNA...

...AND THEY TRIED TO *KILL US.**

*LAST ISH-- MARV.

STOP IT! IT'S *CHRISTMAS,* SCOTT--AND YOU'VE BEEN *TEARING* YOURSELF APART OVER ALEX FOR *WEEKS...*

...CAN'T YOU JUST THIS *ONCE* GIVE IT A *REST...*

...AND *KISS* ME.

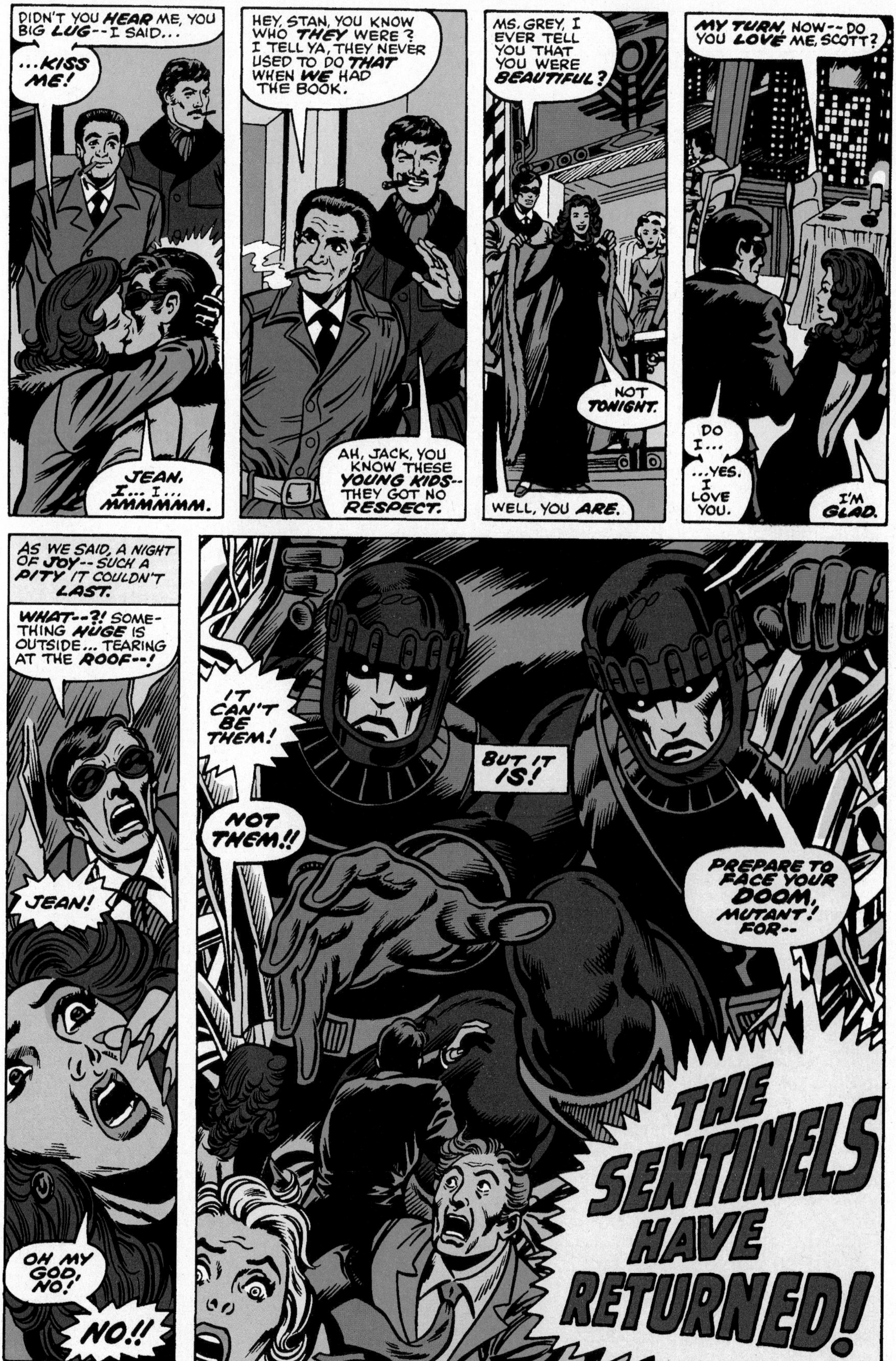
DIDN'T YOU HEAR ME, YOU BIG LUG--I SAID...
...KISS ME!
JEAN, I... I... MMMMMMM.
HEY, STAN, YOU KNOW WHO THEY WERE? I TELL YA, THEY NEVER USED TO DO THAT WHEN WE HAD THE BOOK.
AH, JACK, YOU KNOW THESE YOUNG KIDS-- THEY GOT NO RESPECT.
MS. GREY, I EVER TELL YOU THAT YOU WERE BEAUTIFUL?
NOT TONIGHT.
WELL, YOU ARE.
MY TURN, NOW--DO YOU LOVE ME, SCOTT?
DO I...
...YES. I LOVE YOU.
I'M GLAD.
AS WE SAID, A NIGHT OF JOY--SUCH A PITY IT COULDN'T LAST.
WHAT--?! SOMETHING HUGE IS OUTSIDE... TEARING AT THE ROOF--!
JEAN!
OH MY GOD, NO!
NO!!
IT CAN'T BE THEM!
BUT IT IS!
NOT THEM!!
PREPARE TO FACE YOUR DOOM, MUTANT! FOR--
THE SENTINELS HAVE RETURNED!

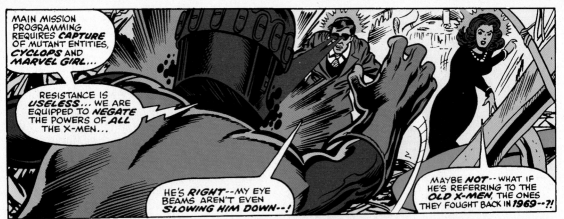

MAIN MISSION PROGRAMMING REQUIRES *CAPTURE* OF MUTANT ENTITIES, *CYCLOPS* AND *MARVEL GIRL*...

RESISTANCE IS *USELESS*... WE ARE EQUIPPED TO *NEGATE* THE POWERS OF *ALL* THE X-MEN...

HE'S *RIGHT*--MY EYE BEAMS AREN'T EVEN *SLOWING HIM DOWN*--!

MAYBE *NOT*-- WHAT IF HE'S REFERRING TO THE *OLD X-MEN*, THE ONES THEY FOUGHT BACK IN *1969*--?!

IT COULD BE THAT THIS UGLY *DOESN'T* KNOW MY TELEKINETIC POWER'S A LOT *STRONGER* NOW THAN IT WAS *THEN*--!

WARNING: MUTANT MINDBLAST HAS THROWN THIS UNIT *OFF-BALANCE...*

BEAUTIFUL MOVE, JEAN--!

THE SENTINEL'S *OUTSIDE* THE BUILDING-- NOW I CAN LET HIM HAVE IT *FULL POWER!*

IN OTHER WORDS, *SCRATCH ONE SENTINEL!*

GOT HIM!

SPA-KOW

THE PROBLEM IS, THERE'S TWO OF THEM.

SCOTT--!!

THE SENTINEL'S BLAST-- SCOTT DIDN'T HAVE A CHANCE--!

TERMINAL DYSFUNCTION RECORDED FROM SENTINEL A7...

...THIS UNIT FORCED TO TAKE EXTREME ACTION AGAINST MUTANT, CYCLOPS.

SVAM!

SENTINEL IF YOU'VE KILLED HIM I'LL... UNNNHHH...

PHHHTT!

THIS UNIT HAS... 'KILLED'... HIM, MUTANT...

...HIS POWER WAS TOO GREAT FOR THIS UNIT TO COPE WITH ALONE.

SENTINEL A3 TO MAIN MISSION... AM RETURNING WITH CAPTIVE, MARVEL GIRL, VIA ULTRA-LINEAR LEAP...

...EVENTS AT TARGET-LOCUS, ROCKEFELLER CENTER NECESSITATED TERMINATION OF MUTANT LIFE-ENTITY, CYCLOPS. MESSAGE ENDS.

WHICH ONLY GOES TO PROVE THAT EVEN A SENTINEL CAN MAKE A MISTAKE.

CHEST... WHOLE BODY FEELS ON FIRE... I...

...GOOD LORD, THE SENTINEL'S LIFT-OFF-- IT'S SHIFTING THE WRECKAGE... THROWING ME OFF THE ROOF!

THIS RADIO MAST... MY ONLY HOPE... I ONLY PRAY IT HOLDS--IT'S GOT TO--'CAUSE IF IT DOESN'T...

...IT'S SIXTY STORIES TO THE STREET. AND NO BANSHEE TO CATCH ME AS I FALL.

IT HELD!

BUT ONLY BY... A THREAD. I MOVE AN INCH AND THIS WHOLE MESS IS GONNA GIVE WAY...

...SO I STAY WHERE I AM AND I HOLD ON. BUT FOR HOW LONG, SCOTT...?

HOW LONG?!?

BACKTRACK A MINUTE NOW, AND WITNESS THE ARRIVAL OF SOME RATHER UNIQUE WRECKAGE RIGHT ON RADIO CITY'S DOOR-STEP...

RUN FOR IT--! EVERYONE FIND SOME COVER-- FAST!!

IT SOUNDS LIKE THE WHOLE BUILDIN'S COMIN' DOWN!!

THAT'S NO BUILDIN', FRIEND-- SAINTS PRESERVE US ALL--

--THAT'S A SENTINEL!

NO TIME FOR SUBTLETY, BANSHEE-ME-BOYO--

--IF THE SENTINELS ARE HUNTIN' MUTANTS AGAIN, SCOTT AN' JEAN ARE GONNA NEED ALL THE HELP THEY CAN GET!

MOIRA--! YE AN' STORM FIND NIGHT-CRAWLER AN' COLOSSUS, WARN 'EM--!

'CAUSE IF THE SENTINELS ARE BACK...

BANSHEE-- WHAT IS A SENTINEL?

TO A MUTANT, ORORO-- SENTINEL'S ANOTHER NAME FOR DEATH!

WAIT UP, BUB-- IF THERE'S A FIGHT BREWIN', THEN THE WOLVER-INE'S GONNA BE IN ON IT--!

DIDJA HEAR--? THAT GREEN GUY SAID THEY WUZ MUTIES--!

AN' THAT BLACK CHICK, SHE'S GLOWIN' LIKE THE SUN--!

WHAT'S GOIN' ON HERE, ANYWAY?!

MORE THAN YOU CAN EVER KNOW, HUMAN!

HEY--!!

BUT IF BANSHEE THINKS *STORM* WILL REMAIN AWAY FROM THE HEART OF THIS BATTLE...

...HE IS *MISTAKEN.*

WAIT--! HANGING FROM THAT RADIO MAST-- IT'S *CYCLOPS!* AND HE'S ABOUT TO *FALL!*

DON'T BE AFRAID, MY FRIEND-- YOU ARE *SAFE* NOW.

STORM! THANK GOD THE *SENTINELS* DIDN'T GET YOU *ALL.*

ALL? I DO NOT *UNDERSTAND.*

A *BUNCH* OF THEM NAILED BANSHEE AND WOLVERINE...

...JUST *PLUCKED* THEM OUT OF THE SKY AND THERE WASN'T A *THING* I COULD DO TO *STOP IT.*

AH, SCOTT... THESE SENTINELS... ARE THEY LARGE, METALLIC *ROBOTS...?*

HUH? OF COURSE THEY ARE... *WHY?*

OH NO.

SENTINEL A3 REPORTED YOUR LIFE FUNCTIONS *TERMINATED,* CYCLOPS-- IT SEEMS A3 WAS IN *ERROR.*

SAID ERROR WILL BE *CORRECTED-- NOW!*

ZPOW!

NO!!

OUR PROGRAMMING IS *SPECIFIC* AND *BINDING,* MUTANT--

--*ALL* WHO RESIST US MUST BE *DESTROYED.*

WELL I AM *STORM,* MONSTER...

...AND *I* RESIST YOU--!

AND I WILL *NOT* BE DESTROYED!!

121

FEMALE, THIS UNIT IS PROGRAMMED TO DEAL WITH ALL *MUTANT POWERS*...THIS UNIT...

...*WARNING*... *WARNING*... WIND VELOCITY *INCREASING*... TURBULENCE THREATENING *SYSTEMS OVERLOAD*...

YOU ARE ONLY A *MACHINE*, SENTINEL--AND HOW CAN A MERE MACHINE *STAND* AGAINST THE POWER OF *STORM*--?

THE POWER OF A RAMPAGING *HURRICANE*!!

CHRIS, LOOK UP IN THE *SKY*-- DO YOU *SEE IT*?

YEAH, I SEE IT, *BONNIE*--BUT I DON'T *BELIEVE IT*!

A *HURRICANE*! A FREAKIN' HURRICANE FLOATING SEVENTY STORIES ABOVE *ROCKEFELLER CENTER*!

AND IN THE *EYE* OF THAT HURRICANE, ONE SLIGHT WIND- CARESSED *WOMAN*, WHO MOLDS THIS *TEMPEST* AS A MASTER SCULPTRESS MOLDS HER *CLAY*...

OH MY GOD.

ORORO-- FOR PITY'S SAKE, *STOP!* BEFORE YOU DESTROY THE *ENTIRE CITY!*

IT IS *DONE*.

THERE WAS NO NEED FOR *WORRY*, SCOTT. I HAVE *TOTAL CONTROL* OVER MY ABILITIES-- *NOTHING* WAS HARMED SAVE THE *SENTINEL*.

SO I SEE...

...BUT IF *PROFESSOR X* WERE HERE, I'M SURE HE'D...

GOOD LORD, THE *PROFESSOR!*

HE DOESN'T KNOW ABOUT THESE NEW *SENTINELS*--HE'S GOT TO BE *WARNED!*

NICE THOUGHT, SCOTT-- BUT YOU'RE A BIT TOO LATE.

AND OUR SCENE SHIFTS DOWN-TIME HALF-A-DAY AND SOUTH A THOUSAND MILES...TO A PRIVATE YACHT TROLLING THE BAHAMA OUT ISLANDS...

...IT'S HERE THAT CHARLES XAVIER HAS COME FOR HIS... VACATION. HERE THAT HE'S COME TO ASK AN OLD FRIEND FOR HELP.

I DON'T KNOW, CHARLES-- IF I DIDN'T KNOW YOU BETTER, I'D FIGURE THIS AS SOME SORT OF PRACTICAL JOKE.

DEJAH THORIS
COCOA BEACH

ENTER PETER CORBEAU, PhD, DSc, TWICE NOBEL PRIZE-WINNER AND DIRECTOR OF THE UN'S PROJECT STARCORE.*

I MEAN, THE BINARY SYSTEM YOU DESCRIBED ISN'T MIZAR A, OR ALSEVAR PRIME, OR DUNSINANE...

* AS READERS OF THE HULK WILL NO DOUBT REMEMBER-- MARV.

FACE IT, CHARLES, STARCORE'S CHARTED OVER HALF THE MILKY WAY... AND YOUR BINARY ISN'T ANYWHERE TO BE FOUND.

ARE YOU SURE, PETER? YOU MIGHT HAVE MISSED SOMETHING.

YOU KNOW ME BETTER THAN THAT. I'VE CHECKED THE PROGRAM A DOZEN TIMES.

BLAZES, MAN, I EVEN RAN A QUERY THRU THE FANTASTIC FOUR AND AVENGERS CHARTS. THE RESULT WAS THE SAME: NOTHING.

CHARLES, LOOK, YOU'VE BEEN UNDER A HELLUVA STRAIN LATELY, MORE THAN ANY MAN CAN RIGHTLY STAND...

...IT COULD BE THAT THIS BINARY OF YOURS ISN'T REAL AT ALL...

...IT COULD BE ALL IN YOUR MIND.

ARE YOU SAYING I'M... INSANE...?

JUST TIRED, IS ALL.

BUT I THINK YOU SHOULD SEEK PROFESSIONAL HELP...

DEJAH THORIS
COCOA BEACH

WHAT THE--?! A BITE, MAN!

123

THAT'S *ONE* WAY OF PUTTING IT, ALL RIGHT.

CHARLES XAVIER, I HAVE COME FOR YOU!

A SENTINEL! BUT THAT'S *IMPOSSIBLE*-- MY MENTAL DEFENSES SHOULD HAVE *SHIELDED* ME...

...BUT THEY *HAVEN'T.*

VERY WELL, SENTINEL-- YOU *HAVE* FOUND ME...

...BUT YOU'LL FIND THAT *CAPTURING* ME IS ANOTHER MATTER *ALTOGETHER!*

DANGER... DANGER... MUTANT MINDBLAST *PENETRATING* SHIELDS...THIS UNIT UNABLE TO *COMPENSATE* IN TIME...

...THIS UNIT IS *FALLING...*

CONSIDER YOURSELF *LUCKY,* SENTINEL--THAT *MINDBLAST* SHOULD HAVE *DESTROYED* YOU.

IT SEEMS THAT MY *DREAM* MUST HAVE *SAPPED* MY POWERS FAR MORE THAN I'D *THOUGHT.*

I'VE DONE MY *BEST,* PETER-- THE REST IS UP TO *YOU!*

YOU'VE GIVEN US *TIME,* CHARLES-- AND WITH THIS LITTLE *HYDROFOIL* O' MINE, TIME IS *ALL* WE NEED.

I *DESIGNED* THIS BABY MYSELF--THERE'S *NOTHING* AFLOAT CAN CATCH HER WHEN SHE'S *RUNNING.*

AND *RIGHT NOW,* SHE'S RUNNING *FINE!*

DO ME A *FAVOR,* THOUGH-- WATCH OUT FOR OUR *TIN PLAYMATE* WHILE I CALL IN THE *AIR FORCE.*

IMAGES...WORDS NEVER TASTED...COLORS NEVER SMELT...WORLDS BEYOND IMAGINING CRASHING TOGETHER AND DYING... SO MANY IMAGES...

...AND THRU THEM ALL, A TERRIBLE, ACHING NEED...

...AND A FACE...

NNOOOO

MAYDAY! MAYDAY! ANY STATION--

WHAT-- CHARLES!!

LORD, THAT SCREAM! THE POOR SOD'S GONE TOTALLY ROUND THE BEND.

CORBEAU WOULD HAVE DONE SOMETHING...

...BUT HE NEVER GOT THE CHANCE.

YOU CANNOT ESCAPE US, MUTANT!

SPRA-KAMM!

IMPACT THRU ME DEEP UNDER... HAVEN'T MUCH AIR IN MY LUNGS...

...CAN'T TELL HOW FAR TO THE SURFACE...INSIDE ...LUNGS STARTING TO BURN...

MADE IT!

BUT WHAT ABOUT XAVIER?!

CHARLES! CHARLES!

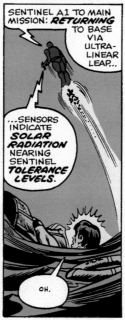

SENTINEL A1 TO MAIN MISSION: RETURNING TO BASE VIA ULTRA-LINEAR LEAP...

...SENSORS INDICATE SOLAR RADIATION NEARING SENTINEL TOLERANCE LEVELS.

OH.

LOOKS BAD, CHUM -- YOU'RE TWO HUNDRED MILES FROM LAND...

...AND IF NO ONE HEARD YOUR MAYDAY, IT'S GOING TO BE ONE LONG SWIM...

TIME-CUT NOW: **FOUR DAYS** UP THE LINE, TO 28 DECEMBER 1975, A **SUNDAY** IN NEW YORK.

EXCEPT THAT THIS **ISN'T** NEW YORK.

WILL YE BE LOOKIN' A' **THAT**-- THE HEAD HONCHO, **DR. STEVEN LANG**, HISSELF...

...COME T'PAY US ALL A **VISIT**. WE'RE **HONORED**, SIR.

I'M GLAD TO FIND YOU IN SUCH **HIGH SPIRITS**, BANSHEE-- YOUR FRIENDS SHOULD **LEARN** FROM YOUR **EXAMPLE**.

DR. LANG-- EXCUSE ME, SIR, BUT THE **SOLAR RADIATION STORMS** SHOW NO SIGNS OF **ABATING**...

...WE'LL HAVE TO **SHUT DOWN** SENTINEL OPERATIONS FOR THE **TIME BEING**.

UNDERSTOOD, TECHNICIAN. WE'LL **MAKE DO** WITH THE MUTANTS WE'VE **GOT**.

I **DUNNO**, SIR-- IS THIS **WOLVERINE** A MUTANT? HIS READINGS ARE **NOTHING** LIKE THE OTHERS'.

THE **SENTINELS** SAY HE IS...

...BUT MUTANT OR **NO**, WHATEVER THE **WOLVERINE** IS, HE **ISN'T HUMAN**.

KEEP IT UP, BUB-- AN' I'LL...

DO **NOTHING**, MUTANT. THOSE **CHROMALLOY** SHACKLES ARE **UNBREAKABLE**.

WHERE'S YOUR **SWASTIKA**, LANG? YOU DON'T LOOK **DRESSED** WITHOUT IT.

I'M NO...**NAZI**, MISS GREY. JUST A MAN DOING HIS **DUTY**.

FOLLOWING **ORDERS**, HUH?

IF YOU LIKE. YOU-- **MUTANTKIND**-- ARE THE **ENEMY**. I'M TO FIND A WAY TO **DESTROY** YOU.

WHY START WITH THE **X-MEN**?

BECAUSE THE X-MEN HAVE BEEN THE MOST **EFFECTIVE** MUTANT OPPOSITION TO THE SENTINELS-- BECAUSE **YOU**, CYCLOPS AND XAVIER ARE THE **HEART** AND SOUL OF THE X-MEN.

CUT OUT THE HEART AND THE BODY **DIES**. DESTROY THE X-MEN, AND THE SENTINELS ARE **UNBEATABLE**.

YOU **SAD**, PATHETIC, **SCREWED-UP** LITTLE MAN-- DO YOU THINK THE X-MEN ARE THAT **EASILY BEATEN**--?

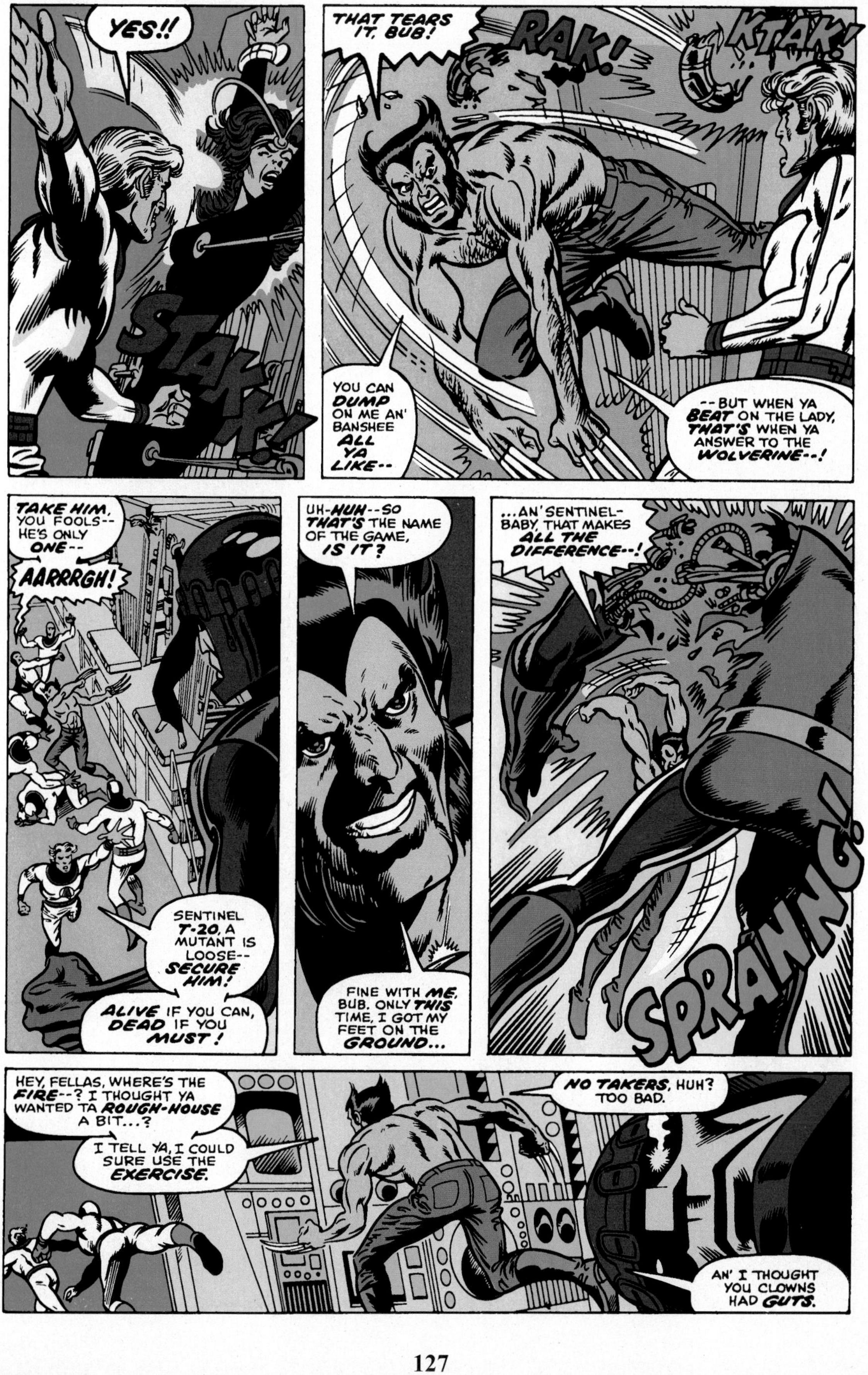
YES!!
STAKK!
THAT TEARS IT, BUB!
RAK!
KTAK!
YOU CAN DUMP ON ME AN' BANSHEE ALL YA LIKE--
--BUT WHEN YA BEAT ON THE LADY, THAT'S WHEN YA ANSWER TO THE WOLVERINE--!
TAKE HIM, YOU FOOLS--HE'S ONLY ONE--
AARRRGH!
SENTINEL T-20, A MUTANT IS LOOSE--SECURE HIM!
ALIVE IF YOU CAN, DEAD IF YOU MUST!
UH-HUH--SO THAT'S THE NAME OF THE GAME, IS IT?
FINE WITH ME, BUB. ONLY THIS TIME, I GOT MY FEET ON THE GROUND...
...AN' SENTINEL-BABY, THAT MAKES ALL THE DIFFERENCE--!
SPRANNG!
HEY, FELLAS, WHERE'S THE FIRE--? I THOUGHT YA WANTED TA ROUGH-HOUSE A BIT...?
I TELL YA, I COULD SURE USE THE EXERCISE.
NO TAKERS, HUH? TOO BAD.
AN' I THOUGHT YOU CLOWNS HAD GUTS.

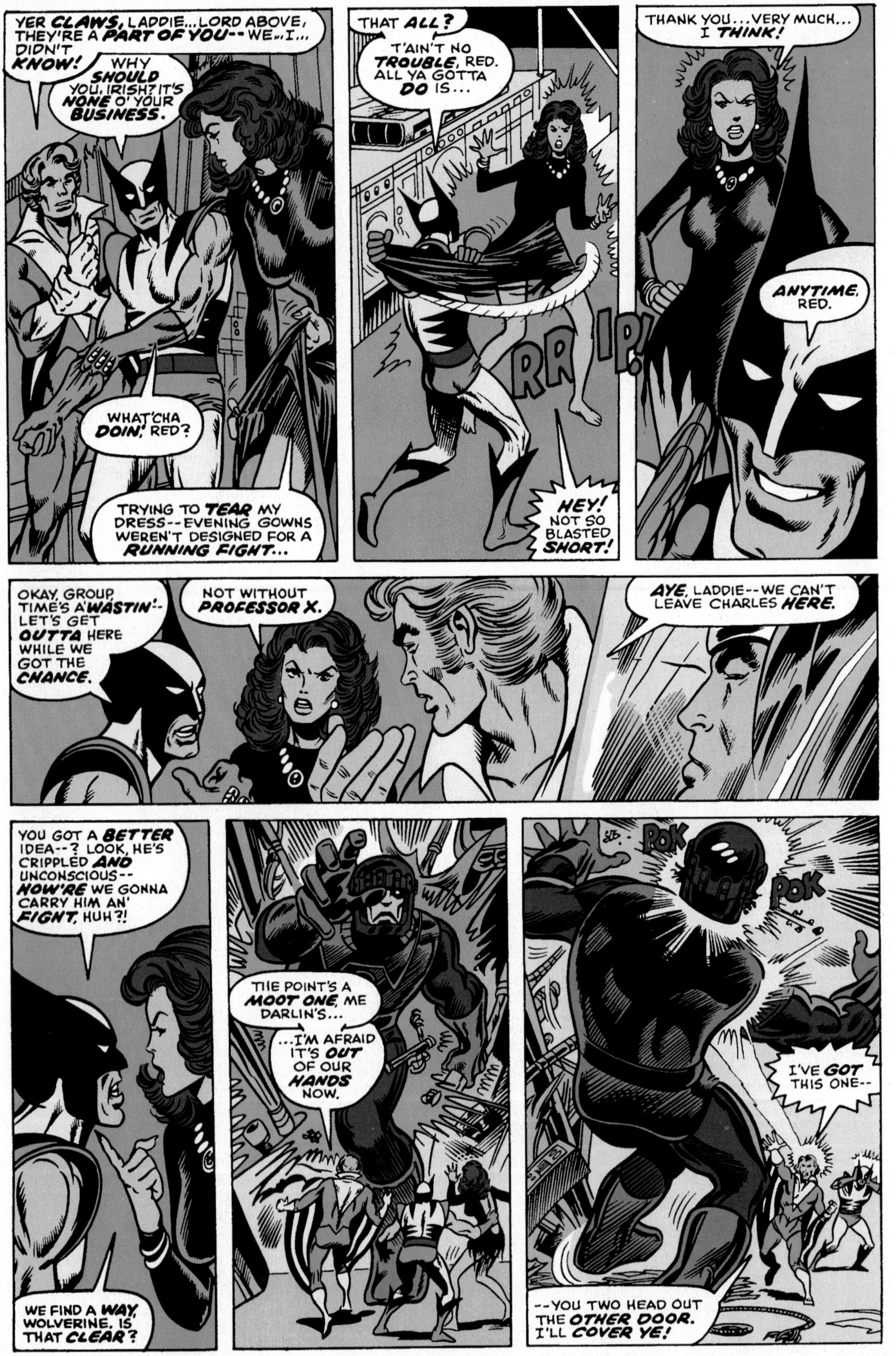
YER CLAWS, LADDIE...LORD ABOVE, THEY'RE A PART OF YOU-- WE..I... DIDN'T KNOW!
WHY SHOULD YOU, IRISH? IT'S NONE O' YOUR BUSINESS.
WHAT'CHA DOIN', RED?
TRYING TO TEAR MY DRESS--EVENING GOWNS WEREN'T DESIGNED FOR A RUNNING FIGHT...
THAT ALL?
T'AIN'T NO TROUBLE, RED. ALL YA GOTTA DO IS...
RRIIP!
HEY! NOT SO BLASTED SHORT!
THANK YOU...VERY MUCH... I THINK!
ANYTIME, RED.
OKAY, GROUP, TIME'S A WASTIN'-- LET'S GET OUTTA HERE WHILE WE GOT THE CHANCE.
NOT WITHOUT PROFESSOR X.
AYE, LADDIE--WE CAN'T LEAVE CHARLES HERE.
YOU GOT A BETTER IDEA--? LOOK, HE'S CRIPPLED AND UNCONSCIOUS-- HOW'RE WE GONNA CARRY HIM AN' FIGHT, HUH?!
WE FIND A WAY, WOLVERINE. IS THAT CLEAR?
THE POINT'S A MOOT ONE, ME DARLIN'S...
...I'M AFRAID IT'S OUT OF OUR HANDS NOW.
POK
POK
I'VE GOT THIS ONE--
--YOU TWO HEAD OUT THE OTHER DOOR. I'LL COVER YE!

MOVE IT BOTH O' YE'S!

THEY'RE POPPIN' OUTTA THE WOODWORK!

TRUER WORDS WERE NEVER SPOKE.

OH LORDY.

TAKE 'EM!!

HIT 'EM WITH EVERYTHIN' YE'VE GOT BEFORE THEY CAN REACT--THAT'S OUR ONLY HOPE--!

WAY TO GO, IRISH!

NO...SOMETHING'S WRONG HERE, BANSHEE-- OUR POWERS ARE CHOPPING THESE SENTINELS INTO BITS...

LISTEN, RED, DON'T LOOK A GIFT HORSE IN THE MOUTH, Y'KNOW?

HEY--!!

WOLVERINE, BEHIND YOU--!

IT'S...GOT MY ARMS PINNED... NO LEVERAGE... CAN'T SLASH FREE...

I'VE GOT TO MOVE FAST OR HE'LL BE CRUSHED...

...FOCUS ALL MY TELEKINETIC POWER INTO A TIGHT BEAM MINDBLAST...TRY TO FUSE THE SENTINEL'S COMPUTER BRAIN...

FZZAKT!

DONE IT!!

129

OH NO...IT'S TOPPLING RIGHT FOR ME...NO TIME...

JEAN!

HAVE NO FEAR, LASS...

...BANSHEE'S HERE.

CUTTIN' IT A LITTLE CLOSE AGAIN, AREN'T YOU, MR. CASSIDY?

NOW IS THAT ANY WAY TA TALK--I SAVED YE, DIDN'T I?

GRAB AHOLD, SHORTIE-- WE'RE BUSTIN' OUTTA HERE--!

AN' NOTHIN' 'TWEEN HEAVEN AN' HELL IS GONNA STOP US--!!

POK!

EEEEEE

EEEEEE*

WANNA BET, BANSHEE?

So NEAR, BANSHEE, AND YET SO FAR...NEW YORK CLOSE ENOUGH TO SEE ON A CLEAR DAY...TANTALIZING... UNREACHABLE...

...IF ONLY YOUR FRIENDS KNEW... BUT PERHAPS IT'S BETTER THAT THEY DON'T.

ANYTHING, CYCLOPS?

HM? OH, KURT-- I DIDN'T HEAR YOU COME IN.

NO. THERE'S NOTHING.

130

CEREBRO'S SCANNED THE ENTIRE WORLD *TWICE OVER* AND THERE'S NOT A SIGN OF THEM *ANYWHERE*...

...NO *THEM*, NO DEFENSIVE SHIELDS, *NOTHING!*

CYCLOPS... *SCOTT*, YOU'VE BEEN WORKING *FOUR DAYS STRAIGHT* WITH NO REST, PRECIOUS LITTLE *FOOD*...

YOU'RE *BURNING* YOURSELF *OUT*, MY FRIEND...

I KNOW WHAT I'M *DOING*, NIGHTCRAWLER-- WHEN I *WANT* YOUR ADVICE, I'LL *ASK* FOR IT-- *EH?!*

INTRUDER ALERT

CEREBRO'S FLASHING *INTRUDER ALERT*-- THERE'S SOMEONE COMING OVER THE *BACK WALL*...

STAY HERE, KURT, I'M GOING TO CHECK...

INTRUDER ALERT

BAMF

...KURT...?

WHERE'D HE *GO*?

OH.

WAIT A MINUTE. I CAN SEE OUR INTRUDER'S *FACE* ON THE MONITOR...

...AND I *KNOW* WHO HE IS... HE'S...

DR. PETER CORBEAU, AN OLD FRIEND OF THE *PROFESSOR'S*.

HE SAYS HE'S HERE TO *HELP* US -- AND I'VE TAKEN THE *LIBERTY* OF BRIEFING HIM ON ALL THAT'S *HAPPENED*.

AND THE *GIST* OF IT, DR. CORBEAU, IS THAT CEREBRO CAN'T *FIND* THEM, NOT EVEN A *RESIDUAL TRACE*... AND THE *ONLY* WAY FOR THAT TO HAPPEN...

...IS FOR *JEAN* AND THE OTHERS... TO BE *DEAD*.

I DON'T *ACCEPT* THAT-- BUT WHAT OTHER CHOICE HAVE *WE*? IT'S LIKE THEY'VE VANISHED OFF THE *FACE OF THE EARTH*...

THAT'S *IT*--! THAT'S WHY THE SENTINEL WAS SO WORRIED ABOUT *SOLAR FLARES*...

DON'T YOU *SEE*, CYCLOPS...?

"THEY'RE NOT *ON* THE EARTH *AT ALL!*"

--TO BE CONTINUED--

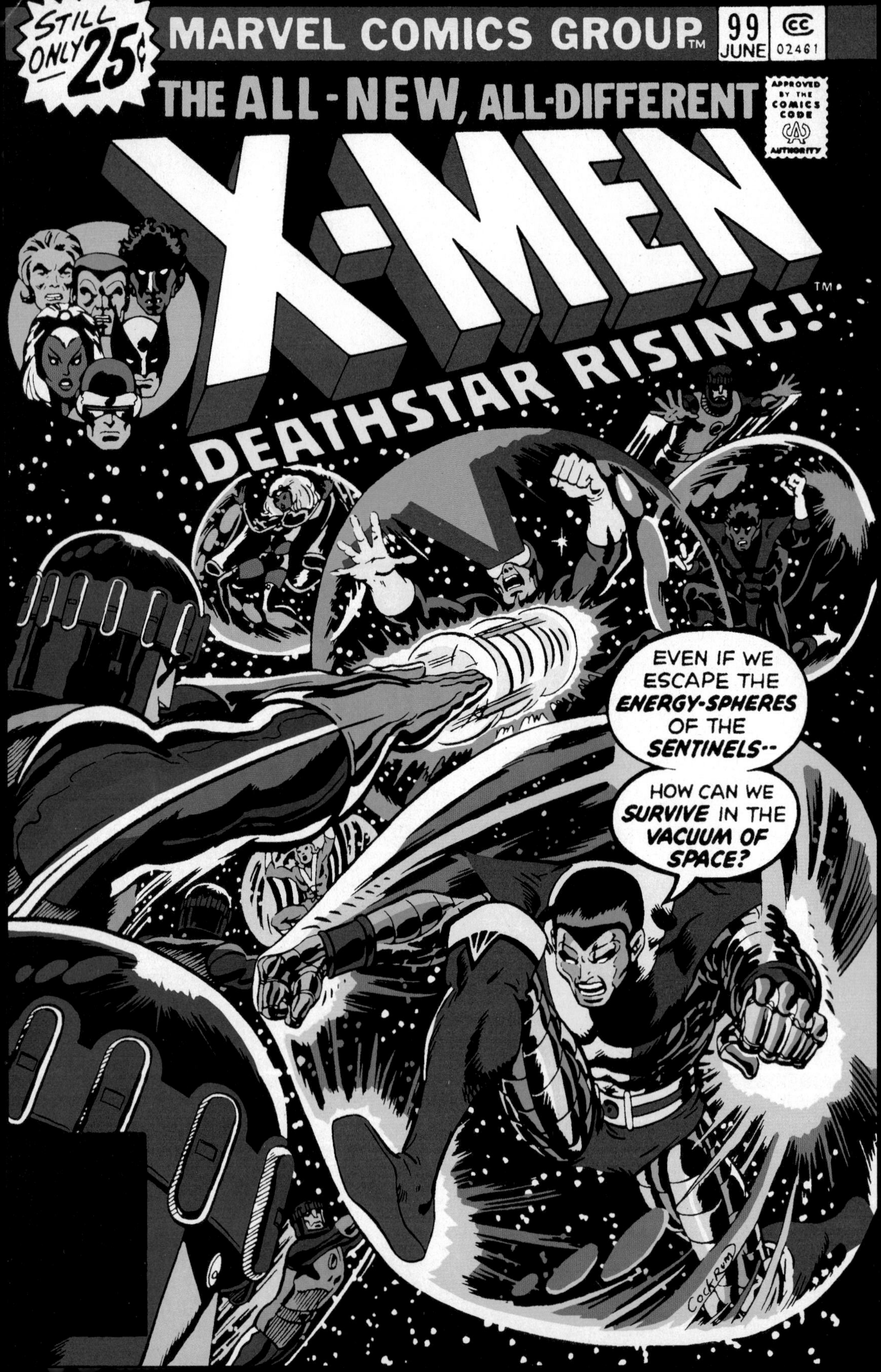

STILL ONLY 25¢
MARVEL COMICS GROUP™
99 JUNE
CC 02461
THE ALL-NEW, ALL-DIFFERENT
APPROVED BY THE COMICS CODE AUTHORITY
X-MEN™
DEATHSTAR RISING!
EVEN IF WE ESCAPE THE ENERGY-SPHERES OF THE SENTINELS--
HOW CAN WE SURVIVE IN THE VACUUM OF SPACE?
COCKRUM

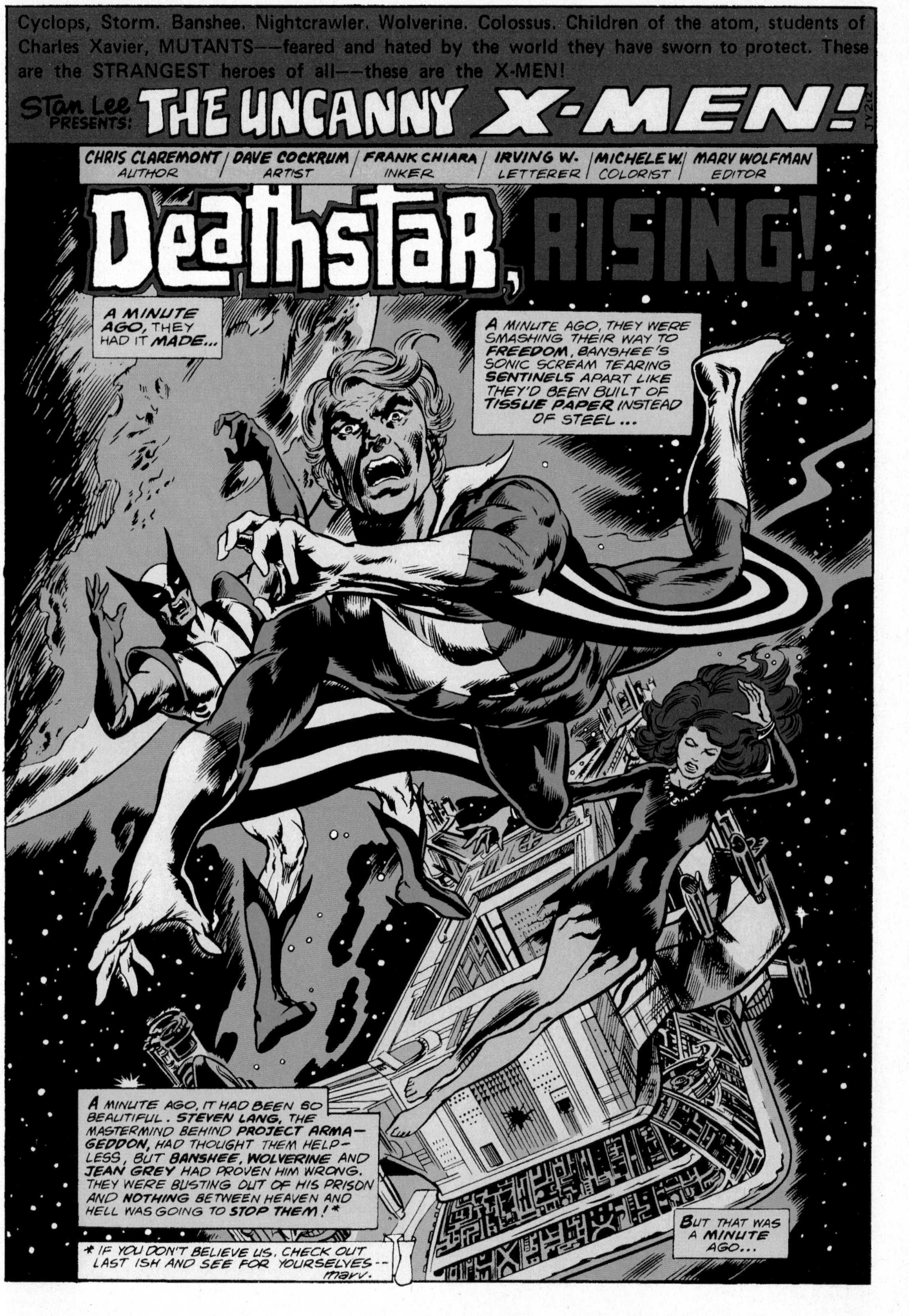

Cyclops, Storm. Banshee. Nightcrawler. Wolverine. Colossus. Children of the atom, students of Charles Xavier, MUTANTS––feared and hated by the world they have sworn to protect. These are the STRANGEST heroes of all––these are the X-MEN!
Stan Lee PRESENTS: THE UNCANNY X-MEN!
CHRIS CLAREMONT AUTHOR / DAVE COCKRUM ARTIST / FRANK CHIARA INKER / IRVING W. LETTERER / MICHELE W. COLORIST / MARV WOLFMAN EDITOR
DEATHSTAR, RISING!
A MINUTE AGO, THEY HAD IT MADE...
A MINUTE AGO, THEY WERE SMASHING THEIR WAY TO FREEDOM, BANSHEE'S SONIC SCREAM TEARING SENTINELS APART LIKE THEY'D BEEN BUILT OF TISSUE PAPER INSTEAD OF STEEL...
A MINUTE AGO, IT HAD BEEN SO BEAUTIFUL. STEVEN LANG, THE MASTERMIND BEHIND PROJECT ARMAGEDDON, HAD THOUGHT THEM HELPLESS, BUT BANSHEE, WOLVERINE AND JEAN GREY HAD PROVEN HIM WRONG. THEY WERE BUSTING OUT OF HIS PRISON AND NOTHING BETWEEN HEAVEN AND HELL WAS GOING TO STOP THEM!*
BUT THAT WAS A MINUTE AGO...
* IF YOU DON'T BELIEVE US, CHECK OUT LAST ISH AND SEE FOR YOURSELVES--MARV.

THINGS HAVE **CHANGED**...

ALERT...ALERT...MUTANT CAPTIVES HAVE **BREACHED** PRIMARY HULL OF ORBITAL PLATFORM...

...MUTANTS NOW FLOATING IN **DEEP SPACE.**

THINGS HAVE **CHANGED**...

YOU SAY BANSHEE, WOLVERINE, AND JEAN **AREN'T** ON EARTH, DR. CORBEAU...

...BUT HOW CAN YOU BE **SURE?**

I'M **NOT.** THAT'S WHERE **CEREBRO** COMES IN.

IT IS IMPERATIVE THAT **RESCUE** BE EFFECTED BEFORE MUTANT LIFE FUNCTIONS **TERMINATE**...

I'VE HOOKED IT INTO **NORAD'S VALHALLA MOUNTAIN** MAIN DATA BANK--I NEVER DREAMED XAVIER HAD **THAT** KIND OF CLEARANCE--

--ANYWAY, ALL THAT'S LEFT TO DO IS ASK VALHALLA THE **RIGHT** QUESTIONS.

USE **ATMOS-SPHERES** TO PROVIDE MUTANTS WITH A **TEMPORARY ENVIRONMENT**...

"YOU SEE, CYCLOPS, ACCORDING TO YOUR RECORDS, SENTINELS ARE COMPOSED OF SPECIAL ALLOYS, **UNIQUE** CIRCUIT ELEMENTS, **STRATEGIC** MATERIALS-- NORAD'LL HAVE A RECORD OF THOSE...

SENTINEL R-71 TO MAIN MISSION: RESCUE OPER- ATION **COMPLETED**...

...PRELIMINARY **SENSOR SCAN** OF PRISONERS INDICATES LIFE FUNCTIONS OPERATIONAL AT **MINIMUM SUPPORT LEVELS**...ALL SUFFERING FROM **EXTREME EXPOSURE**...

"BY ASKING **SPECIFIC** QUESTIONS, WE CAN DISCOVER THE **ORIGIN** OF THOSE ELEMENTS, THEIR **DESTINATION**--EVEN A NEGATIVE RESPONSE WILL TELL US **SOMETHING**...

SEARCH **NEGATIVE!**

"EVENTUALLY, WITH PATIENCE, AND A LOT OF **LUCK**..."

...IN SHORT, CONSIDER YOURSELVES **LUCKY** TO BE ALIVE.

BUT I TRUST YOU'VE LEARNED YOUR **LESSON**-- THAT THERE IS **NO ESCAPE** FROM HERE...

...NOT NOW, NOT **EVER.**

...WE GET THE ANSWER I **EXPECTED,** AND...**FEARED.**

OH, MY LORD. THE SENTINELS **ARE** STAGING FROM AN ORBITAL PLATFORM...

...**SHIELD'S** ORBITAL PLATFORM!

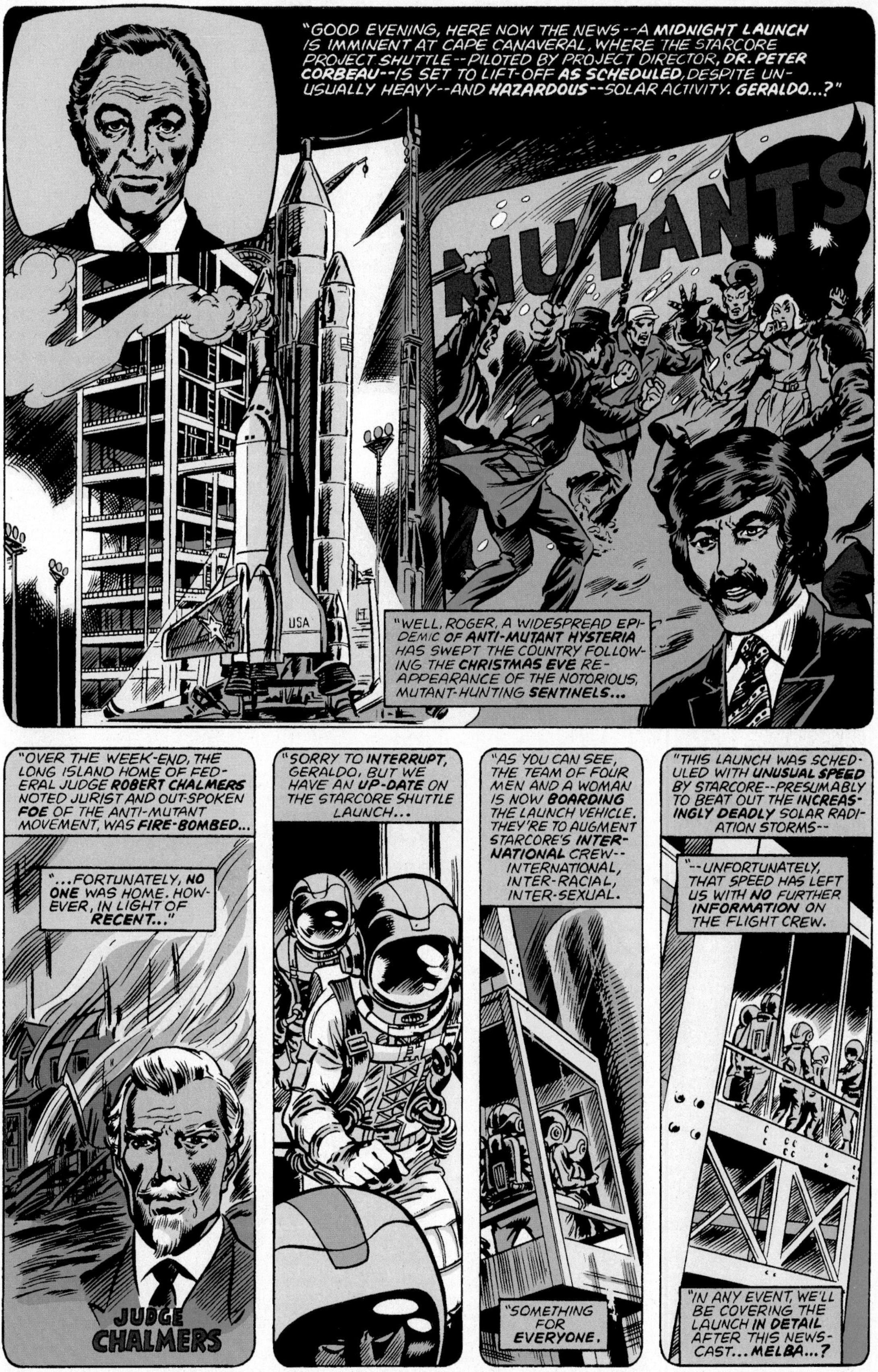
"GOOD EVENING, HERE NOW THE NEWS--A MIDNIGHT LAUNCH IS IMMINENT AT CAPE CANAVERAL, WHERE THE STARCORE PROJECT SHUTTLE--PILOTED BY PROJECT DIRECTOR, DR. PETER CORBEAU--IS SET TO LIFT-OFF AS SCHEDULED, DESPITE UNUSUALLY HEAVY--AND HAZARDOUS--SOLAR ACTIVITY. GERALDO...?"
MUTANTS
USA
"WELL, ROGER, A WIDESPREAD EPIDEMIC OF ANTI-MUTANT HYSTERIA HAS SWEPT THE COUNTRY FOLLOWING THE CHRISTMAS EVE REAPPEARANCE OF THE NOTORIOUS, MUTANT-HUNTING SENTINELS...
"OVER THE WEEK-END, THE LONG ISLAND HOME OF FEDERAL JUDGE ROBERT CHALMERS NOTED JURIST AND OUT-SPOKEN FOE OF THE ANTI-MUTANT MOVEMENT, WAS FIRE-BOMBED...
"...FORTUNATELY, NO ONE WAS HOME. HOWEVER, IN LIGHT OF RECENT..."
JUDGE CHALMERS
"SORRY TO INTERRUPT, GERALDO, BUT WE HAVE AN UP-DATE ON THE STARCORE SHUTTLE LAUNCH...
"AS YOU CAN SEE, THE TEAM OF FOUR MEN AND A WOMAN IS NOW BOARDING THE LAUNCH VEHICLE. THEY'RE TO AUGMENT STARCORE'S INTERNATIONAL CREW--INTERNATIONAL, INTER-RACIAL, INTER-SEXUAL.
"SOMETHING FOR EVERYONE.
"THIS LAUNCH WAS SCHEDULED WITH UNUSUAL SPEED BY STARCORE--PRESUMABLY TO BEAT OUT THE INCREASINGLY DEADLY SOLAR RADIATION STORMS--
"--UNFORTUNATELY, THAT SPEED HAS LEFT US WITH NO FURTHER INFORMATION ON THE FLIGHT CREW.
"IN ANY EVENT, WE'LL BE COVERING THE LAUNCH IN DETAIL AFTER THIS NEWSCAST... MELBA...?

BY ALL THE GODS, IT FEELS *MARVELOUS* TO GET THIS *HELMET* OFF...

MARVELOUS...? IS THAT *REALLY* THE WORD...?

ANOTHER SECOND *TRAPPED* INSIDE THIS CURSED SUIT AND I'D HAVE STARTED *SCREAMING*...

DR. CORBEAU, WON'T YOUR *REAL* CREW BE *UPSET* THAT WE HAVE TAKEN THEIR PLACE?

YOU *ARE* THE REAL CREW, NIGHT-CRAWLER.

THIS IS ALL FOR *SHOW*... A VERY ELABORATE AND EXPENSIVE *DECEPTION*.

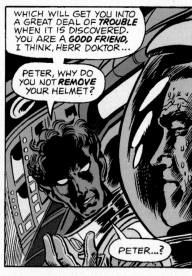

WHICH WILL GET YOU INTO A GREAT DEAL OF *TROUBLE* WHEN IT IS DISCOVERED. YOU ARE A *GOOD FRIEND*, I THINK, HERR DOKTOR...

PETER, WHY DO YOU NOT *REMOVE* YOUR HELMET?

PETER...?

T MINUS TEN MINUTES AND *COUNTING*--VENT ALL PRIMARY *FUEL TANKS*...

SSSSS

TCHANG!

PETER, ARE YOU--

GODS BELOW!!

MIKHAIL!!

WHAT *IS* IT, MY FRIEND-- WHAT'S THE *MATTER*?

N-NOTHING, TOVARISCH ...I...I'M *SORRY*, KURT, I DID NOT MEAN TO...

I...I WAS AFRAID, KURT. *AFRAID*.

I SIT HERE, INSIDE A *ROCKET*, AND ALL I CAN THINK OF IS MY BROTHER, *MIKHAIL* ...A TEST PILOT, ONE OF RUSSIA'S FIRST *COSMONAUTS*...

...MIKHAIL...*DYING*, MY FRIEND. *BURN-ING* TO DEATH ON A BAIKONUR LAUNCH PAD WHEN HIS ROCKET...*EXPLODED*...

WE WERE SO... *CLOSE*, MIKHAIL AND I-- WE WERE ALL WE *HAD*...

...AND EVER SINCE THAT DAY...

I UNDERSTAND, COLOSSUS--I REMEMBER THE *APOLLO I* FIRE... THE FRIENDS *I* LOST THAT DAY...

T MINUS *ONE MINUTE* AND COUNTING--ALL SYSTEMS *GO*...

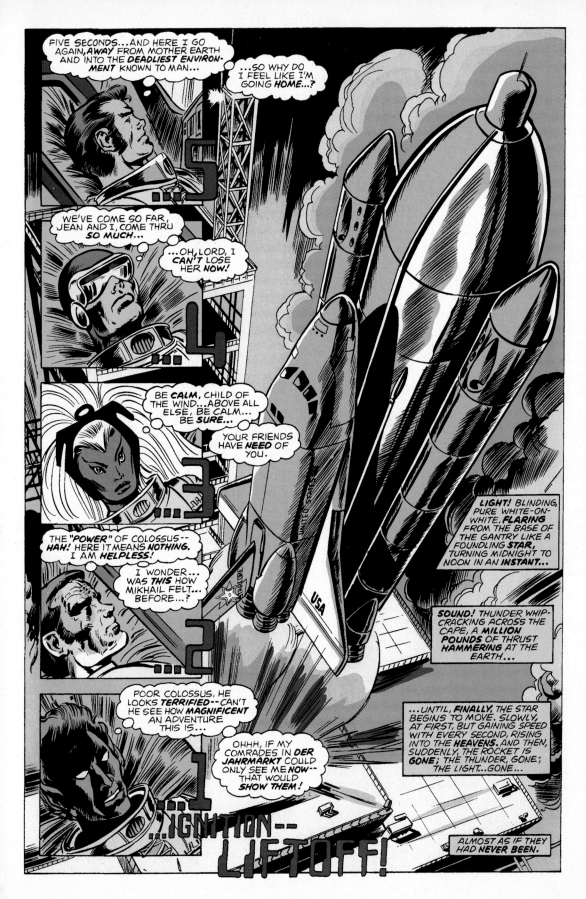

FIVE SECONDS...AND HERE I GO AGAIN, *AWAY* FROM MOTHER EARTH AND INTO THE *DEADLIEST ENVIRONMENT* KNOWN TO MAN...

...SO WHY DO I FEEL LIKE I'M GOING *HOME*...?

WE'VE COME SO FAR, JEAN AND I, COME THRU *SO MUCH*...

...OH, LORD, I *CAN'T* LOSE HER *NOW!*

BE *CALM*, CHILD OF THE WIND...ABOVE ALL ELSE, BE CALM... BE *SURE*...

YOUR FRIENDS HAVE *NEED* OF YOU.

THE *"POWER"* OF COLOSSUS-- HAH! HERE IT MEANS *NOTHING*. I AM *HELPLESS!*

I WONDER... WAS *THIS* HOW MIKHAIL FELT...*BEFORE*...?

POOR COLOSSUS, HE LOOKS *TERRIFIED*--CAN'T HE SEE HOW *MAGNIFICENT* AN ADVENTURE THIS IS...

OHHH, IF MY COMRADES IN *DER JAHRMARKT* COULD ONLY SEE ME *NOW*-- THAT WOULD *SHOW THEM!*

LIGHT! BLINDING, PURE WHITE-ON-WHITE. *FLARING* FROM THE BASE OF THE GANTRY LIKE A FOUNDLING *STAR*, TURNING MIDNIGHT TO NOON IN AN *INSTANT*...

SOUND! THUNDER WHIP-CRACKING ACROSS THE CAPE, A *MILLION POUNDS* OF THRUST HAMMERING AT THE EARTH...

...UNTIL, *FINALLY*, THE STAR BEGINS TO MOVE. SLOWLY, AT FIRST, BUT GAINING SPEED WITH EVERY SECOND, RISING INTO THE *HEAVENS*. AND THEN, SUDDENLY, THE ROCKET IS *GONE*; THE THUNDER, GONE; THE LIGHT...GONE...

...IGNITION-- LIFTOFF!

ALMOST AS IF THEY HAD *NEVER BEEN.*

STARCORE, THIS IS *CAPCOM*: AT T PLUS TWO MINUTES, YOU ARE ON TRACK, ON SKED, ALL TELEMETRY READING *NOMINAL*.

BEAUTIFUL? FOR THE *MOMENT*, PERHAPS...

...BUT LET'S SHIFT OUR ATTENTION TO *ANOTHER* SOLAR ORBIT, TO THE VAST *U.N.* SPONSORED RESEARCH STATION KNOWN AS *STARCORE ONE*...

...AND WE'LL HEAR A SLIGHTLY *DIFFERENT* TALE.

IN OTHER WORDS, A *BEAUTIFUL* FLIGHT.

I THOUGHT I *SAID* THAT, CORBEAU.

HILARY--THAT *SUNFLARE*!! MY INSTRUMENTS ARE GOING *OFF THEIR SCALES*--!

THEN *RE-CALIBRATE*, COLONEL KUTUZOV, AND *FAST*! THE WAY OL' *SOL'S* ACTING UP, WE'RE WORKING WITH *NO MARGIN FOR ERROR*!

COME *ON*, DMITRI, WHAT'S HOLDING UP THOSE *SOLAR FORECASTS*?!

THEY'RE JUST COMING THRU NOW...

...AND THEY ARE... *VERY BAD*. WORSE THAN WE'D *ANTICIPATED*.

"PETER CORBEAU IS FLYING STRAIGHT INTO THE *WORST* SOLAR STORM IN *LIVING MEMORY*...!"

ACH, PETER, WE ARE IN *SPACE* AND WE ARE ALL *STILL ALIVE*...

...ARE YOU *DISAPPOINTED*, MY FRIEND?

PLEASE, KURT WAGNER, *NO JOKES*...I AM NOT IN THE *MOOD*...

I FEEL...VERY ...*STRANGE*...

I ALMOST WISH I *WAS* DEAD...

A MILD FORM OF *SPACE-SICKNESS*, COLOSSUS--YOUR BODY REACTING AND ADAPTING TO *ZERO-GRAVITY*-- NOTHING TO *WORRY* ABOUT...

...MEANTIME, *PIPE DOWN*, THE LOT OF YOU. I'VE GOT A *PRIORITY MESSAGE* COMING THRU FROM STARCORE...

EARLY MORNING NOW, HALF-A-WORLD REMOVED FROM CAPE CANAVERAL AND STARCORE...

THE VILLAGE OF DAL'ROON, A HALF-HOUR DRIVE OUT OF CENTRAL DUBLIN. A SMALL VILLAGE, OFF THE BEATEN TRACK, THE LOCAL FARM HOLDINGS JUST NOW BEGINNING TO GIVE WAY TO INDUSTRIAL PARKS...

...BUT STILL--ALL THINGS CONSIDERED --A NICE PLACE TO LIVE.

OR DIE. WILL YE BE SHUTTIN' THE DOOR, YE FLAMIN' IDJIT--!

THERE'S A WINTER GALE BLOWIN'--OR HAVEN'T YE NOTICED...?

I...I'M SORRY.

MY NAME IS FLAHERTY. I'M A SOLICITOR. THIS LETTER IS FOR A CLIENT OF MINE IN AMERICA.

IT'S IMPERATIVE IT GET TO HIM WITH-OUT DELAY.

Mr Sean Cassidy
c/o Prof. Xavier's Sch...
for Gifted Young...
1407 Greymalkin...
Scarsdale, New...
SPECIAL DELI...
U.S.A.

WITHOUT DELAY, YOU UNDERSTAND--!

I'LL BE KNOWIN' HOW T' DO ME OWN JOB, THANK YE VERY MUCH--I BEEN DOIN' IT NIGH ON FORTY YEARS.

NOW, FER THE LAST TIME, CLOSE THAT FLAMIN' DOOR.!!

WELL, MY JOB'S DONE-- AND GLAD I AM IT IS...

A LONG WAY FROM COUNTY MAYO, AREN'T YE, MR. FLAHERTY?

YOU!!

YOU'RE TOO LATE-- YOUR COUSIN'S BEEN WARNED AND HE'LL STOP YOUR MAD PLANS!

AA RRG!!

POOR, FOOLISH LAWYER FLAHERTY...

...MY COUSIN COULD SOONER STOP THE MORNING SUN FROM RISING.

AYE, COUSIN SEAN, YOU'LL STOP BLACK TOM, WON'T YE...?

AT LEAST, YOU'LL DIE TRYING!!

"1,347 MILES ABOVE OUR TOUSLED HEADS, IT CIRCLES THE EARTH..."

"...AND TO IT HAVE COME DICTATORS AND DIGNITARIES-- PHYSICISTS AND FOOLS--" AND, ONCE UPON A TIME, AVENGERS...

BUT THAT WAS YEARS AGO, BEFORE BUDGET CUTS FORCED SHIELD TO ABANDON ITS SPACE PLATFORM...BEFORE PROJECT ARMAGEDDON...

WHAT'S THAT ON THE VID-SCREEN, MISTER?

THIS IS STARCORE-EAGLE-ONE. SOLAR RADIATION LEVELS ARE MOVING INTO THE DANGER ZONE...

...WE'RE REQUESTING SANCTUARY.

THIS IS STEVEN LANG SPEAKING-- WE ARE A TOP SE-CRET U.S. GOVERN-MENT INSTALLATION, CORBEAU, AND YOU HAVE FOREIGN PERSONNEL ABOARD...

...SANCTUARY DENIED.

DR. LANG--THE MUTANT DETECTOR! IT'S GOIN' CRAZY!

THAT SHIP OUT THERE MUST BE CRAMMED WITH MUTIES!

"THEN ORDER OUT THE SENTINELS, TECHNICIAN--I'M SURE THEY'LL GIVE OUR CRAFTY GUESTS THE WELCOME THEY DESERVE..."

HEADS UP, TROOPS, WE'VE BEEN RUMBLED! BOGIES AT TWELVE O'CLOCK HIGH AND COMING FAST!

EVERYONE INTO FULL PRESSURE SUITS --ON THE DOUBLE!!

BUT WHAT ABOUT COLOSSUS--?!

HE HAS NO PRESSURE SUIT-- IF WE'RE HIT, HE WON'T STAND A CHANCE!

"THEN WE JUST BETTER PRAY WE DON'T GET HIT!"

NICE TRY, DR. CORBEAU...

...BUT NO DICE.

CORBEAU! CYCLOPS! THE SHIP'S HULL IS **OPEN TO SPACE**--!

STORM, **LOOK OUT**--! THE ENERGY BEAM HAS CUT YOUR **LIFELINE**!!

HELP ME, SOMEONE--! THE EXPLOSIVE DECOMPRESSION IS PULLING STORM OUT OF THE **SHIP**--!

I **CAN'T** GET TO HER IN TIME!!

STORM!

CORBEAU, COLOSSUS IS **SUFFOCATING**! WE'VE NO TIME FOR **SUBTLETY**, MAN-- GET US **INSIDE** THAT STATION--

--AND GET US INSIDE **NOW**!

OKAY, CYCLOPS, BUT JUST BEAR **ONE THING** IN MIND: WE SMASH **THIS** BABY UP AND WE DON'T **GO** HOME. GOT THAT?

SO HERE GOES **NOTHING**--

--**GERONIMO**!!

ALERT! ALERT! TARGET VEHICLE MAKING **UNAUTHORIZED ENTRY** INTO ARMAGEDDON COMMAND BASE...

...THESE UNITS **UNABLE** TO PREVENT MUTANT INCURSION INTO **MAIN MISSION SECURITY ZONE.**

TRANSLATION: STEVE LANG'S ORBITAL ANTHILL IS BEING **RAMMED** AND INVADED-- AND THERE'S NOT A **BLESSED** THING HIS SENTINELS CAN **DO** ABOUT IT...

SP'KA

DAMM!!

L-1 TO MAIN MISSION...AM IN PURSUIT OF *LONE FEMALE MUTANT*...

AS PER *LATEST PROGRAM-MING*, THIS UNIT'S MISSION IS TO SEEK OUT...AND *DESTROY!*

A *SENTINEL*...COMING STRAIGHT FOR ME...!

AND I AM *STUCK* HERE...AS HELPLESS AS AN ANTELOPE IN A *LION SNARE*...

...UNLESS...I AM *MISTRESS* OF THE WIND AND STORM...BUT WHAT IF MY POWER INCLUDES THE *COSMIC STORM* AS WELL...?

A *SLIM HOPE*... BUT IF I COULD ONLY *FLY* ON THE *SOLAR WINDS*...

AND I *CAN!*

HO, SENTINEL, YOU THOUGHT ME AN *EASY* TARGET--YOU WOULD HAVE SLAIN ME *WITHOUT MERCY*...

...THEREFORE, *MACHINE*, STORM GIVES YOU WHAT YOU WOULD HAVE GIVEN *ME*--

--AND *MORE!!*

WARNING...UNIT L-1 BEING BUFFETED BY UNKNOWN *ENERGY MATRICES*...

...THIS UNIT'S MEMORY BANKS HAVE *NO DATA* ON THIS PHENOMENON... *CANNOT COPE*...

AAAAAIIIIIEEEE

OF *COURSE NOT*, SENTINEL...

...BECAUSE YOUR MAKERS NEVER CONCEIVED OF YOU FACING A *FORCE 12* GALE IN DEEPEST SPACE, A GALE *BACKED* BY THE FULL POWER OF THE *RAGING SUN* ITSELF!

HIS *SCREAM*...THE FEAR IN IT...THAT SENTINEL SOUNDED ALMOST... *HUMAN*...

IS *THIS* HOW YOU HONOR YOUR PARENTS' *MEMORY*, ORORO? BY *BREAKING* THE OATH YOU SWORE SO LONG AGO, THAT YOU WOULD *NEVER* TAKE ANOTHER'S *LIFE*?

AND YET, SOONER OR LATER, YOUR DUTY AS AN *X-MAN* MAY REQUIRE YOU TO DO *JUST THAT*.

PERHAPS, THEN, IT WOULD BE BETTER IF YOU... *CEASED*...BEING AN *X-MAN*...

AND YET AGAIN, ORORO, **HOW** DO YOU DESERT FRIENDS WHO NEED YOU?

THOUGH, AT THE MOMENT, WE MUST ADMIT THAT YOUR MUTANT **COMRADES** SEEM TO BE DOING **WELL ENOUGH** ON THEIR OWN.

CURSE YOU, MONSTER--!

WERE IT NOT FOR **YOUR KIND,** STORM WOULD BE **SAFE** NOW!

BD ROW!

MEIN GOTT-- COLOSSUS IS FIGHTING LIKE A MAN **BERSERK**...

...LIKE A MAN FIGHTING FOR THE **WOMAN HE LOVES**...

BUT PAY ATTENTION TO THE **JOB AT HAND,** NIGHTCRAWLER-- THAT SENTINEL HAS CAPTURED **CYCLOPS**...

THIS **ANESTHETIC GAS** WILL SOON RENDER YOU UNCONSCIOUS, CYCLOPS --AND OUR PRISONER...

PRISONER FOR THIS **INSTANT,** SENTINEL, BUT YOU HAVE **NIGHT-CRAWLER'S** PLEDGE...

...THAT YOU'LL NOT HOLD CYCLOPS **FOR LONG!!**

KD AM

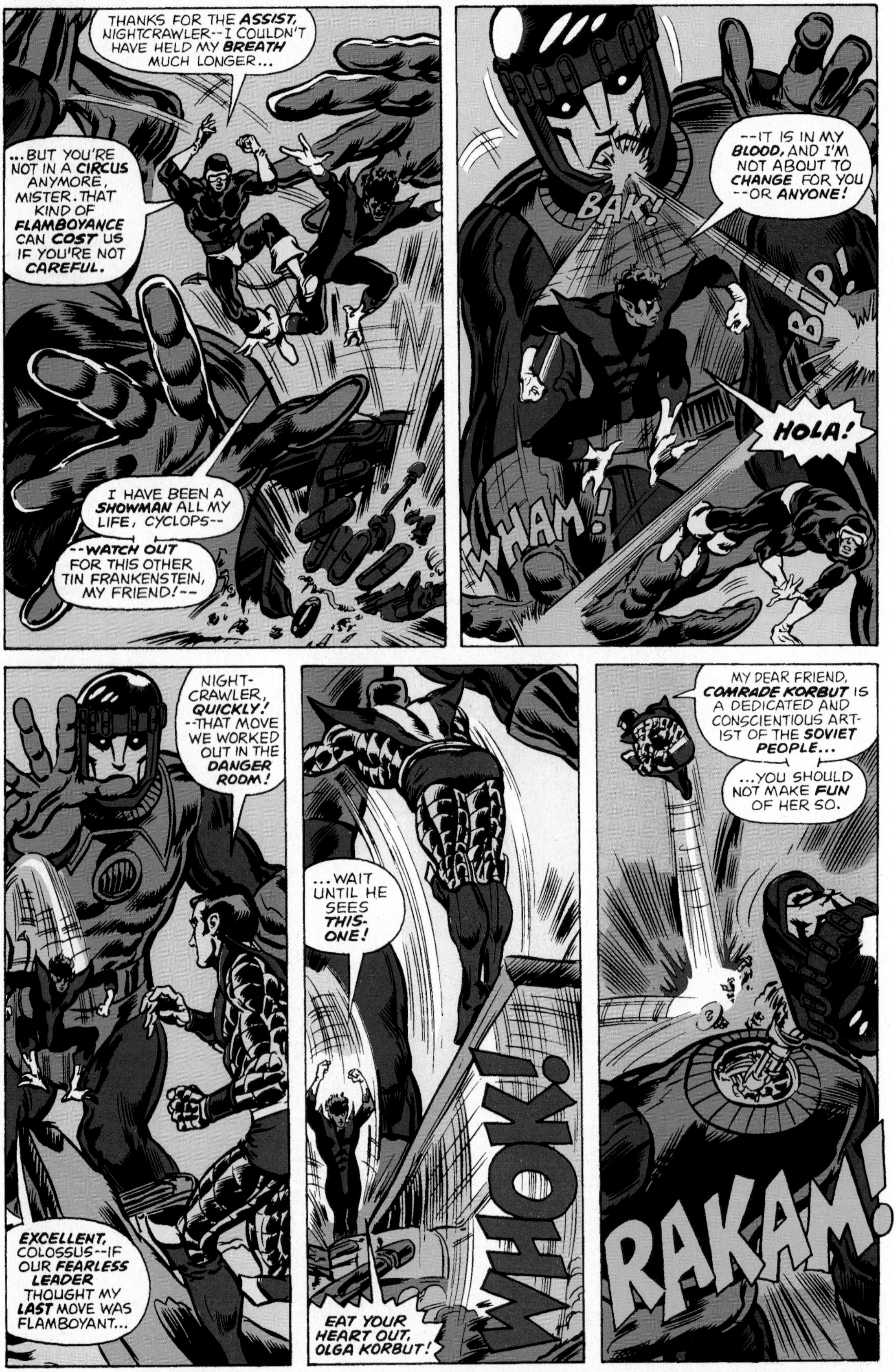
THANKS FOR THE ASSIST, NIGHTCRAWLER--I COULDN'T HAVE HELD MY BREATH MUCH LONGER...
...BUT YOU'RE NOT IN A CIRCUS ANYMORE, MISTER. THAT KIND OF FLAMBOYANCE CAN COST US IF YOU'RE NOT CAREFUL.
I HAVE BEEN A SHOWMAN ALL MY LIFE, CYCLOPS--
--WATCH OUT FOR THIS OTHER TIN FRANKENSTEIN, MY FRIEND!--
--IT IS IN MY BLOOD, AND I'M NOT ABOUT TO CHANGE FOR YOU --OR ANYONE!
BAK!
BIP!
HOLA!
WHAM!
NIGHT-CRAWLER, QUICKLY! --THAT MOVE WE WORKED OUT IN THE DANGER ROOM!
EXCELLENT, COLOSSUS--IF OUR FEARLESS LEADER THOUGHT MY LAST MOVE WAS FLAMBOYANT...
...WAIT UNTIL HE SEES THIS ONE!
EAT YOUR HEART OUT, OLGA KORBUT!
WHOK!
MY DEAR FRIEND, COMRADE KORBUT IS A DEDICATED AND CONSCIENTIOUS ARTIST OF THE SOVIET PEOPLE...
...YOU SHOULD NOT MAKE FUN OF HER SO.
RAKAM!

FZAM!

THAT'S THE **LAST ONE**--OVER A **DOZEN** SENTINELS SCRAGGED IN **HALF** AS MANY MINUTES...

THIS IS **INSANE**--THE DANGER ROOM GIVES US MORE **TROUBLE** THAN THESE STEEL DUMMIES HAVE. IT'S ALL A BIT **TOO EASY**...

YOU CALL **THIS**... EASY?

COMPARED TO THE **TRASK** SENTINELS, THIS MODEL'S A WALKING **JOKE**.

WHICH BEGGARS THE QUESTION: WHAT'S THE **REAL** THREAT IN ALL OF THIS...?

JEAN GREY AND THE OTHERS--WHAT ABOUT **STORM**?

SHE IS **ADRIFT** OUT THERE-- SHE COULD BE **HURT**!

I HAVE A FEELING THAT THE **SOONER** WE FIND JEAN AND THE OTHERS, THE SOONER WE'LL **KNOW**.

BACK OFF, COLOSSUS-- I **KNOW** HOW YOU FEEL...

YOU KNOW **NOTHING**! SHE IS OUR **FRIEND**, OUR COMRADE IN BATTLE--SHE COULD BE... **DEAD**!

AND **YOU** ACT AS IF YOU DO NOT EVEN **CARE**! WELL, COLOSSUS **CARES**!!

YOU DO ME **GREAT HONOR**, MY FRIEND...

...AND I AM **GRATEFUL**.

EH--?!

STORM--**ORORO**!! YOU'RE **HERE**--!

AND YOU'RE **ALIVE**!!

SO IT WOULD APPEAR.

I CAN'T **BELIEVE IT**...THIS IS TOO WONDERFUL TO BE **TRUE**--!

WHEN I SAW YOU BLOWN **OUT** OF THE SPACESHIP, I THOUGHT YOU WERE **TRULY DOOMED**!

I'VE ALWAYS BEEN VERY...*DIFFICULT*...TO KILL, YOUNG ONE...

...BUT I MUST ADMIT, I FIND THE *SENTINELS* EASIER TO SURVIVE THAN YOUR *BEAR HUGS.*

OH, I AM *SORRY*...IT'S JUST THAT I AM SO *GLAD* TO SEE YOU. WE *ALL* ARE, EH, CYCLOPS? *CYCLOPS...?*

SCOTT...

IMAGES... INSIDE MY MIND...I CAN'T... *JEAN...!*

HELP US, SCOTT. TIME IS *RUNNING OUT* FOR THE PROFESSOR AND ME...CAN BARELY *HOLD CONTACT...*

BANSHEE AND WOLVERINE ARE IN THE "*B*"-DECK DETENTION CELLS...

...PROFESSOR X AND I ARE IN MAIN MISSION...

BUT HURRY, SCOTT, *HURRY!* STEVEN LANG IS COMING--HE MEANS TO...*MURDER US...!*

COLOSSUS, STORM, NIGHTCRAWLER--FOLLOW THE *ROUTE SIGNS* DOWN TO "*B*"-DECK; YOU'LL FIND *WOLVERINE* AND *BANSHEE* THERE.

BREAK THEM *FREE* AND THEN *JOIN ME* IN MAIN MISSION!

MOVE IT, PEOPLE --WE'VE *NO TIME* TO WASTE!

BUT, CYCLOPS, THAT WILL LEAVE YOU *ON YOUR OWN...*

...SUPPOSE THERE ARE MORE *SENTINELS...?*

THEN I'LL *HANDLE* THEM, STORM.

RIGHT NOW, I'VE GIVEN YOU AN *ORDER* --*OBEY IT!*

AS FOR MR. *STEVEN LANG,* SO-CALLED *HEAD HONCHO* OF THIS BALL OF WAX...

...HE'S MINE, X-MEN. *MINE ALONE!!*

I'LL SAY THIS FOR THE **LAST TIME**, PEOPLE-- GET **OUT** OF HERE! YOU COME WITH **ME**, DR. CORBEAU. CAN'T HAVE YOU RUNNING INTO A **STRAY SENTINEL** IN THE DARK.

UH...YES, OF COURSE... LOOK, CYCLOPS, DON'T YOU THINK YOU WERE A LITTLE **ROUGH** ON THEM...

...BUT...I GUESS YOU'VE GOT MORE **IMPORTANT** THINGS ON YOUR MIND, **HAVEN'T** YOU...?

CYCLOPS DOESN'T **ANSWER** --HE DOESN'T REALLY **HAVE** TO.

IT SEEMS THE **TRASK NOTES** I USED TO RECONSTRUCT THE SENTINELS WERE **IN-COMPLETE**...THE SENTINELS **SECOND-RATE**...

...NOT THAT IT **MAT-TERS**. I HAVE ALL THE DATA I **NEED** FROM YOU MUTANTS. WHICH MAKES YOU **EXPENDABLE**...

YOUR FRIENDS MAY HAVE **TAKEN** THIS STATION, MISS GREY--

--BUT I'M AFRAID **YOU** WON'T BE ALIVE TO **SHARE** IN THEIR "VICTORY"--

FTHOM.

--MY GOD!

ZZZZZ

SHE'LL BE A LOT **MORE** ALIVE THAN **YOU**, SCUM--!

FREE **JEAN** AND THE **PROFESSOR**, CORBEAU...

...I'LL DEAL WITH MR. LANG, **PERSONALLY**!

HOW DOES IT **FEEL**, YOU **ANIMAL**--FACING SOMEONE **ONE-ON-ONE**, SOMEONE WHO CAN **FIGHT BACK**!?

BRAK!

ANSWER ME, LANG-- **ANSWER ME**!!

CYCLOPS, FOR PITY'S SAKE, **STOP**! YOU'RE **KILLING** HIM!

ANSWER!!

SUDDENLY...

SCOTT--*BEHIND YOU!!* THERE'S SOMEONE IN THE *NEXT ROOM!*

WHAT *IS* IT, JEAN-- ANOTHER *SENTINEL?*

NOT QUITE.

AAARRRGH!

NO. OH NO--IT *CAN'T* BE YOU...

...PLEASE DON'T LET IT BE YOU.

BUT IT *IS,* MISS GREY...THE *ULTIMATE* IRONY...

...THE ULTIMATE, *UNDEFEATABLE* ENEMY.

THIS IS THE HEART OF PROJECT ARMAGEDDON, MY DEAR--NOT THOSE RATHER *PATHETIC* SENTINELS...

...THOUGH I ADMIT I HAD *HOPES* FOR THEM.

RESISTANCE, AS THEY SAY, IS *FUTILE--* YOUR MENTAL POWERS ARE BEING *NEUTRALIZED* BY A MIND NOT... *UNLIKE* YOUR OWN...

"TAKE HER AWAY, MY PETS. *PREPARE* HER."

"WHICH MEANS, OF COURSE, THAT YOU *WON'T* BE ABLE TO *WARN* YOUR FELLOW X-MEN UNTIL IT'S *TOO* LATE..."

"BECAUSE OUR *FINAL* ACT IS ABOUT TO *BEGIN.*"

BANSHEE-- ALL OF YOU-- *LOOK!*

I'M *LOOKIN',* BUT I'M A FAR, *FAR* PIECE FROM *BELIEVIN'!*

ACH, THIS IS A *JOKE,* IS IT NOT? IT *MUST* BE A JOKE. OR A *NIGHTMARE.*

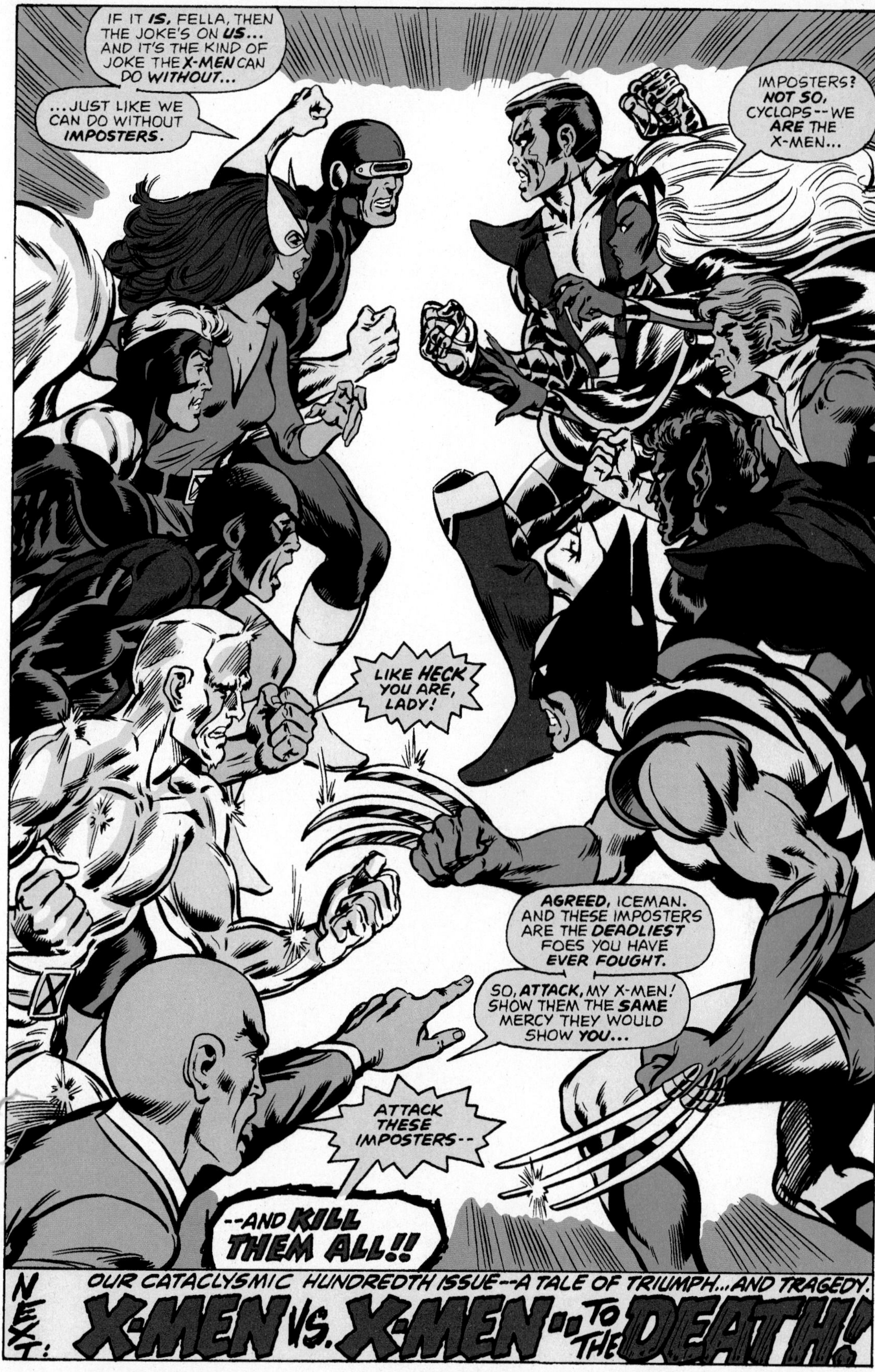
IF IT IS, FELLA, THEN THE JOKE'S ON US... AND IT'S THE KIND OF JOKE THE X-MEN CAN DO WITHOUT...
...JUST LIKE WE CAN DO WITHOUT IMPOSTERS.
IMPOSTERS? NOT SO, CYCLOPS--WE ARE THE X-MEN...
LIKE HECK YOU ARE, LADY!
AGREED, ICEMAN. AND THESE IMPOSTERS ARE THE DEADLIEST FOES YOU HAVE EVER FOUGHT.
SO, ATTACK, MY X-MEN! SHOW THEM THE SAME MERCY THEY WOULD SHOW YOU...
ATTACK THESE IMPOSTERS--
--AND KILL THEM ALL!!
NEXT: OUR CATACLYSMIC HUNDREDTH ISSUE--A TALE OF TRIUMPH...AND TRAGEDY.
X-MEN VS. X-MEN -- TO THE DEATH!

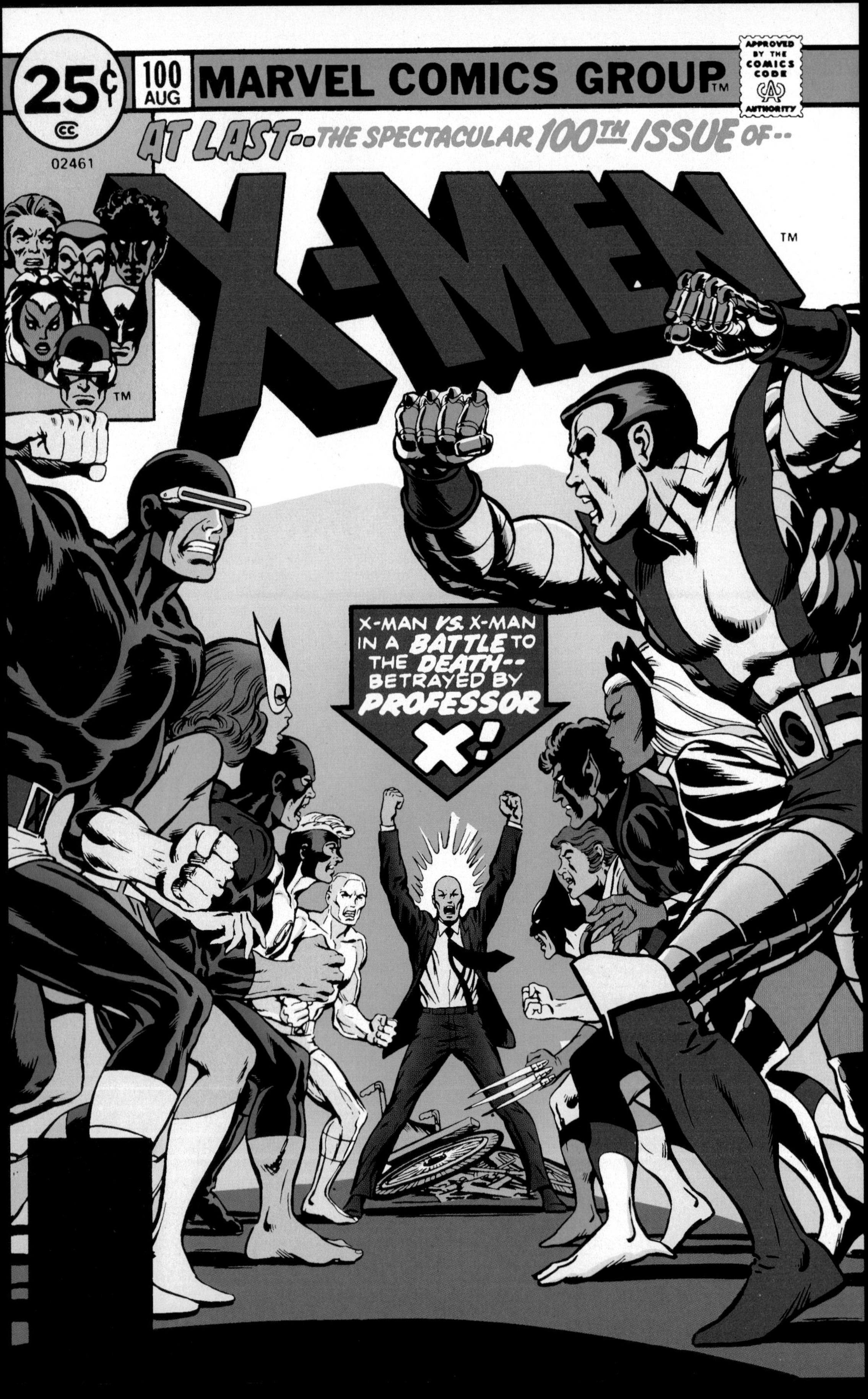

25¢
CC
02461
100
AUG
MARVEL COMICS GROUP™
APPROVED BY THE COMICS CODE AUTHORITY
AT LAST--THE SPECTACULAR 100TH ISSUE OF--
X-MEN™
X-MAN VS. X-MAN IN A BATTLE TO THE DEATH--BETRAYED BY PROFESSOR X!

Cyclops. Storm. Banshee. Nightcrawler. Wolverine. Colossus. Children of the atom, students of Charles Xavier, MUTANTS——feared and hated by the world they have sworn to protect. These are the STRANGEST heroes of all!

Stan Lee PRESENTS: THE UNCANNY X-MEN! TM

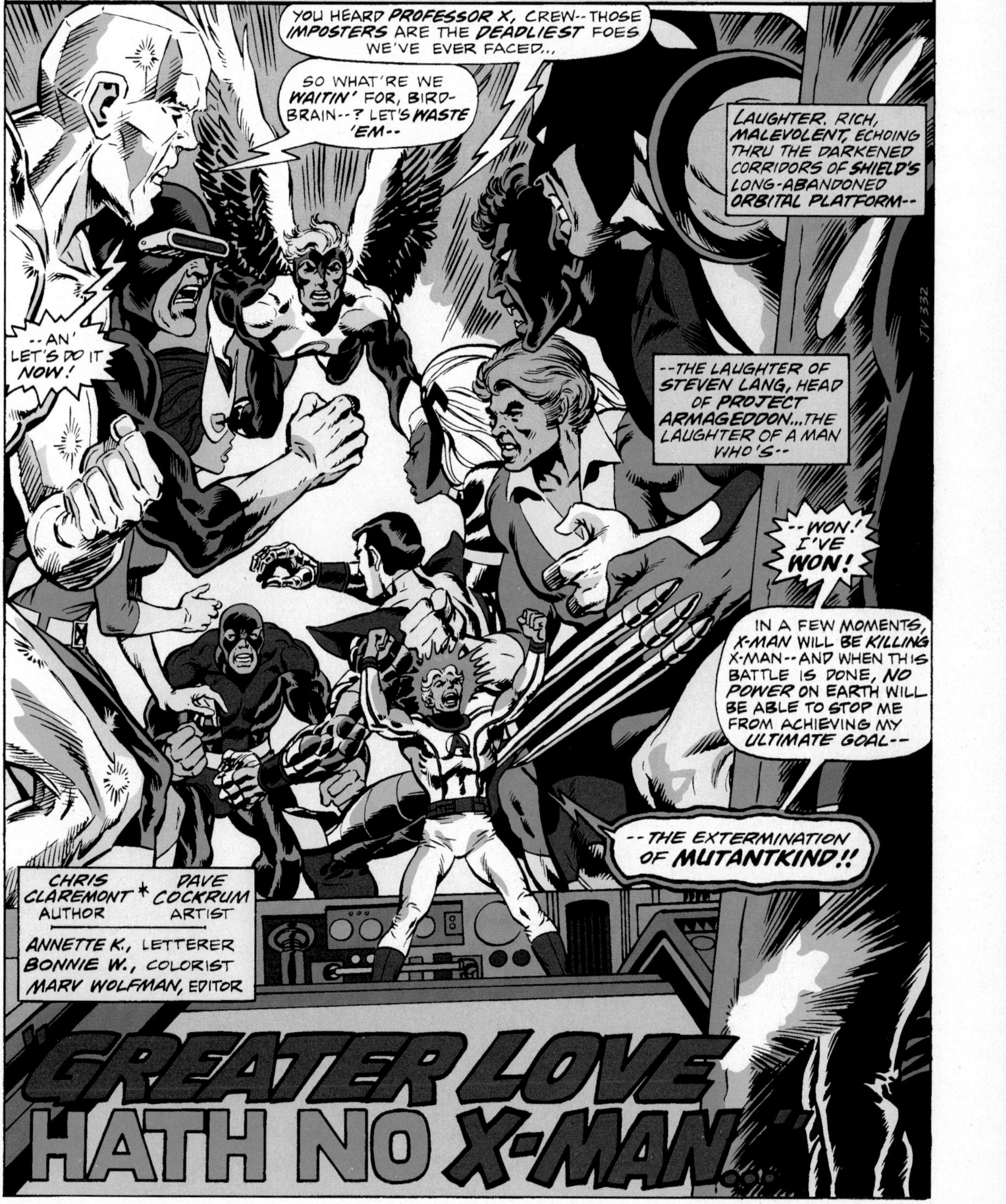

YOU HEARD PROFESSOR X, CREW-- THOSE IMPOSTERS ARE THE DEADLIEST FOES WE'VE EVER FACED...
SO WHAT'RE WE WAITIN' FOR, BIRD-BRAIN--? LET'S WASTE 'EM--
--AN' LET'S DO IT NOW!
LAUGHTER. RICH, MALEVOLENT, ECHOING THRU THE DARKENED CORRIDORS OF SHIELD'S LONG-ABANDONED ORBITAL PLATFORM--
--THE LAUGHTER OF STEVEN LANG, HEAD OF PROJECT ARMAGEDDON...THE LAUGHTER OF A MAN WHO'S--
--WON! I'VE WON!
IN A FEW MOMENTS, X-MAN WILL BE KILLING X-MAN--AND WHEN THIS BATTLE IS DONE, NO POWER ON EARTH WILL BE ABLE TO STOP ME FROM ACHIEVING MY ULTIMATE GOAL--
--THE EXTERMINATION OF MUTANTKIND!!
CHRIS CLAREMONT AUTHOR * DAVE COCKRUM ARTIST
ANNETTE K., LETTERER
BONNIE W., COLORIST
MARV WOLFMAN, EDITOR
"GREATER LOVE HATH NO X-MAN..."

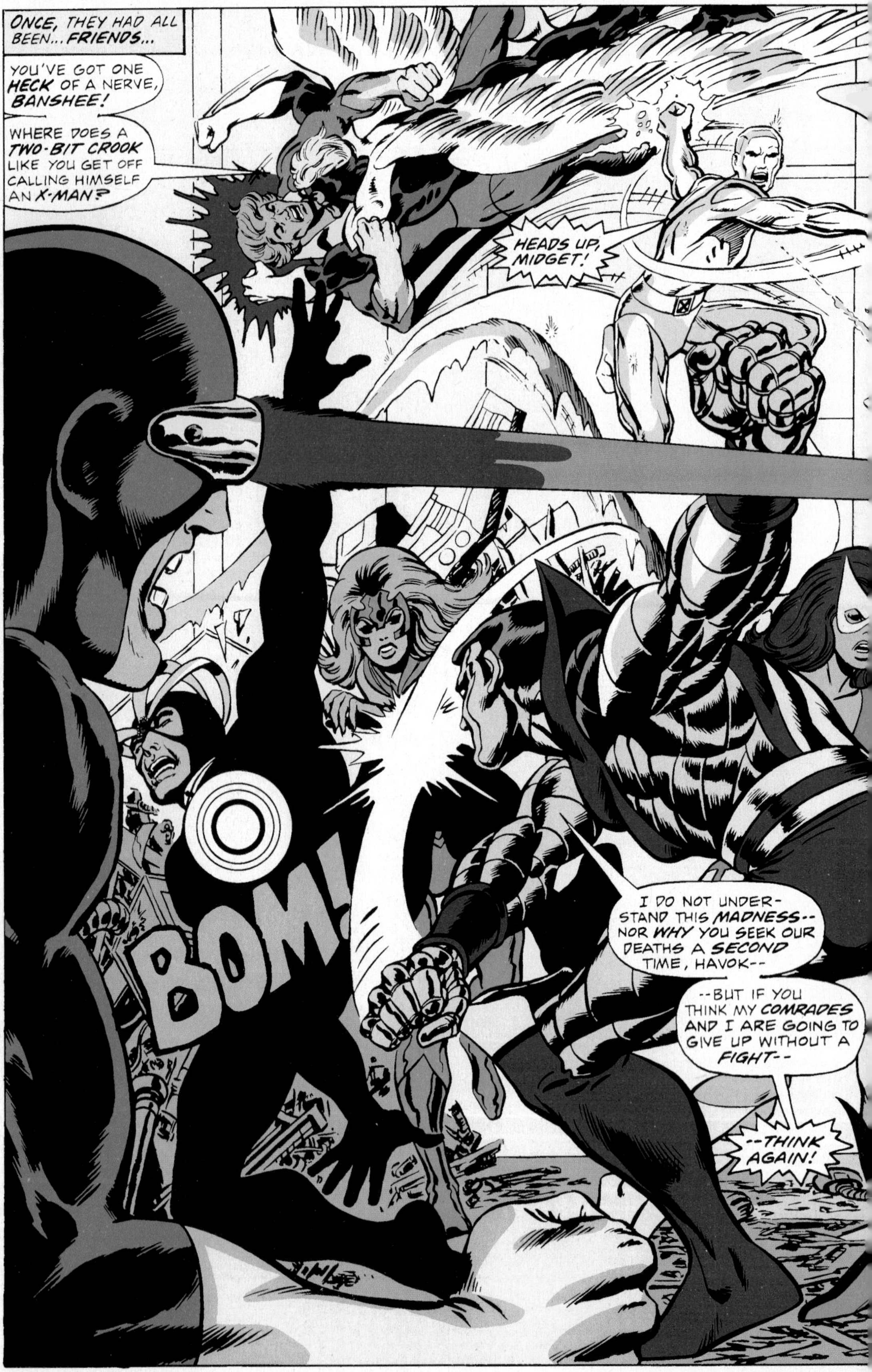
ONCE, THEY HAD ALL BEEN... FRIENDS...
YOU'VE GOT ONE HECK OF A NERVE, BANSHEE!
WHERE DOES A TWO-BIT CROOK LIKE YOU GET OFF CALLING HIMSELF AN X-MAN?
HEADS UP, MIDGET!
BOM!
I DO NOT UNDERSTAND THIS MADNESS-- NOR WHY YOU SEEK OUR DEATHS A SECOND TIME, HAVOK--
--BUT IF YOU THINK MY COMRADES AND I ARE GOING TO GIVE UP WITHOUT A FIGHT--
--THINK AGAIN!

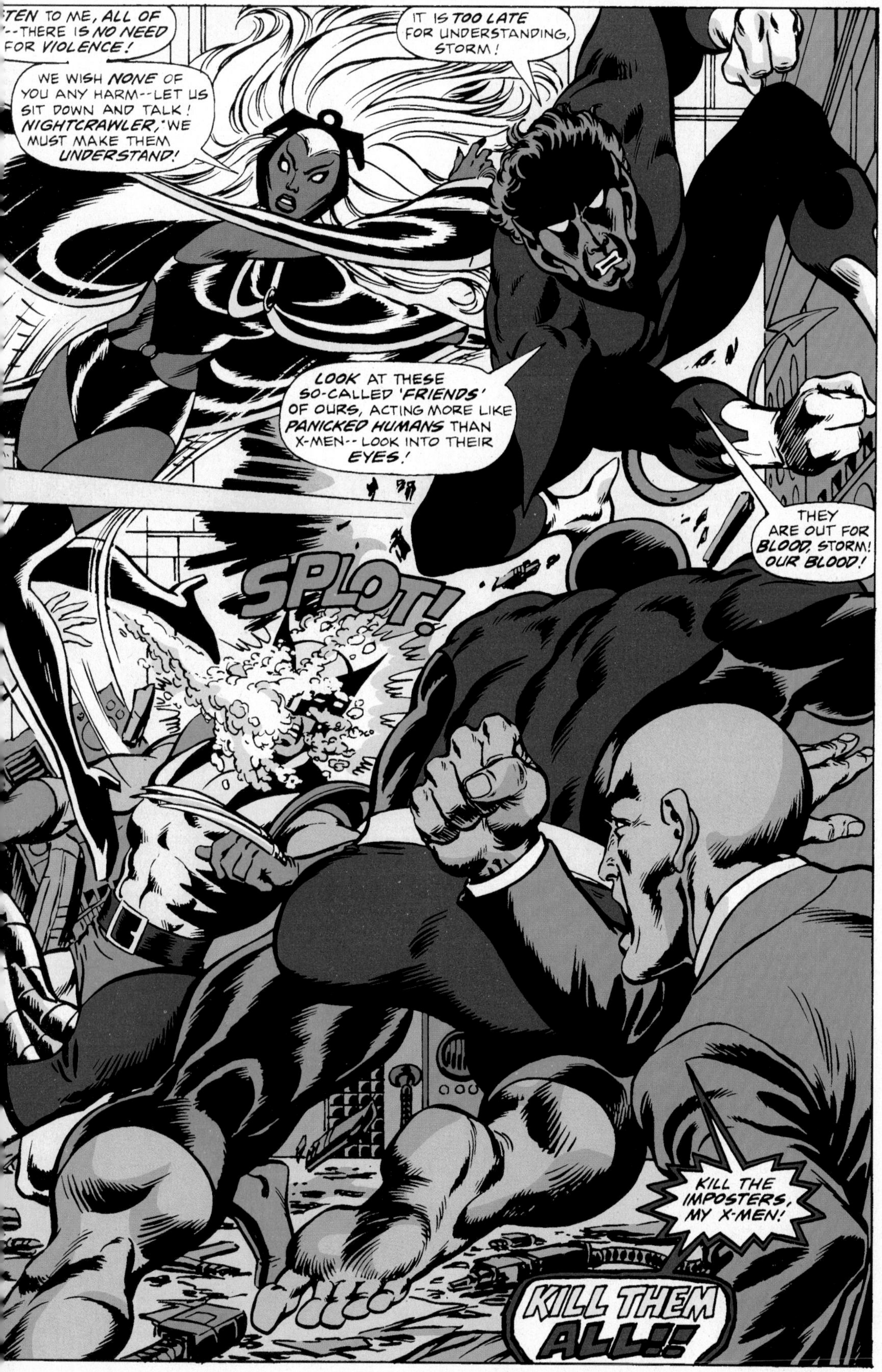

-TEN TO ME, ALL OF --THERE IS NO NEED FOR VIOLENCE!
WE WISH NONE OF YOU ANY HARM--LET US SIT DOWN AND TALK! NIGHTCRAWLER, WE MUST MAKE THEM UNDERSTAND!
IT IS TOO LATE FOR UNDERSTANDING, STORM!
LOOK AT THESE SO-CALLED 'FRIENDS' OF OURS, ACTING MORE LIKE PANICKED HUMANS THAN X-MEN--LOOK INTO THEIR EYES!
THEY ARE OUT FOR BLOOD, STORM! OUR BLOOD!
SPLOT!
KILL THE IMPOSTERS, MY X-MEN!
KILL THEM ALL!!

INDEED, *ONE* OF THEM IS AFTER *ME.*

YOU ARE CALLED THE *BEAST,* ARE YOU NOT?

I *RECOGNIZE* YOU FROM SOME OLD *PHOTOGRAPHS.*

BUT I'D THOUGHT YOU'D GONE ALL *HAIRY* AND JOINED THE *AVENGERS.*

YOU ANTHRO-POMORPHIC *ELF!* THE BASHFUL *BEAST* HAS NEVER BEEN *HIRSUTE...*

...AND AS FOR THE REST--

THEY THREW YOU *OUT--?* ~ULP.~

SORRY, MY FRIEND--

--BUT SINCE YOU *WILL NOT* COME TO ME, THE *BEAST* AND HIS *DEXTEROUS DIGITS* MUST OF A SURETY--

COME UP TO YOU!!

HIS SPEED... *AGILITY...*IT IS PHENOMENAL--I HAVE NEVER SEEN THE *LIKE--* ~UNNGHN!~

WOK!

OOPS. SORRY, O *DAUNTLESS LEADER--*

--IT SEEMS THE FLOOR IS MORE *CROWDED* THAN I'D THOUGHT.

HEY!

CYCLOPS, *WHY* ARE WE FIGHTING AMONG *OUR-SELVES?* WHAT OF THE THREAT OF *STEVEN LANG* -- OF HIS *SENTINELS?*

WAIT... WHAT'S *HAPPENED* TO YOUR *VISOR--?*

YOU'VE GOT IT *WRONG,* MISTER.

YOU'RE THE *THREAT--*

--AND *HERE'S* WHERE YOU GET *ELIMINATED!*

154

NIGHTCRAWLER!

HE TOOK CYKE'S BLAST HEAD ON!

HE'S DOWN-- AN' HE AIN'T MOVIN'!

WORRY ABOUT YOURSELF, FELLA! ANOTHER SECOND AND YOU'LL BE ON ICE --PERMANENTLY!

WELL, YOU AIN'T GOT THAT SECOND, BUB!

SHAKT!

HEY, NOW, LET'S BE NICE TO THE KID, PINT-SIZE!

HE MAY BE KINDA DUMB AT TIMES...

...BUT WE THINK HE'S LOVEABLE.

PUT ME DOWN, YA FEATHERED CREEP-- OR I'LL CLIP YOUR WINGS FOR GOOD!

THREATS. ALWAYS THREATS.

YOU WANT DOWN, MIDGET--? THEN THE ANGEL WILL BE GLAD TO OBLIGE YOU.

HERE, TINHEAD-- CATCH!

WOLVERINE, NO--! I CANNOT GET OUT OF YOUR WAY IN TIME--!

FLAM!

WOLVERINE--THE HATRED IN HIS VOICE--DID YOU HEAR--?

I HEARD IT, A'READY--

AS YOU WISH, MY FRIEND...

OKAY, THEN, JUST LIKE WE DID IT IN THE DANGER ROOM--!

--NOW GET US OUTTA HERE, COLOSSUS --THAT WINGED YO-YO OWES ME A REMATCH!

THE FASTBALL SPECIAL-- EXECUTE--

--NOW!

WHAT THE--?

THAT LITTLE STUNT IS *ALL SHE WROTE*, PAL!

AND IF YOU'RE WONDERING *WHICH* X-MAN HAS THE *PLEASURE* OF BLASTING YOU FROM HERE TO *HADES*, ALL YOU HAVE TO DO IS--

--CRY *HAVOK!*

I...*KNOW* WHO YOU ARE... *ASSASSIN!*

SUCH *POWER*--I NEVER *DREAMED*--WERE I HUMAN, THAT BLAST WOULD HAVE BURNED ME TO A *CRISP.*

BUT EVEN MY *ARMORED* BODY HAS ITS *LIMITS*--BY ALL THAT I HOLD *DEAR*, HE IS CAUSING ME-- *PAIN!*

I CANNOT STAND MUCH *MORE* OF THIS.

BUT I *WILL*...STAND, I WILL--I *MUST*--SURVIVE!

HEAR ME, HAVOK--*COLOSSUS* IS COMING FOR YOU--

--AND--I--WILL--NOT--BE-- STOPPED!

TWICE NOW, YOU HAVE TRIED TO KILL US IN *COLD BLOOD*-- KILL THOSE WHO CALLED YOU COMRADE AND...*FRIEND*..*

...NO *REASON*, NO EXPLANATION, NO...*MERCY*-- JUST MAD, UNCONTROLLED *BUTCHERY!*

YOU ARE *BENEATH CONTEMPT!*

* ANYONE REMEMBER X-MEN #97 ? --MARV.

AND COLOSSUS *SWEARS* THAT FROM *THIS DAY FORTH*, YOU WILL BUTCHER--

KROM!

--*NO MORE!*

JEAN GREY'S POWER SEEMS MUCH *WEAKER* THAN USUAL-- I COULD DEAL WITH HER *EASILY*, BUT I CANNOT BRING MYSELF TO *HARM* HER.

I MUST USE *REASON* INSTEAD...

JEAN, *WHY* HAVE YOU TURNED AGAINST YOUR *FRIENDS*?

YOU'RE *NO* FRIEND OF MINE, *WITCH*!

THEN WHAT OF THE *HOURS* WE'VE SPENT TOGETHER-- THE CONFIDENCES WE'VE *SHARED*--?

LIAR! I DON'T *KNOW* YOU! NEVER *TALKED* TO YOU, NEVER SHARED A *CONFIDENCE*!

IT'S A *CHEAP SHOT*, LADY, AND IT WON'T WORK!

HOW CAN YOU DENY THE *TRUTH*--AND WITH SUCH *HATRED*--?

HOW COULD YOUR *BRIEF CAPTIVITY* HAVE MADE YOU SO UNLIKE *YOURSELF* ...UNLESS...

...YOU'RE *NOT* YOUR...'SELF' AT ALL... YOUR *TRUE* SELF.

OF COURSE, THAT *MUST* BE IT! *YOU'RE* THE IMPOST--

AARRRGH!

BROK!

BEAUTIFUL MOVE, LORNA.

I KEPT THIS "STORM" CHARACTER *OCCUPIED* WHILE YOU SLIPPED IN AND LET HER HAVE IT WITH A *MAGNETIC FORCE BLAST*.

AND NOW THAT THE LADY'S *DOWN* AND *HELPLESS*--

--LET'S *FINISH* HER!

LEGS... *PINNED* UNDER THE DEBRIS... CAN'T PULL *FREE*...

NO CHANCE FOR... *ESCAPE*... NO CHANCE AT ALL...

EEEEE

MARVEL GIRL--! WE'RE BEING ATTACKED FROM BEHIND!

BUT *WHO*--?!

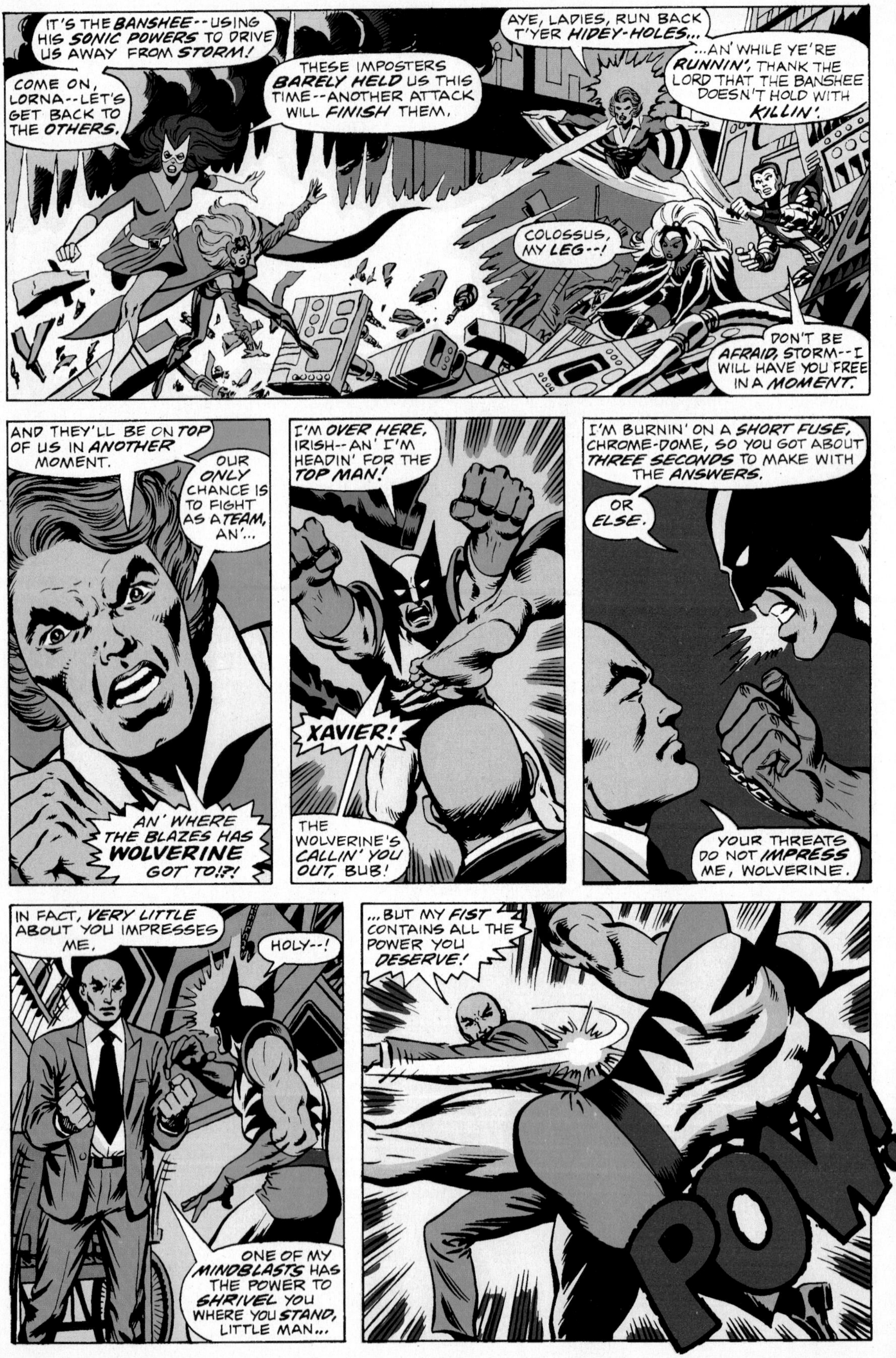
IT'S THE BANSHEE--USING HIS SONIC POWERS TO DRIVE US AWAY FROM STORM!
COME ON, LORNA--LET'S GET BACK TO THE OTHERS.
THESE IMPOSTERS BARELY HELD US THIS TIME--ANOTHER ATTACK WILL FINISH THEM.
AYE, LADIES, RUN BACK T'YER HIDEY-HOLES...
...AN' WHILE YE'RE RUNNIN', THANK THE LORD THAT THE BANSHEE DOESN'T HOLD WITH KILLIN'.
COLOSSUS, MY LEG--!
DON'T BE AFRAID, STORM--I WILL HAVE YOU FREE IN A MOMENT.
AND THEY'LL BE ON TOP OF US IN ANOTHER MOMENT.
OUR ONLY CHANCE IS TO FIGHT AS A TEAM, AN'...
AN' WHERE THE BLAZES HAS WOLVERINE GOT TO!?!
I'M OVER HERE, IRISH--AN' I'M HEADIN' FOR THE TOP MAN!
XAVIER!
THE WOLVERINE'S CALLIN' YOU OUT, BUB!
I'M BURNIN' ON A SHORT FUSE, CHROME-DOME, SO YOU GOT ABOUT THREE SECONDS TO MAKE WITH THE ANSWERS.
OR ELSE.
YOUR THREATS DO NOT IMPRESS ME, WOLVERINE.
IN FACT, VERY LITTLE ABOUT YOU IMPRESSES ME.
HOLY--!
ONE OF MY MINDBLASTS HAS THE POWER TO SHRIVEL YOU WHERE YOU STAND, LITTLE MAN...
...BUT MY FIST CONTAINS ALL THE POWER YOU DESERVE!
POW!

ON YOUR **FEET**, MY FRIEND. I WANT THE **SATISFACTION** OF KNOCKING YOU DOWN **AGAIN**.

NICE PUNCH, PROF--I'LL GIVE YA THAT...

...BUT I AIN'T GOIN' DOWN A **SECOND** TIME.

ON THE **CONTRARY**, WOLVERINE! YOU **ARE** GOING DOWN.

ONLY YOU **WON'T** BE GETTING UP AGAIN-- **EVER!**

GOOD GIRL, JEAN-- THIS ARROGANT FOOL HASN'T A CHANCE AGAINST YOUR **MENTAL POWERS.**

LORD... MY BRAIN... FEELS LIKE IT'S **BURNIN'**--CAN'T **THINK** FOR THE PAIN--

--ONLY MY **INSTINCTS** LEFT TO... GUIDE ME...

YEAH... MY **INSTINCTS**... MY... **SENSES**...

IT WON'T BE LONG NOW, PROFESSOR.

RIGHT... **THERE**, LADY...

...ONLY YOU GOT IT **BACKWARDS**...JUS' COULDN'T **SEE** 'TIL NOW...

Y'SEE, FOLKS, I'M LIKE AN **ANIMAL**--

--I DON'T KNOW FROM **FACES.**

I KNOW FROM **SCENTS**, VOICES... FEELINGS...

I **ALSO** KNOW JEAN GREY.

AN', LADY, WHATEVER YOU **ARE**--

--YOU **AIN'T** JEAN GREY!!

THERE ISN'T EVEN TIME FOR A **SCREAM.**

LENIN'S GHOST... NO...

WOLVERINE--YE BLOODY **HOMICIDAL MANIAC**--

WHAT HAVE YE **DONE?!**

COMPUTER, SHIFT TO CAMERA 3, IMMEDIATE-LY!

I MUST SEE WHAT'S **HAPPENING.**

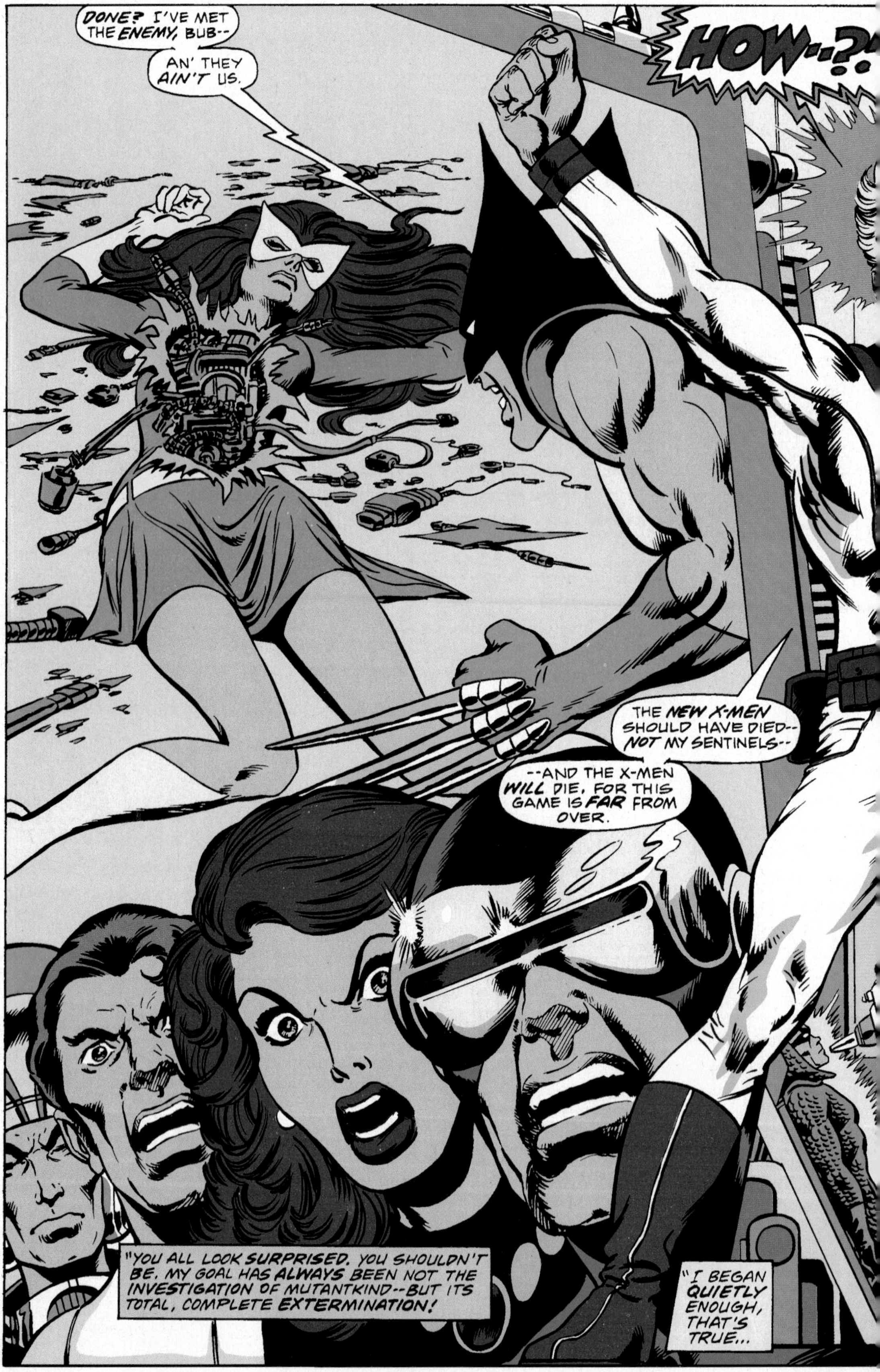
DONE? I'VE MET THE ENEMY, BUB--
AN' THEY AIN'T US.
HOW--?!
THE NEW X-MEN SHOULD HAVE DIED-- NOT MY SENTINELS--
--AND THE X-MEN WILL DIE, FOR THIS GAME IS FAR FROM OVER.
"YOU ALL LOOK SURPRISED. YOU SHOULDN'T BE. MY GOAL HAS ALWAYS BEEN NOT THE INVESTIGATION OF MUTANTKIND--BUT ITS TOTAL, COMPLETE EXTERMINATION!
"I BEGAN QUIETLY ENOUGH, THAT'S TRUE...

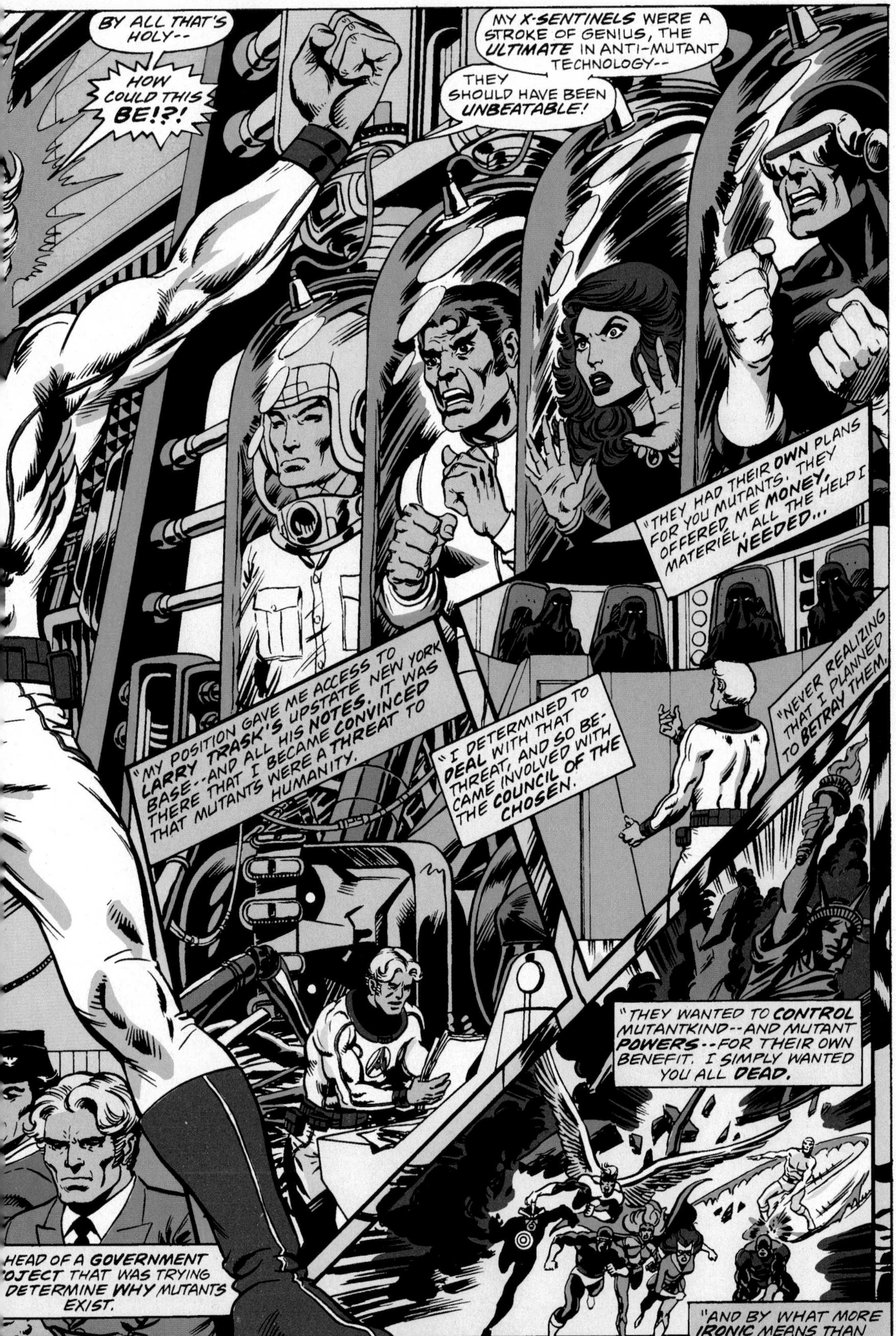
BY ALL THAT'S HOLY--
HOW COULD THIS BE!?!
MY X-SENTINELS WERE A STROKE OF GENIUS, THE ULTIMATE IN ANTI-MUTANT TECHNOLOGY--
THEY SHOULD HAVE BEEN UNBEATABLE!
HEAD OF A GOVERNMENT OJECT THAT WAS TRYING DETERMINE WHY MUTANTS EXIST.
"MY POSITION GAVE ME ACCESS TO LARRY TRASK'S UPSTATE NEW YORK BASE--AND ALL HIS NOTES. IT WAS THERE THAT I BECAME CONVINCED THAT MUTANTS WERE A THREAT TO HUMANITY.
"I DETERMINED TO DEAL WITH THAT THREAT, AND SO BECAME INVOLVED WITH THE COUNCIL OF THE CHOSEN.
"THEY HAD THEIR OWN PLANS FOR YOU MUTANTS. THEY OFFERED ME MONEY, MATERIEL, ALL THE HELP I NEEDED...
"NEVER REALIZING THAT I PLANNED TO BETRAY THEM.
"THEY WANTED TO CONTROL MUTANTKIND--AND MUTANT POWERS--FOR THEIR OWN BENEFIT. I SIMPLY WANTED YOU ALL DEAD.
"AND BY WHAT MORE IRONIC MEANS THAN THE X-SENTINELS--?"

--USING MUTANTKIND'S **STRONGEST DEFENDERS** AS THEIR **EXECUTIONERS!**

AND WHO **BETTER** FOR THE X-SENTINELS' FIRST VICTIMS THAN THE **REAL X-MEN?**

STILL, **ONE** DEFEAT DOESN'T MEAN THE WAR IS...EH?!?

LORD, THE **NEGA-TUBE**-- IT-- IT'S GLOWING **WHITE-HOT!**

RRAK!

DR. LANG--

--I THINK YOU'VE SAID **ENOUGH!**

OH, MY GOD.

LIBERATION DAY, FOLKS-- EVERYBODY OUT!

FRAK!

PROFESSOR X--

NOT TO WORRY, MS. GREY, I'LL CATCH HIM.

--HE'S STILL **UNCONSCIOUS!**

LEAVING SO **SOON**, LANG? THAT'S AWFULLY **RUDE** OF YOU...

...BUT THEN, WHAT ELSE CAN YOU **EXPECT** FROM A **MURDERING COWARD?**

SKOW!

COWARD--?! YOU DARE CALL ME **COWARD?!**

I'M A **MAN**, CYCLOPS--

--WHICH IS **MORE** THAN YOU'LL **EVER** BE, YOU MUTANT SWINE!

D'YOU **HEAR** ME, HOMO-SO-CALLED SUPERIOR?! **A MAN!**

I'M BETTER THAN ANY OF YOU, BETTER THAN **ALL** OF YOU!

AND NOW THAT I'VE REACHED MY **FLYING GUNSHIP,** I'LL **PROVE** IT!

YOU'RE NOT PROVING A **THING**, LANG, EXCEPT HOW **SICK** AND TWISTED YOU ARE **INSIDE**!

SKRAZ!

I'VE FOUGHT A LOT OF **VILLAINS** IN MY TIME, MISTER--

-- BUT UNTIL I MET **YOU**, I NEVER **HATED** BEFORE.

YOU'D **HOUND** US WITHOUT MERCY, **EXTERMINATE** US--

-- FOR **NO** OTHER REASON THAN THAT WE'RE **DIFFERENT** FROM YOUR CONCEPTION OF **HUMANITY**!

JUST WHO DO YOU THINK YOU **ARE**?!

AND FOR YOUR **INFORMATION**, DR. LANG--

--YOU WON'T BE KILLING **ANYONE** TODAY.

MY **CONTROLS**-- THEY'RE MOVING BY **THEMSELVES**.

GOT TO TRY TO **BREAK** FREE, GET AWAY BEFORE I'M **CAPTURED**!

I CAN **DO** IT--I'M A **MAN**--MY WILL IS **STRONGER** THAN ANY **MUTANT WITCH'S**.

ALL I HAVE TO DO IS HIT **FULL POWER** ON THE **THRUSTERS**...

OH, NO! THE CONTROLS ARE JAMMED--I CAN'T **TURN**--!

HELP ME, SOMEBODY--X-MEN, **HELP ME**! I'M HEADING RIGHT FOR THE **SCREEN**!

I'M GOING TO--

CRASH!

COMRADES, I'VE *FOUND* THEM! AND THEY STILL *LIVE!*

THEN QUIT *JABBERIN'*, COLOSSUS, AN' LET'S GET 'EM *OUTTA* HERE, THIS WHOLE SECTION O' THE SPACE PLATFORM'S *ABLAZE*, AN' THE FIRE'S *SPREADIN'.*

LANG'S *FREEBOOTIN'* GOONS HAVE ALREADY *EVACUATED* IN RE-ENTRY LIFEBOATS -- WE'RE THE ONLY PEOPLE *LEFT.*

AN' WE'RE ABOARD A STATION THAT COULD *BLOW* ITSELF T'BITS ANY MINUTE NOW!

A FEW MINUTES LATER...

THE FIRE'S ALMOST REACHED THE *HYPERGOLIC FUEL CELLS,* DR. CORBEAU --

-- WE HAVEN'T MUCH *TIME.*

WRONG, CYCLOPS, WE HAVE *ALL* THE TIME IN THE WORLD.

'CAUSE WE'RE SURE NOT *GOING* ANYWHERE -- AT LEAST IN *THIS* CRATE.

THE *FLIGHT CONTROL COMPUTER* MUST'VE GOTTEN SLAGGED DURING OUR LITTLE FRACAS WITH THE *SENTINELS* * -- AND WITHOUT IT, WE'RE AS GOOD AS *FINISHED.*

*LAST ISH. --MARV.

WHAT ABOUT A *MANUAL RE-ENTRY?*

WHAT *ABOUT* IT, WOLVERINE?

IN CASE YOU HADN'T *NOTICED...*

...WE'VE GOT A *THUMPING* GREAT *HOLE* IN THE SHUTTLE'S HULL, AND -- THANKS AGAIN TO THE SENTINELS -- NO FUNCTIONAL *PRESSURE* SUITS.

BUT THAT'S THE *LEAST* OF OUR PROBLEMS.

ICH...VERST'HEN, HERR DOKTOR...

...THE *SOLAR FLARE.*

YOU GOT IT, NIGHTCRAWLER. THE *WORST* FLARE IN YEARS. THE *COMPUTER* WAS SUPPOSED TO FLY US THROUGH IT WHILE WE SAT *SAFE-AND-SOUND* IN THE SHUTTLE'S SHIELDED 'LIFE-CELL.'

ONLY WE HAVE *NO* COMPUTER.

SURE, *I* CAN FLY A RE-ENTRY, *NO SWEAT,* BUT I WOULDN'T LAST *THIRTY SECONDS* IN THAT FLARE.

ONE OF *YOU* MIGHT SURVIVE THE FLARE, BUT YOU CAN'T *PILOT* THE SHUTTLE WE NEED SOMEONE WHO CAN DO *BOTH,* AND THERE'S *NO* SUCH ANIMAL.

WRONG, DR. CORBEAU... ...I CAN DO BOTH.

ARE YOU *CRAZY,* JEAN--?

SINCE WHEN ARE YOU A *QUALIFIED ASTRONAUT?*

SINCE *NOW.*

HOLD STILL, DOCTOR, THIS WILL ONLY HURT A *LITTLE.*

I'M A *TELEPATH,* SCOTT, REMEMBER? I CAN *ABSORB* ALL DR. CORBEAU KNOWS ABOUT FLYING THE SPACE SHUTTLE. I WON'T BE A *GREAT PILOT,* BUT I'LL BE GOOD ENOUGH TO GET US *DOWN.*

AND *HOW* WILL YOU SURVIVE THE *SOLAR FLARE,* YOU LITTLE--!

MY *TELE-KINETIC* POWERS WILL SCREEN OUT THE HARMFUL *RADIATION*-- I'LL BE ALL RIGHT!

FOR *HOW LONG*--?! EVEN *YOUR* POWER CAN'T HANDLE THAT MUCH--

UNNNGNH!

PERHAPS NOT--

--BUT IT *CAN* DO THIS.

TAKE HIM AFT TO THE *LIFE-CELL,* BANSHEE.

YE HIT HIM PRETTY *HARD,* LASSIE.

I *MEANT* TO.

BY THE TIME HE WAKES UP, WE'LL BE *COMMITTED.*

NICE SHOT, LADY--YOU BUCKIN' FOR *MARTYR O' THE YEAR* OR SOMETHIN'?

MAKE IT QUICK, WOLVERINE--I'M *BUSY.*

WHAT'RE YA TRYIN' TA *PROVE*--THAT YOU'RE AS *GOOD AN' NOBLE* AS *BIG DADDY X*? IT'S *SUICIDE*, JEANNIE!

THE NAME IS *JEAN*, MISTER-- AND I HAVE JUST ABOUT *HAD IT* WITH YOU!

I HAVE *TRIED* TO LIKE YOU, WOLVERINE--OBNOXIOUS LITTLE *UPSTART* THAT YOU ARE--BUT FOR THE *LIFE* OF ME, I DON'T KNOW WHY I MADE THE *EFFORT!*

SO SHUT YOUR *MOUTH*, AND GET INTO THE LIFE CELL--*NOW!* --BEFORE I LOSE MY *TEMPER!*

JEAN...

NOT YOU, TOO, ORORO-- I COULDN'T *BEAR* IT.

LOOK, *I* HAVE THE BEST CHANCE OF *SURVIVAL*-- THAT'S IT, *PURE AND SIMPLE.*

IT'S *ME*--OR IT'S *NONE* OF US.

THEN--MAY THE GODS *PROTECT* YOU, JEAN GREY.

THANK YOU, ORORO.

A LAST *FAVOR*, MY FRIEND...?

WOULD YOU... TELL *SCOTT*...

...TELL HIM I *LOVED* HIM.

OKAY, LADY, IT'S TIME TO DO YOUR *STUFF...*

...NAMELY, *SEALING* THE HULL TELE-KINETICALLY WITH THIS PIECE OF *WRECKAGE.*

--AND AWAY WE GO.

RCS TO TWENTY PERCENT *REAR THRUST*-- AND WE SLIDE *FREE* OF THE STATION, EASY AS *PIE.*

I'M SURE *GLAD* THEY BUILT THIS BIRD TO TAKE *PUNISHMENT*--LOOKS LIKE ITS *COLLISION* WITH THE STATION DIDN'T EVEN SCRATCH THE *PAINT.*

ENOUGH *MUSING*, JEAN, LOVE--THE LIFE-CELL WAS DESIGNED TO TAKE A *LOT* OF RADIATION, BUT IN A FLARE LIKE THIS, ALL BETS ARE *OFF.* THE SOONER WE'RE ON EARTH, THE *BETTER.*

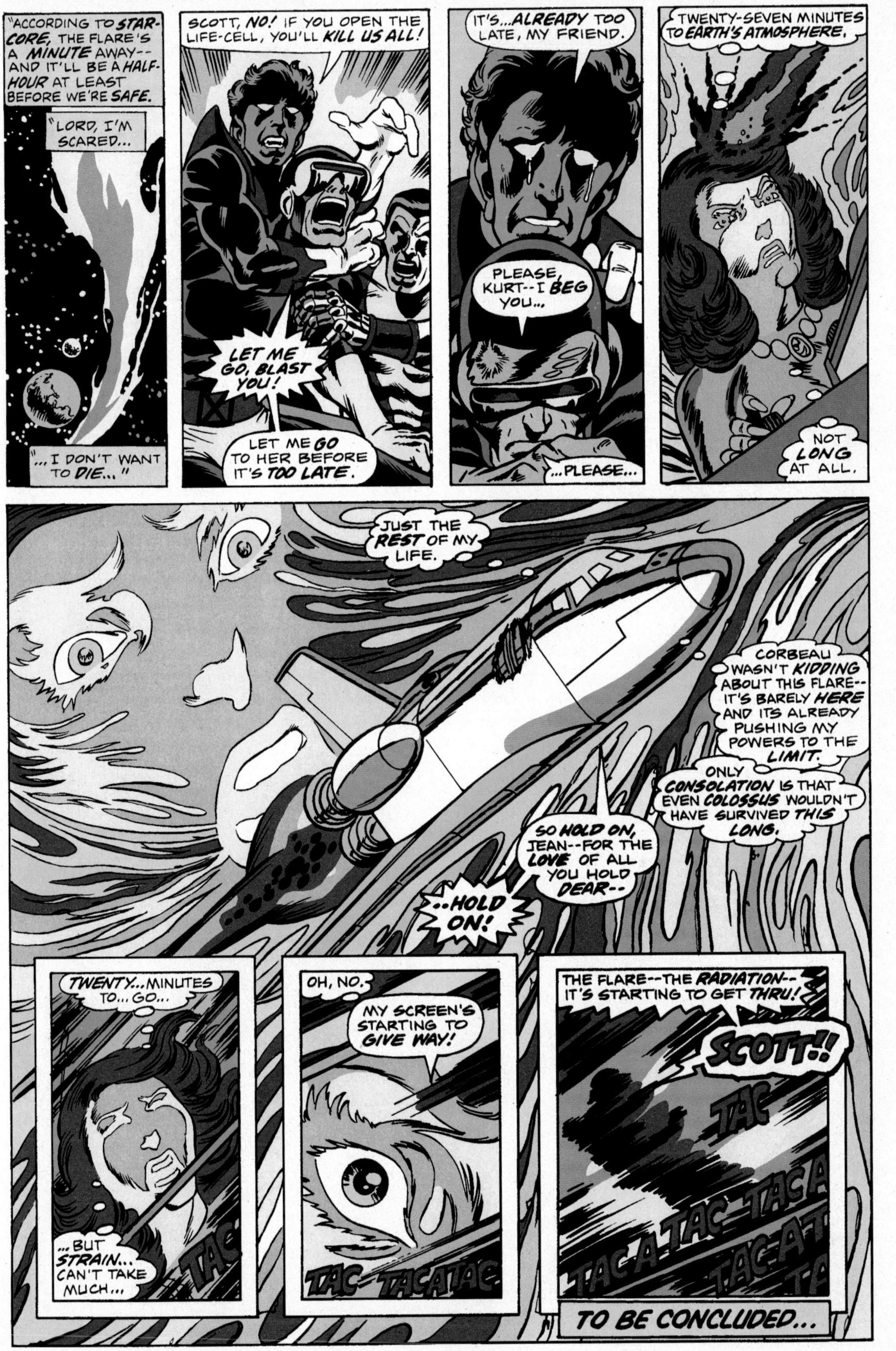
"ACCORDING TO STAR-CORE, THE FLARE'S A MINUTE AWAY-- AND IT'LL BE A HALF-HOUR AT LEAST BEFORE WE'RE SAFE.
"LORD, I'M SCARED...
"...I DON'T WANT TO DIE..."
SCOTT, NO! IF YOU OPEN THE LIFE-CELL, YOU'LL KILL US ALL!
LET ME GO, BLAST YOU!
LET ME GO TO HER BEFORE IT'S TOO LATE.
IT'S...ALREADY TOO LATE, MY FRIEND.
PLEASE, KURT--I BEG YOU...
...PLEASE...
TWENTY-SEVEN MINUTES TO EARTH'S ATMOSPHERE.
NOT LONG AT ALL.
JUST THE REST OF MY LIFE.
CORBEAU WASN'T KIDDING ABOUT THIS FLARE-- IT'S BARELY HERE AND ITS ALREADY PUSHING MY POWERS TO THE LIMIT.
ONLY CONSOLATION IS THAT EVEN COLOSSUS WOULDN'T HAVE SURVIVED THIS LONG.
SO HOLD ON, JEAN--FOR THE LOVE OF ALL YOU HOLD DEAR--
--HOLD ON!
TWENTY...MINUTES TO...GO...
...BUT STRAIN... CAN'T TAKE MUCH...
TAC
OH, NO.
MY SCREEN'S STARTING TO GIVE WAY!
TAC TACATAC
THE FLARE--THE RADIATION-- IT'S STARTING TO GET THRU!
SCOTT!!
TAC
TACATAC TACA
TACA TAC TACAT
TA
TO BE CONCLUDED...

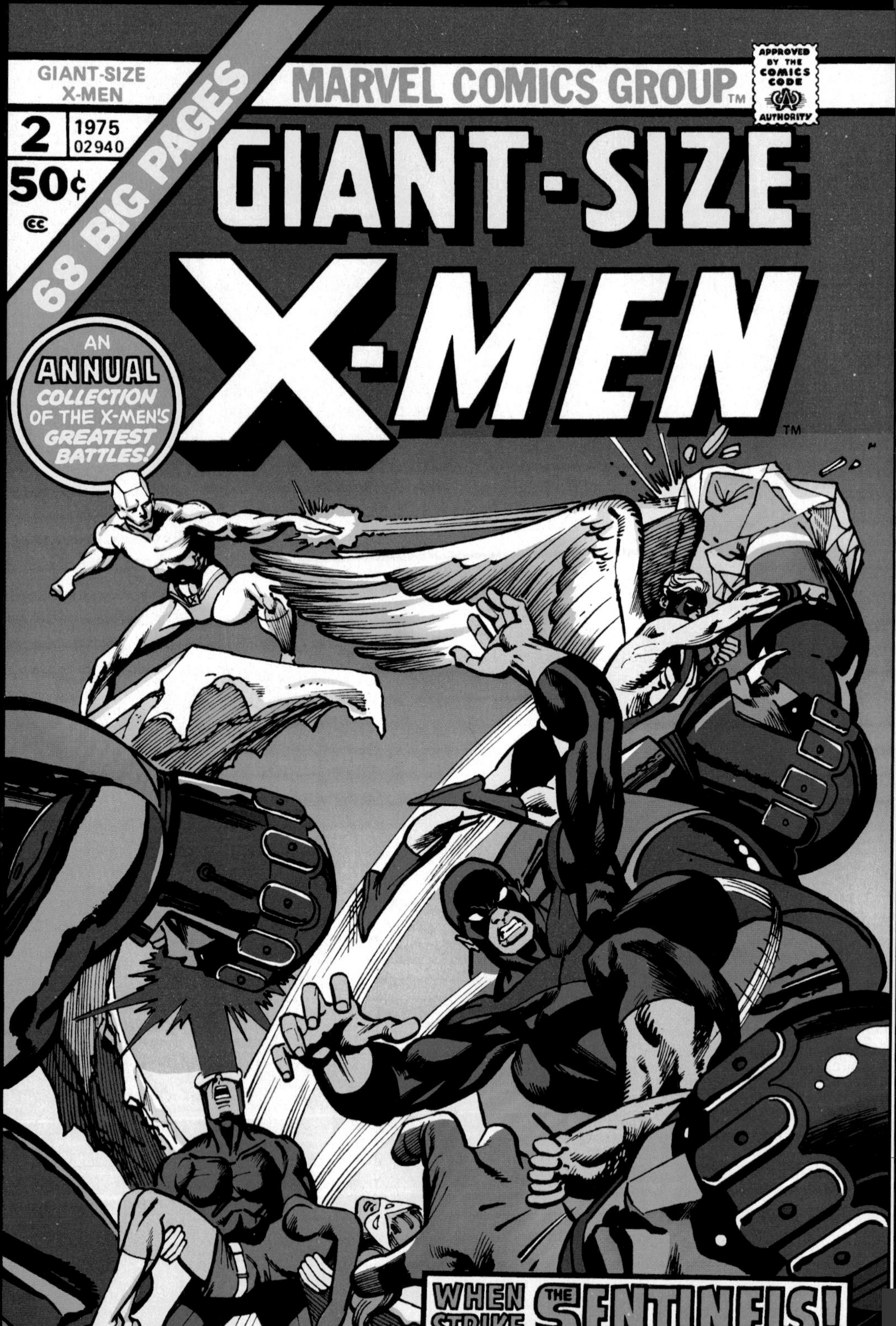
GIANT-SIZE X-MEN
2
1975
02940
50¢
68 BIG PAGES
MARVEL COMICS GROUP™
APPROVED BY THE COMICS CODE AUTHORITY
GIANT-SIZE
X-MEN™
AN ANNUAL COLLECTION OF THE X-MEN'S GREATEST BATTLES!
WHEN STRIKE THE SENTINELS!

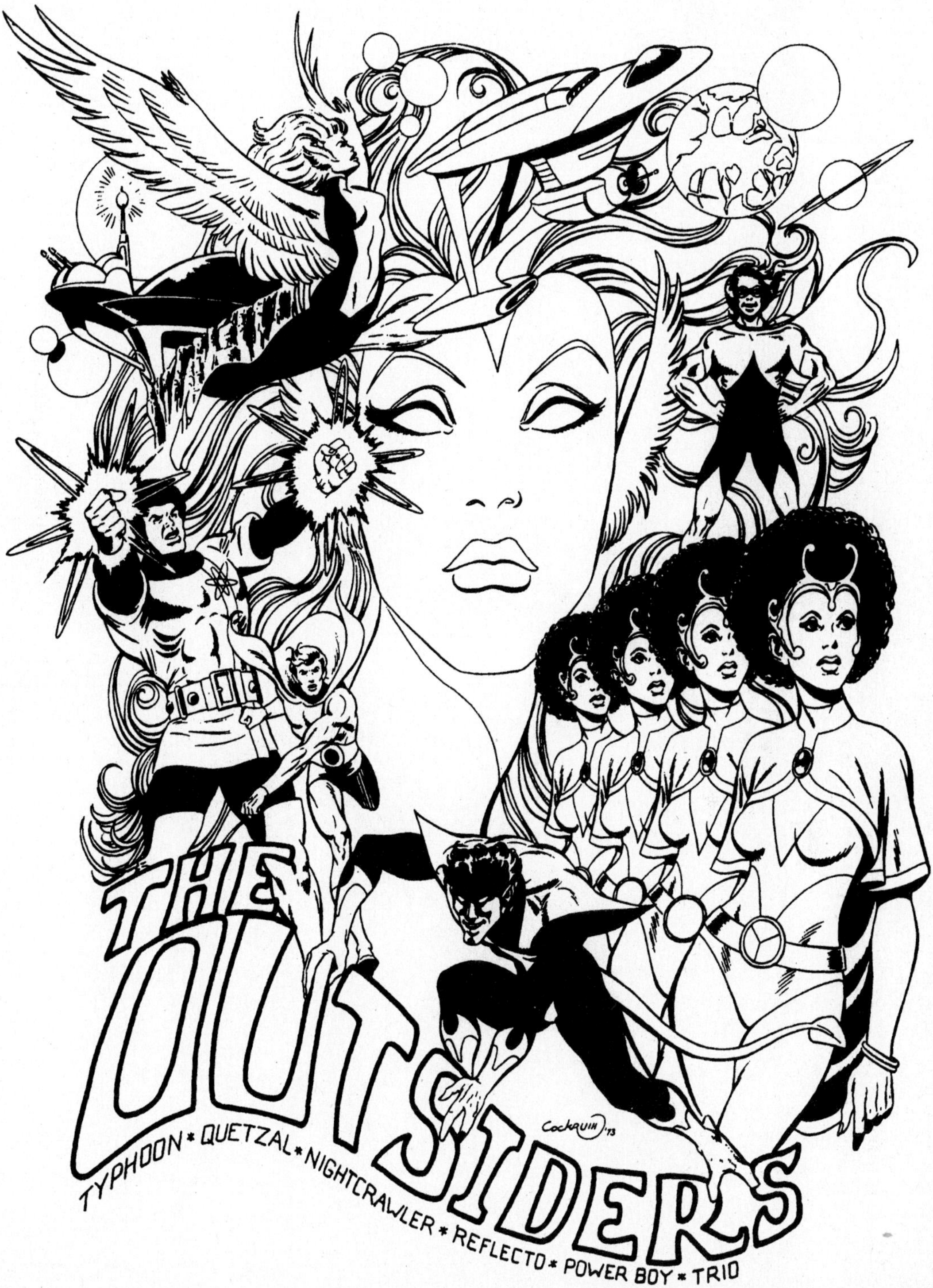
THE OUTSIDERS
TYPHOON * QUETZAL * NIGHTCRAWLER * REFLECTO * POWER BOY * TRIO
COCKRUM '73

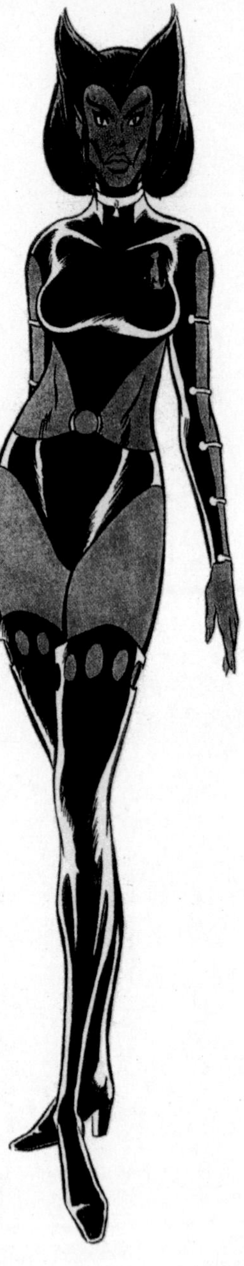
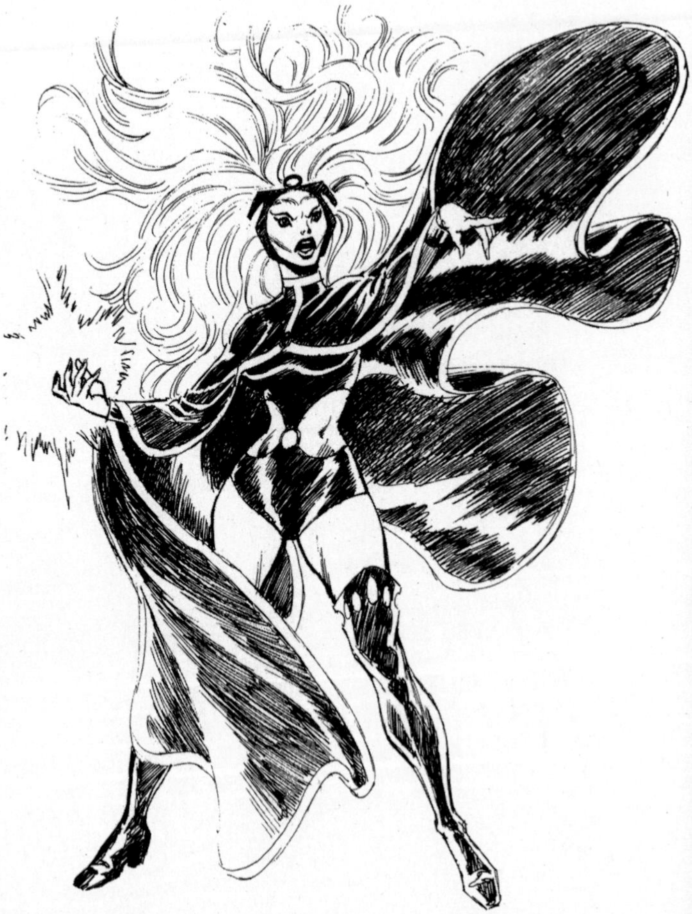

Character design for Vampyre by Dave Cockrum, another almost-X-Man who didn't make the grade. She was discarded for being too similar to Wolverine and Nightcrawler in look and concept. The original take on the doomed X-Man, Thunderbird, was set aside when it was decided to stress the character's Native American roots.

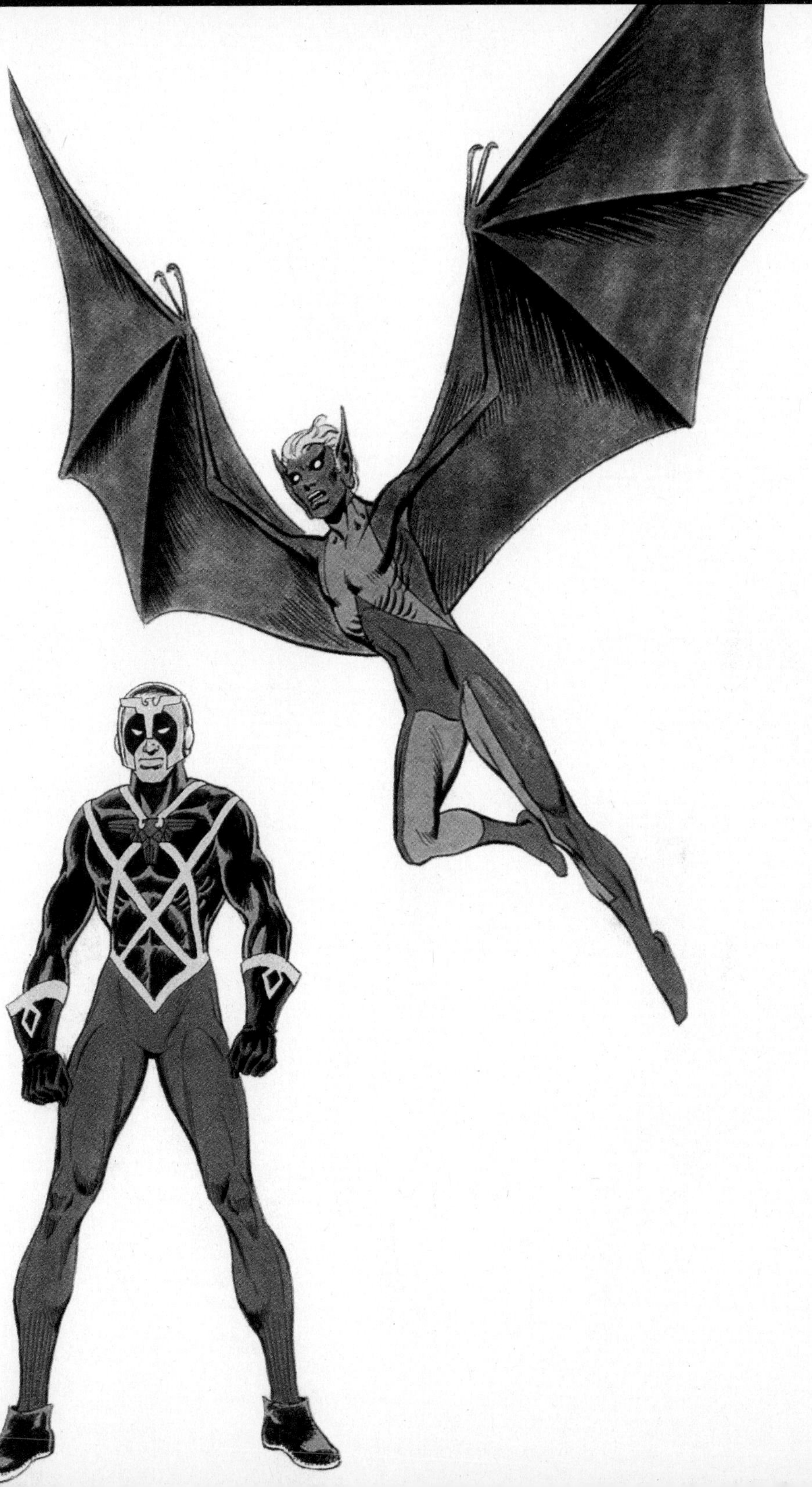

Unused costume redesign for Marvel Girl. The look was ultimately rejected, although the cloak idea was incorporated into Storm. Jean Grey was instead transformed into Phoenix as seen in the accompanying costume designs by Dave Cockrum.

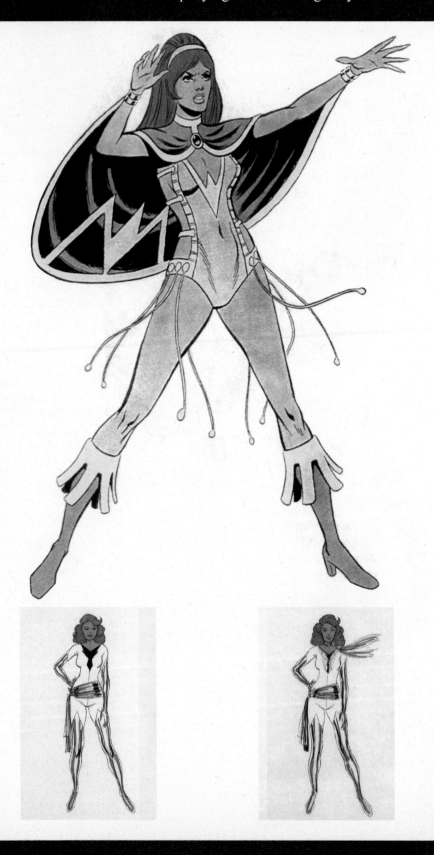

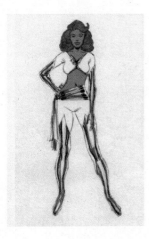

PHOENIX IS APPROX. 5'4", WEIGHS ABOUT 110 LBS.

PHOENIX/JEAN GREY IS A SCHIZOID PERSONALITY; THE CHARACTER AS SEEN HERE IS THE JEAN GREY ASPECT. PHOENIX IS MUCH WILDER, LESS UNDER CONTROL.

WHEN THE PHOENIX PERSONALITY IS DOMINANT HER HAIR IS LONGER AND FREE-FLOWING, EYES FIREY AND FACE LIT WITH DRAMATIC LIGHTING.

THE JEAN GREY HAIRSTYLE IS MORE-OR-LESS A FARRAH FAWCETT-MAJORS CUT.

PHOENIX CLASP RESTS ON RIGHT HIP; SASH FANS OUT AS IT PASSES AROUND LEFT HIP.

ALTHOUGH JEAN IS RELATIVELY SHORT, SHE HAS LONG LEGS (PROPORTIONATELY).

GLOVES, BOOTS AND SASH ARE HIGHLY-METALLIC GOLD; ALMOST A 'LIQUID METAL' LOOK.

JEAN GREY -- IN PRIVATE LIFE -- DRESSES IN THE COLORFUL, FLOWING, CLINGY, SEXY-TYPE STUFF YOU SEE IN COSMOPOLITAN. LOTS OF FULL SKIRTS AND BELL-BOTTOMS.

HOW TO DRAW THE X-MEN: PHOENIX!

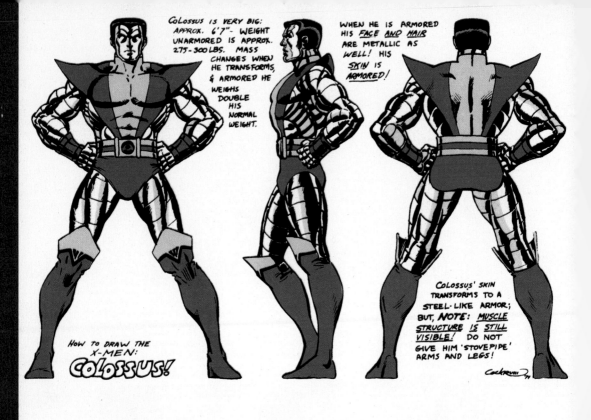

COLOSSUS IS VERY BIG: APPROX. 6'7"- WEIGHT UNARMORED IS APPROX. 275-300 LBS. MASS CHANGES WHEN HE TRANSFORMS, & ARMORED HE WEIGHS DOUBLE HIS NORMAL WEIGHT.

WHEN HE IS ARMORED HIS FACE AND HAIR ARE METALLIC AS WELL! HIS SKIN IS ARMORED!

HOW TO DRAW THE X-MEN: **COLOSSUS!**

COLOSSUS' SKIN TRANSFORMS TO A STEEL-LIKE ARMOR; BUT, *NOTE: MUSCLE STRUCTURE IS STILL VISIBLE!* DO NOT GIVE HIM 'STOVEPIPE' ARMS AND LEGS!

COCKRUM '77

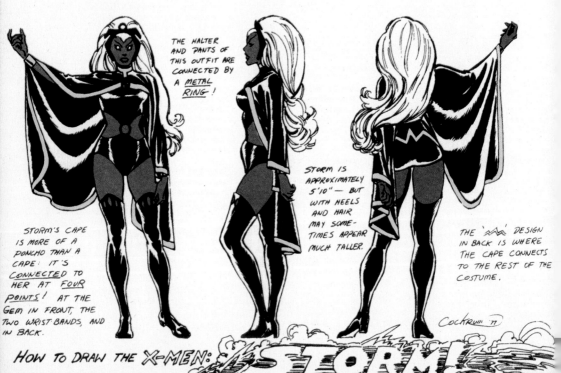

THE HALTER AND PANTS OF THIS OUTFIT ARE CONNECTED BY A METAL RING!

STORM IS APPROXIMATELY 5'10" — BUT WITH HEELS AND HAIR MAY SOMETIMES APPEAR MUCH TALLER.

STORM'S CAPE IS MORE OF A PONCHO THAN A CAPE: IT'S CONNECTED TO HER AT FOUR POINTS! AT THE GEM IN FRONT, THE TWO WRIST BANDS, AND IN BACK.

THE 'ʌʌ' DESIGN IN BACK IS WHERE THE CAPE CONNECTS TO THE REST OF THE COSTUME.

COCKRUM '77

HOW TO DRAW THE X-MEN: **STORM!**

NIGHTCRAWLER!

NIGHTIE'S FACE IS ALWAYS IN SHADOW. IT'S AN EFFECT HE CREATES HIMSELF: DO IT LIKE WALLY WOOD DRAMATIC LIGHTING, BUT FROM THE FRONT VIEW THE WHOLE FOREHEAD IS DARK.

NIGHTCRAWLER STANDS ABOUT 5'10", BUT MAY LOOK A BIT SHORTER BECAUSE HE DOESN'T STAND UP STRAIGHT.

NIGHTIE'S HANDS ARE THE SAME SIZE AND PROPORTIONS AS NORMAL HUMAN HANDS. THE FINGERS ARE THICK, & SPACED WIDE APART.

THE TAIL IS CONNECTED TO THE BASE OF THE SPINE... IT DOES NOT GROW OUT OF HIS ASS!

THE TAIL IS PREHENSILE, BY THE WAY...

NIGHTIE HAS FANGS, UPPER AND LOWER: BE SUBTLE, JUST LEAVE WHITE 'BREAKS' OR 'GAPS'... BIG, BLATANT TEETH MAKE HIM LOOK RIDICULOUS!

WHEN DRAWING NIGHTIE FROM THE FRONT: DO NOT CONNECT THE TAIL DIRECTLY TO HIS CROTCH -- YOU'LL GIVE THE CODE FITS, & JOHN ROMITA

FOOM TEN

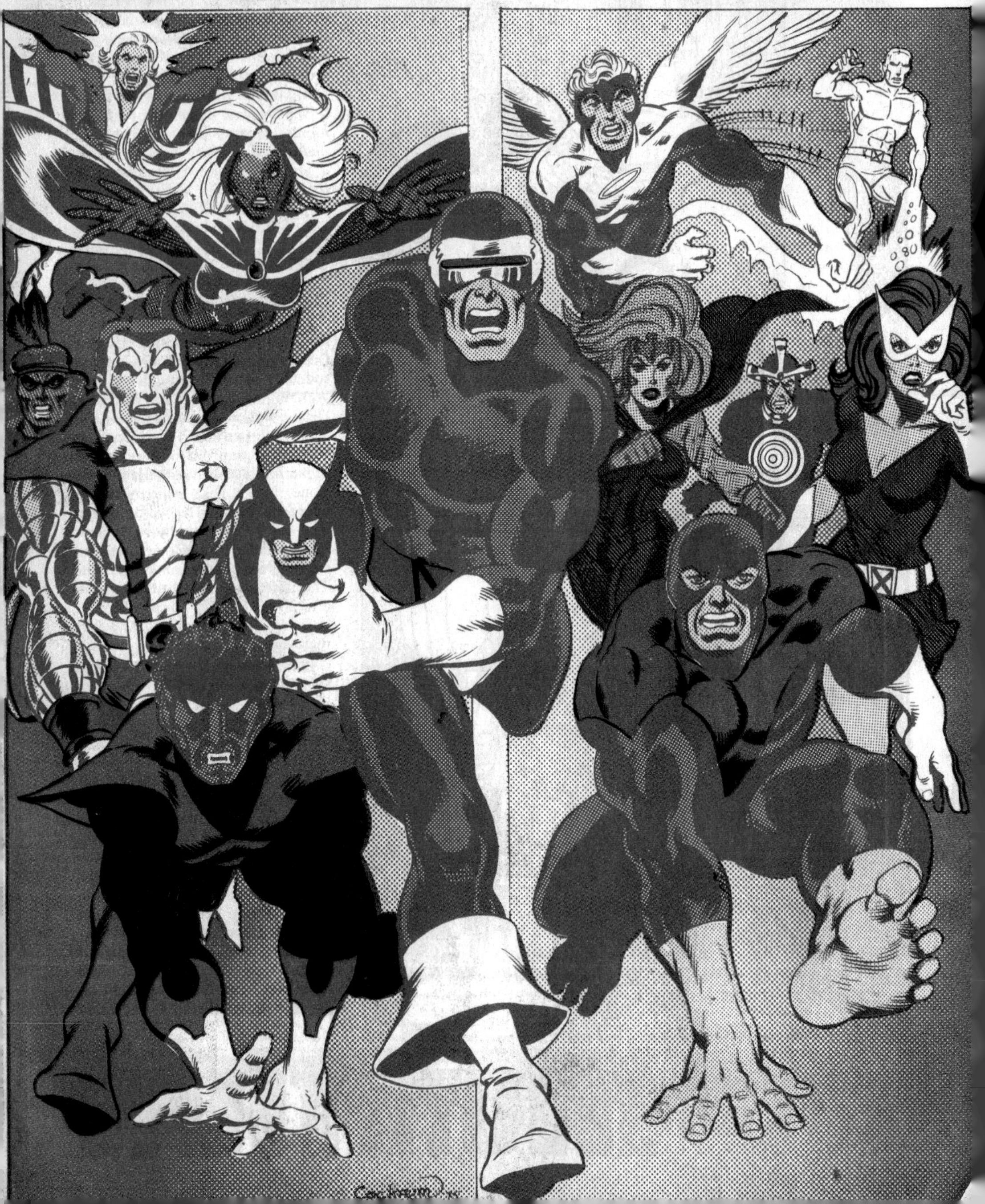

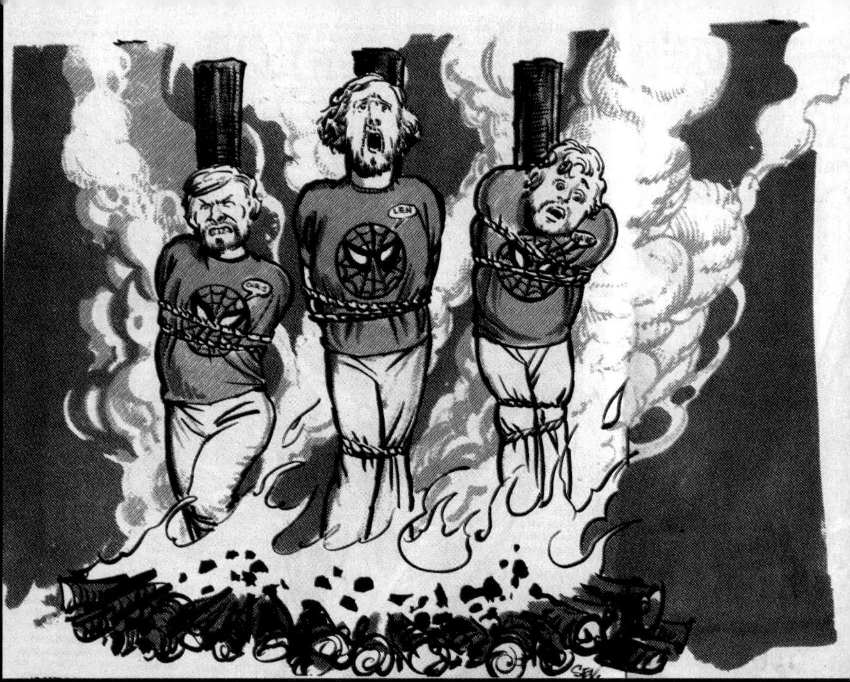

LEN

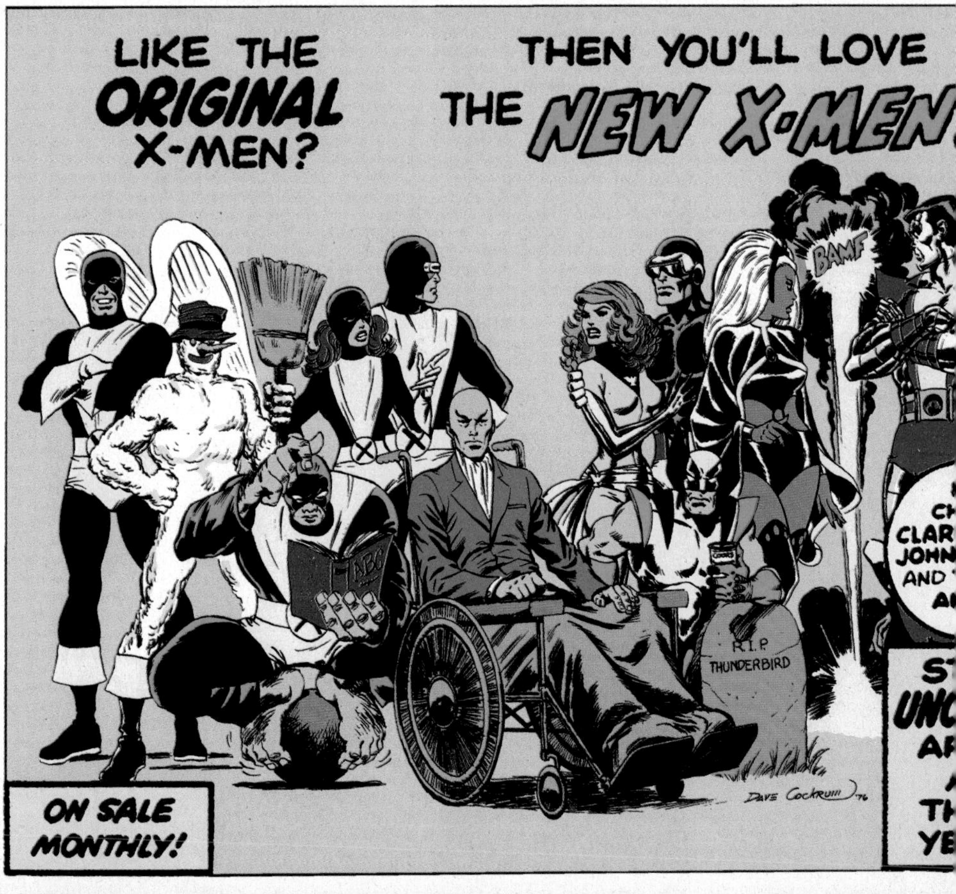

LIKE THE ORIGINAL X-MEN?
THEN YOU'LL LOVE THE NEW X-MEN
BAMF
R.I.P. THUNDERBIRD
DAVE COCKRUM '76
ON SALE MONTHLY!

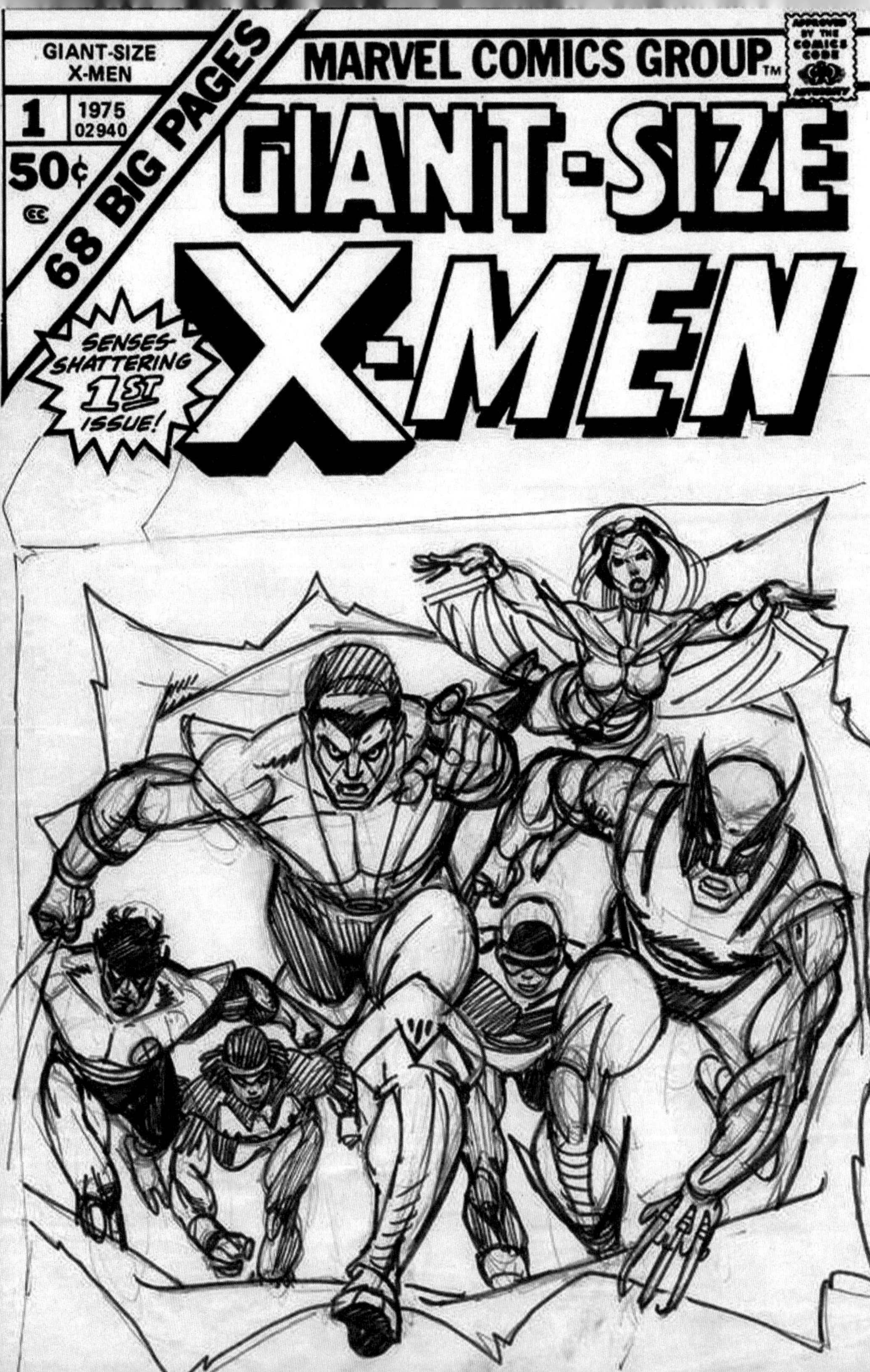
GIANT-SIZE
X-MEN
1
1975
02940
50¢
68 BIG PAGES
MARVEL COMICS GROUP™
APPROVED BY THE COMICS CODE AUTHORITY
GIANT-SIZE
X-MEN
SENSES-SHATTERING 1ST ISSUE!

Giant-Size X-Men #1 cover original art
by Gil Kane & Dave Cockrum

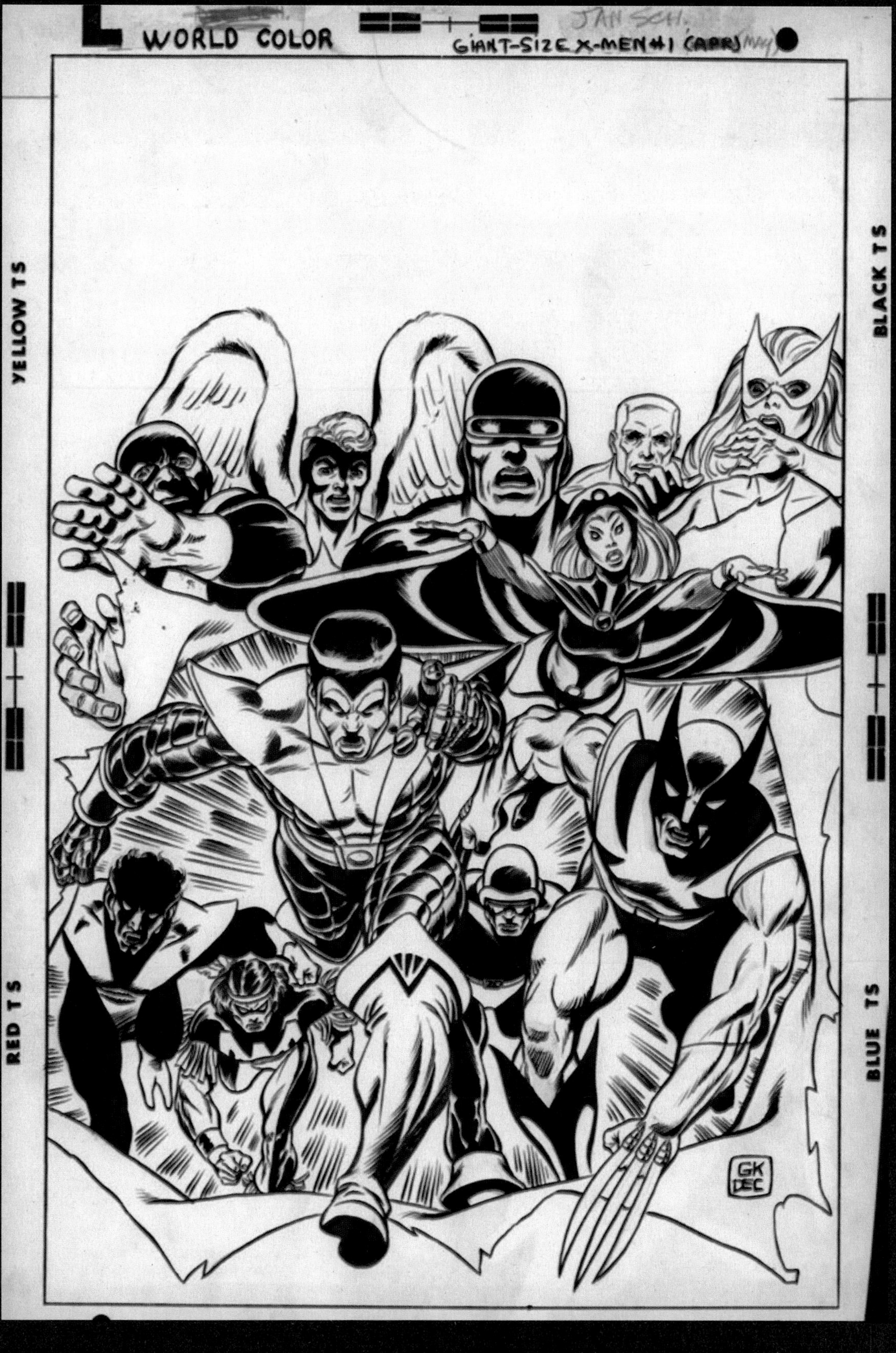
WORLD COLOR
GIANT-SIZE X-MEN #1 (APR)
YELLOW TS
BLACK TS
RED TS
BLUE TS
GK DEC

Giant-Size X-Men #1, page 18 original art
by Dave Cockrum

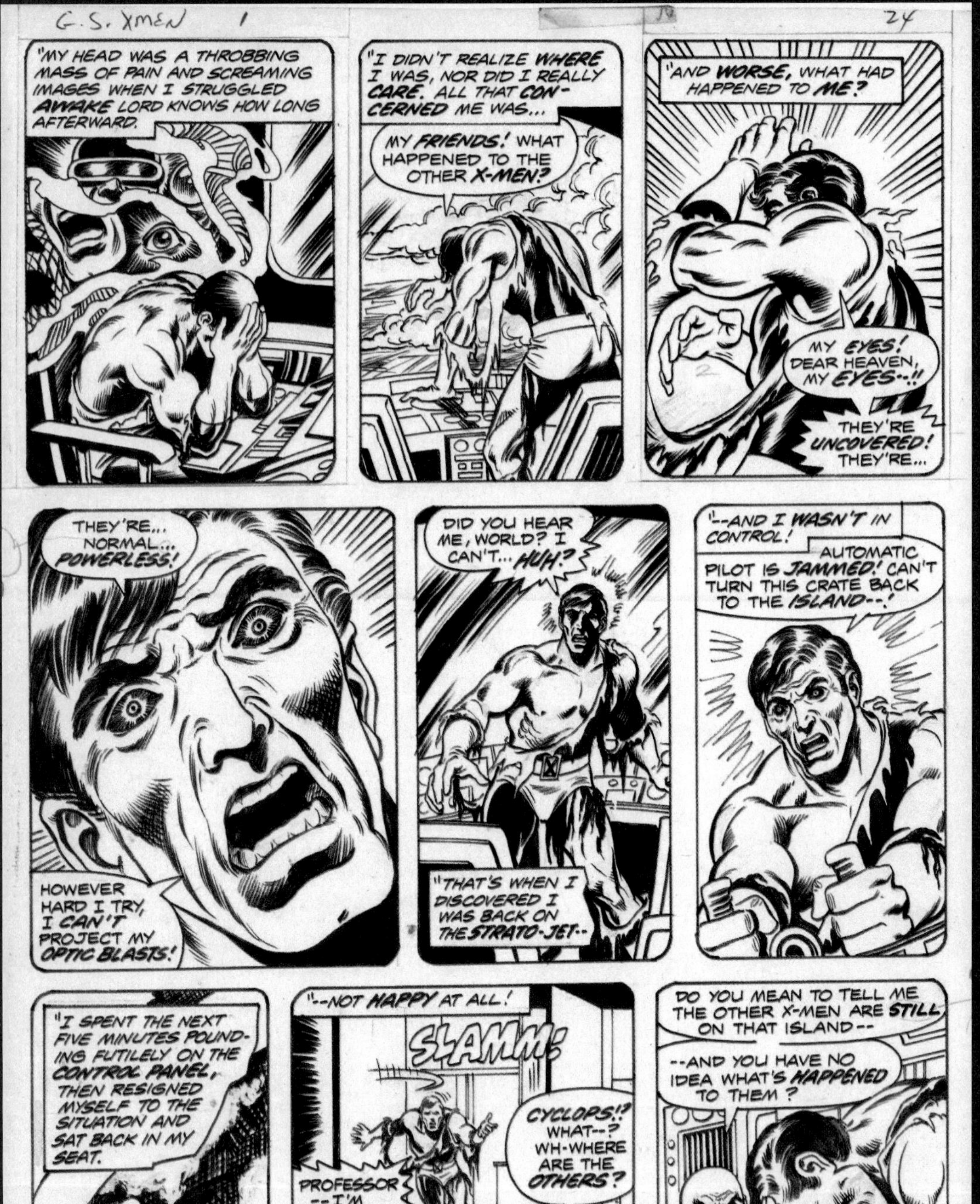
G.S. XMEN 1
24
"MY HEAD WAS A THROBBING MASS OF PAIN AND SCREAMING IMAGES WHEN I STRUGGLED AWAKE LORD KNOWS HOW LONG AFTERWARD.
"I DIDN'T REALIZE WHERE I WAS, NOR DID I REALLY CARE. ALL THAT CONCERNED ME WAS...
MY FRIENDS! WHAT HAPPENED TO THE OTHER X-MEN?
"AND WORSE, WHAT HAD HAPPENED TO ME?
MY EYES! DEAR HEAVEN, MY EYES--!!
THEY'RE UNCOVERED! THEY'RE...
THEY'RE... NORMAL... POWERLESS!
HOWEVER HARD I TRY, I CAN'T PROJECT MY OPTIC BLASTS!
DID YOU HEAR ME, WORLD? I CAN'T... HUH?
"THAT'S WHEN I DISCOVERED I WAS BACK ON THE STRATO-JET--
"--AND I WASN'T IN CONTROL!
AUTOMATIC PILOT IS JAMMED! CAN'T TURN THIS CRATE BACK TO THE ISLAND--!
"I SPENT THE NEXT FIVE MINUTES POUNDING FUTILELY ON THE CONTROL PANEL, THEN RESIGNED MYSELF TO THE SITUATION AND SAT BACK IN MY SEAT.
"I WASN'T HAPPY BY THE TIME I REACHED WESTCHESTER--
"--NOT HAPPY AT ALL!
SLAMM!
PROFESSOR --I'M BACK!
CYCLOPS!? WHAT--? WH-WHERE ARE THE OTHERS?
"THE PROFESSOR WAS NO HAPPIER THAN I AFTER I TOLD HIM...
DO YOU MEAN TO TELL ME THE OTHER X-MEN ARE STILL ON THAT ISLAND--
--AND YOU HAVE NO IDEA WHAT'S HAPPENED TO THEM?
I KNOW NOTHING, PROFESSOR--EXCEPT THAT SOMETHING ON KRAKOA CURED MY EYES AND DEPOSITED ME BACK IN THAT...
WITNESS THE FRIGHTFUL FATE OF GLENN TALBOT IN HULK #188!
24

Courtesy Heritage Auctions

Giant-Size X-Men #1, page 22 original art
by Dave Cockrum

GIANT SIZE X-MEN
30
YOU FOOL-- YOU CANNOT FLY!
OF COURSE NOT--BUT I CAN LAND WITH THE BEST OF THEM!
THE CHICK AND THE RUSSKIE HAVE LANDED-- AND IT LOOKS LIKE THEY'RE ARGUING--
--WHICH IS ABOUT PAR FOR THIS OUTFIT!
WE'RE GOING DOWN NEXT, THUNDERBIRD-- STRAP IN!
ONCE MORE, THE STRATO-JET'S VTOL SYSTEM LOWERS IT TO EARTH-- AND THOUGH HE TRIES, THE MAN CALLED CYCLOPS CANNOT SUPPRESS A SHUDDER.
HOW MANY MORE WILL WE LOSE THIS TIME, HE WONDERS MORBIDLY. WILL I EVEN LIVE LONG ENOUGH TO FIND OUT?
BUT HE'S A PROFESSIONAL, THIS STAR-CROSSED MUTANT. THE QUESTIONS FOLLOW HIM AS HE STEPS OUT UPON THE LANDSCAPE--
--BUT HE LEAVES HIS FEAR IN THE SHIP.
EAST IS THAT WAY, THUNDERBIRD-- AND THE SOONER WE GET STARTED, THE SOONER WE'LL GET THERE!
YES SIR, GENERAL ONE-EYE SIR! I JUST HOPE YOU'RE NOT LEADING ME INTO ANOTHER LITTLE BIG HORN!
IT'D BE JUST MY LUCK TO BE THE FIRST INDIAN TO GET MASSA-CREED BY...
HOLD IT! I LEFT THE MINI-CEREBRO UNIT BACK IN... HUH?
I DON'T BELIEVE IT!
DON'T BELIEVE WHAT?
THE STRATO-JET--!
IT'S-- GONE!
THE SHATTERING SECRET OF THE FALCON— REVEALED IN CAPTAIN AMERICA #186!
BEST - DAVE COCKRUM
30

Courtesy Heritage Auctions

BIOGRAPHIES

CHRIS CLAREMONT

It is hard to remember a time when the word "mutant" didn't correspond with the largest and most-ardently followed franchise in comics, but in the mid-'70s, the "All-New, All-Different" *X-Men* were naught but forgotten team of misfits with a small audience of holdovers from the book's first era. Chris Claremont took this formerly failed property and turned it into the kind of book for which the fan appetite could not easily be sated, thereby creating a milestone event in comics history that still holds sway decades later.

Chris his career in comics in the early '70s writing issues of *Avengers, Daredevil*, and *Incredible Hulk*, while also delivering several text stories to the black and white Marvel monster and kung fu mags. His first regular writing gig was *War Is Hell*, a "weird war" title which came to a close just as his run on *X-Men* and *Iron Fist* began. *Iron Fist*, which rolled out in the pages of *Marvel Premiere* before getting its own title, was done in concert with artist John Byrne, forming a key partnership that would pay big dividends a few years later. Other high-profile projects from Chris' first full decade in comics included *Marvel Preview: Starlord, Ms. Marvel*, a substantive run on *Marvel Team-Up* (again with Byrne), and *John Carter: Warlord of Mars*.

But it was in the pages of *X-Men* where Chris would gain his own personal fame and, at the same time, change comics history. In tandem with artists Dave Cockrum and John Byrne, Chris helped create a cornerstone franchise for Marvel—one which couldn't have been more different in style and tone than the other superstar phenom in their stable, Spider-Man. After writer Len Wein launched the newly updated series in 1975 with the seminal *Giant-Size X-Men #1*, Chris was tasked with guiding the new adventures of the mutant misfits, and he did so by crafting layered stories that balanced crisp, felt dialogue with high-octane action. Chris placed a premium on characterization, which was a lofty goal in a team book with many players, but he did so deftly enough to spin a wide-ranging tapestry of characters, each of whom became fan favorites.

Leading breathless fans down the path of several timeless tales ("The Dark Phoenix", "Days of Future Past", and *God Loves, Man Kills* to name a few), he helped build such an intense loyalty that it only made sense to spin-off the X-Men's success into new books. The first such spin-off was *New Mutants*, in which Chris brought in some new blood to Xavier's school with a raft of new characters. Later in the decade, Chris and Alan Davis co-created *Excalibur*, another spin-off team of mutants, and established a regular series for Wolverine with John Buscema.

In 1990, he launched a new sister title for the main team of mutants with Jim Lee; *X-Men #1* premiered to numbers that made it the highest selling comic ever. After a long break from the company, Chris returned to Marvel in 2000, writing the novelization of Bryan Singer's X-Men film and taking on the Fantastic Four monthly. He is still active today, writing *Excalibur* and *Exiles* and worthy of his standing as proud papa of the X-Universe.

DAVE COCKRUM

The late Dave Cockrum's legacy as an artist with a vibrant and creative handle on character design is best shown in his indelible influence on the casts of *Legion of Super-Heroes* and *Uncanny X-Men*. Born an Air Force brat in Pendleton, Oregon, Dave Cockrum moved around from town to town in the early years of his life. Perhaps a stable home life wasn't in the cards for young Dave, but comics were a consistent preoccupation for the lad. Proven by his earliest writing in comics: A fan letter to Stan Lee printed in *Fantastic Four #36!*

His first *real* job in the comics business was for Warren Publishing, then purveyors of such black and white magazine fare as *Vampirella*, which enabled him to prove adept enough to be hired on as a background inker for the legendary Murphy Anderson. This position was key for him, as he not only learned the ropes of comic art with one of its hardest workers, it put him in an advantageous position to lobby for the job of artist on *Legion of Super-Heroes*, a strip that backed up the monthly tales of *Superboy*. Cockrum on the *Legion* was a defining time for both the book and its artist: It allowed Dave to blossom behind the boards of a super hero adventure strip with a large and varied cast, and his style helped reinvigorate the teen-age super heroes with a vibrancy replete with flashy costumes and cool-looking characters.

A dispute with DC Comics over the maintenance of original artwork led him to leave the company and his beloved Legion and head over to Marvel. His standing on *Legion* was put to good use on the revival of the X-Men in *Giant-Size X-Men #1*. Working with writer Len Wein, this double-sized extravaganza was an attempt to bring back Marvel's mutants from obscurity. After the Giant-Size issue, a regular series featuring the writing of Chris Claremont and Cockrum's able pencil art began appearing at bi-monthly intervals. An enthusiastic fanbase remained for this band of misunderstood heroes, but nobody could have imagined the response to Claremont and Cockrum's overhaul of the mutant ethos.

By keying the revival of the X-Men to the debut of several new, exotic mutants, Cockrum and Claremont were able to tap into an excitement that would slowly build over the next few years. Cockrum's inventive designs included the stunningly beautiful goddess, Storm; the Russian dynamo Colossus; the raw power of Thunderbird; and Nightcrawler, a character that was actually a holdover from his sketchbook of unused Legion designs. Together with the portrayal of the Phoenix, Jean Grey's new identity, Cockrum's work had a flash that made sure X-Men's new direction would be an eye-grabber.

After handing the book over to Byrne with issue #108, Cockrum worked on his own concepts with *The Futurians*, first published in Marvel Graphic Novel, and then as a regular series for Lodestone. A return to *The Uncanny X-Men* was in the cards during '80s, and after that, Cockrum let his imagination to many projects for indie companies like Valiant and Claypool. Sadly, Cockrum passed away in 2006 from complications due to diabetes.

LEN WEIN

Len Wein's career is highlighted by successes from co-creating Swamp Thing, to launching the "All-New, All-Different" X-Men, and editing *Watchmen*, but few fans know that the award-winning writer and editor started out as a comic book artist.

As a teenager, Wein was tied to the hip with fellow fanzine writer Marv Wolfman, regularly skipping school to tour the DC Comics offices. After building a rapport with artists and execs like Dick Giordano, Carmine Infantino and Joe Orlando, Wein was able to credibly pitch original work to the editors. Though his artwork was politely passed upon, a script for the *House of Mystery* series was accepted and a career as a writer was born. The freelancer attacked his new occupation with gusto, writing for DC, Marvel, Gold Key and Skywald, across all genres from Western to horror, and licensed properties from Hot Wheels to Star Trek.

Although his desired career as an artist didn't quite pan out, it did give Wein insight into his collaborator's creative process and helped him garner acclaim as a writer that was "easy to draw." After dabbling with super heroes in the early '70s (Daredevil, Superman, Flash), he teamed with artist Bernie Wrightson to create Swamp Thing. Originally conceived in the pages of *House of Secrets*, the concept was too great to stay in the horror anthology and soon got its own title to great critical reception. Other notable achievements from his tenure at DC include a run with Dick Dillin on *Justice League of America*, and co-creating the Human Target.

Hopping over to Marvel in 1974, Wein got busy scribing several series, particularly *Incredible Hulk*, where he and artist Herb Trimpe co-created one of comics' most famous characters—Wolverine. That wasn't the end of his mutant doings, as with artist Dave Cockrum, he revived the dormant X-Men property, recasting them as the "All-New, All-Different" X-Men. Its cadre of characters, including Storm, Nightcrawler and Colossus, were ushered into existence by Wein and handed off to writer Chris Claremont, who would shortly turn them into a phenomenon.

Returning to DC, Wein helped spur a creative revival at the company, editing *New Teen Titans, Camelot 3000*, and *Swamp Thing*, which gave writer Alan Moore a platform to share his talents; shortly thereafter, Wein would preside over Moore and Dave Gibbon's ground-breaking *Watchmen*. Since then, Wein's credits in comics, animation and television writing have been numerous and well received. His latest comics work includes a run as writer of *Justice League of America*.

Biographical material researched and written by John Rhett Thomas

THE
MARVEL MASTERWORKS
ALSO AVAILABLE IN HARDCOVER